ALWAYS A
COMMANDO

Clarence meets then-President Wee Kim Wee during a visit to the commando camp in 1986 or 1987.

ALWAYS A
COMMANDO

THE LIFE OF SINGAPORE ARMY
PIONEER CLARENCE TAN

THOMAS A. SQUIRE

Marshall Cavendish Editions

© 2019 Thomas A. Squire

Published by Marshall Cavendish Editions
An imprint of Marshall Cavendish International

A member of the
Times Publishing Group

The publisher makes no representation or warranties with respect to the contents of this book, and specifically disclaims any implied warranties or merchantability or fitness for any particular purpose, and shall in no event be liable for any loss of profit or any other commercial damage, including but not limited to special, incidental, consequential, or other damages.

Other Marshall Cavendish Offices: Marshall Cavendish Corporation. 99 White Plains Road, Tarrytown NY 10591-9001, USA • Marshall Cavendish International (Thailand) Co Ltd. 253 Asoke, 12th Flr, Sukhumvit 21 Road, Klongtoey Nua, Wattana, Bangkok 10110, Thailand • Marshall Cavendish (Malaysia) Sdn Bhd, Times Subang, Lot 46, Subang Hi-Tech Industrial Park, Batu Tiga, 40000 Shah Alam, Selangor Darul Ehsan, Malaysia.

Marshall Cavendish is a registered trademark of Times Publishing Limited

National Library Board, Singapore Cataloguing-in-Publication Data

Name(s): Squire, Thomas A.
Title: Always a commando : the life of Singapore army pioneer Clarence Tan / Thomas A. Squire.
Description: Singapore : Marshall Cavendish Editions, [2017] | Includes bibliographical references.
Identifier(s): OCN 1001426718 | ISBN 978-981-4779-31-9 (paperback)
Subject(s): LCSH: Tan, Clarence, 1941- | Singapore. Armed Forces—Officers—Biography. | Malaysia. Tentera Darat—Officers—Biography. | Singapore. Armed Forces—History.
Classification: DDC 355.0092—dc23

Printed in Singapore

Illustrations by Alvin Mark Tan (www.alvinmark.com)

Photographs courtesy of the author and his family, except on page 82 (Saint Patrick's School) and page 270 (David Yeoh).

For Emma and Luke, the raisons d'être

CONTENTS

Part Three: An Independent Singapore (1965 – Today)

Foreword

"Always A Commando" is a biography of one of Singapore's pioneer army officers, LTC (Retired) Clarence Tan. Clarence's son-in-law, Thomas Squire, has written this as a story for his children, about their grandfather's life journey.

Clarence's experience reflects that of our pioneer generation. They had come from all walks of life, and together, helped to lay the foundation for a strong, united and harmonious Singapore.

Clarence joined the Singapore Volunteer Corps in 1959 and contributed to our defence and security during the Malayan Emergency fighting the Communists. He and his comrades from the First Battalion, Singapore Infantry Regiment were also deployed during Konfrontasi to an island off the east coast of Borneo.

But Clarence is best remembered for his role in developing our Commandos. As the first commanding officer of the Commandos in the newly-formed Singapore Armed Forces (SAF), Clarence worked closely with his colleagues to train new recruits and build a capable and cohesive formation, who wear their distinctive red berets and serve proudly, "For Honour and Glory". He was a legend in his own time, identified by all in the SAF with the Commandos. He had seen action in the turbulent times of the 1960s and 70s, and was called upon for the Laju hijack incident.

I came to know Clarence as a fellow officer and colleague in the SAF, and his wife Judy. Though Clarence was several years my senior in the service, he was always willing to offer his views, ideas and advice in a practical, direct and useful way, based on his actual operational experience and closeness to his men and the ground. When he served as our Defence Adviser in Canberra, I spent two days with him, just the two of us, as he drove us from Sydney to Nowra, and then on to Canberra as we visited several defence installations. Several of the stories in this book have a familiar ring to them, as he reminisced about his experiences over those two days. We also spent quite a lot of that time going through all the different things that he had eaten and how to prepare them – told with all seriousness but also with a sense of humour and self-deprecation that is Clarence.

The stories in this book are not only those of a Singapore army pioneer, but also reflect the aspirations of his fellow pioneer generation for Singapore. It was a delight to meet Clarence, Judy and the children and grandchildren as this book became ready for publication. I hope that these anecdotes will inspire his grandchildren Emma and Luke, and more youths to contribute to society and build a better future for all Singaporeans.

Teo Chee Hean
Deputy Prime Minister
and Coordinating Minister for National Security

A Letter (and a few disclaimers)

Dear Emma and Luke,

It was August 1998 when I first met Kong Kong, your maternal grandfather. Mummy had just finished her posting to Wellington and I had joined her on her return to Singapore. We were not yet married so at that stage I simply addressed him as Uncle Clarence. Kong Kong and Mama were kind enough to let me stay under their roof when I first arrived, so from the moment I stepped off our flight from New Zealand I was immersed into a part of Singapore culture.

Some of the most prominent memories of my early days in Singapore were the meals we all shared at their house in Kembangan. Kong Kong, Mama, Ku Ku Mel, and Mummy and I. The food was all very exotic for me, with much that I had never seen before. All of it delicious – though it did take me a while to appreciate bittergourd – and all washed down with copious amounts of water, thanks to the hot, humid weather and all those spices.

After many of these meals, I often found myself remaining at the dinner table for long periods of time, listening to Kong Kong tell me stories of his life: his days growing up as a child, his days at school, his days in the army. He spoke of his own Peranakan culture, his experiences interacting with the other cultures of Singapore, and of many of the changes that Singapore had gone through in his time – politically, socially, and geographically. I always found these stories fascinating.

Most of the time, your Mummy, Mama, and Ku Ku Mel would disappear as Kong Kong started his stories, leaving me alone with him at the table. Once he started his reminiscing, they would all excuse themselves. I asked your mum once why they never hung around to listen, because to me (aside from it seeming rude to just get up and leave the table mid-conversation) it seemed strange that they did not want to hear these intriguing tales. "We have heard it all before," was her reply.

These post-meal encounters were not dialogues. They were not conversations. They were storytelling time, and Kong Kong was the storyteller. Every now and then I would interject with a question to direct him into an area I was interested in learning more about, or I would say something to indicate my tenuous grasp of the history, but for the most part, he did the talking and I did the listening. Many times, my questions revealed an understandable ignorance of this culture I eventually married into. During one of our early meals, names of relatives like Marco and Giko were being thrown around. So, feeling clever, I said, "Interesting, so you have some Italian blood in the family?" I was to learn, to my humiliation, that these "names" were Chinese terms used to refer to the oldest paternal aunt, Mak Ko, and second oldest paternal aunt, Ji Ko.

From these discussions, I learnt much of what I know about the Peranakan culture, half of your heritage. Most of it was told to me by Kong Kong, but Mama has also provided a significant wealth of information – sometimes while she was still at the table, and sometimes as a corrective interjection to Kong Kong from elsewhere in the house. Your Peranakan heritage is something quite special, and one that you should be proud of. It is a heritage that you share with a relatively small community. Your heritage is more than this bloodline, however. It is also a history that you share with all Singaporeans of other races and creeds who can trace their ancestry back a number of generations on this island, and with those of more recent immigration.

One day, as Kong Kong was finishing yet another story after a Christmas lunch at our old East Grove apartment, I looked over to you, Emma (you were not yet born, Luke), and it struck me how the Singapore that you were growing up in was so different to the one into which your Mama and Kong Kong were born. It was then I first suggested to Kong Kong that we work together to write his stories down for you, his grandchildren. That moment was the genesis for the pages that follow.

As is the case for all of his generation, Kong Kong's life spans the formative years of the Singapore that you know: from his birth at a kampong bungalow on a rubber plantation in 1941, just a year before the Japanese occupation, in a Singapore that was still a British colony, to the development of the proud, progressive and independent nation that it is today. What makes his life particularly interesting is that he spent his professional life as a military officer, as a pioneer of Singapore's fledgling army when the nation became independent. Unsurprisingly, a good number of the stories he shared with me came from his military days.

This book is not the story of a man's involvement in politics or of an independence movement. Kong Kong was neither a politician nor an activist. This is the story of a regular kampong kid, an ordinary rural boy who, through hard work and circumstance, rose to prominence in his career and has now retired to a humble life. One might say he always has been, and still is, a kampong kid at heart. His younger self often emerges when you venture outside with him and he shows you the grasshoppers jumping amongst the grass, the touch-me-nots closing when brushed by a finger, the dragonflies buzzing around the bushes, the armies of ants making their way up the trunk of a tree, and the other fauna and flora around Singapore.

None of us are the result of our acts alone. Our lives are the summation of the world around us and how we respond to it. With this in mind, throughout these pages I have tried my best to summarise the historical events and cultural influences comprising the backdrop to

Kong Kong's life experiences. And what a complex world it was. If at times such discussions seem a little long, or divergent from Kong Kong's life story, stay with me, for I do believe it important to understand the historical context behind many of Kong Kong's stories.

While I am at it, let me add a few disclaimers. I am not a historian, nor am I a military man. I have tried my best to retell the relevant history as I have interpreted it through my research. It will not be perfectly accurate and some may question it, but it should at least provide you with a broad overview of the challenging times that Singapore and the surrounding region have faced. I hope you will read more widely on the historical topics that I have covered. Kong Kong has guided me in much of the military terminology, including ranks and how different army units relate to each other, but even then, I am sure a military expert will find inaccuracies. Furthermore, these words are based on one man's recollections of the past seventy-seven years of his life – inaccuracies in some memories, dates, sequences of some events, and so forth are understandable. On all accounts, I ask that you do not get bogged down by such technicalities, but look beyond them to the collection of stories that this is. Lastly, there is a saying amongst the Peranakan community: "For as many families that identify themselves as Peranakan, there are as many interpretations of the culture." This interpretation is but one.

At the time I first met your Mama and Kong Kong they were living in a house at Lengkong Lima in Kembangan, in the east of Singapore, very near the place where Kong Kong was born into this world. And while not in the same house, as much has changed since then, it is near that same location, in the house on top of Kembangan Hill, where this story begins.

The story that follows is your Kong Kong's. The words are mine.

Love,
Papa

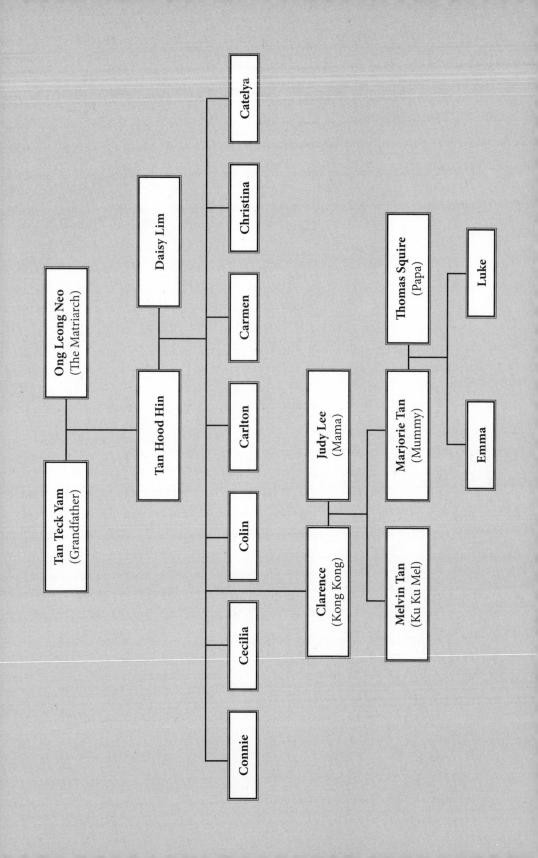

PROLOGUE

The House on Kembangan Hill

Day breaks over the island of Singapore. From the veranda of the house seated on top of Kembangan Hill, the vista of another tranquil morning dawns. Over the treetops of the rubber plantation stretching out from the house halfway down to the sea, the rising sun begins to light up the green land and the calm waters of the Singapore Strait that kiss the southern coast along Marine Parade beach around two miles away. What had appeared at night to be the scattered lights of lowly populated townships now reveal themselves to have been the lights of a myriad of ships anchored in the harbour awaiting the transfer of goods to and from the port down town. On the other side of the Strait, around ten miles away, can be seen Pulau Batam, the island of Batam. The cumulonimbus clouds that had unleashed their thunderous electrical fury over the southern portions of Malaya, including Singapore, in the early hours of the morning now tower over that Indonesian island, drenching it with the rains its lush green jungles thrive on.

Immediately surrounding the house itself, as if forming a fence between the homestead and the surrounding plantation, fruit trees of numerous kinds provide some shade from the low morning sun. Duku, langsat, chiku, rambutan, durian, quinine, jambu, pomelo. Enough varieties to ensure something is available regardless of the season. Clumps of wild orchids, many nestled in the tree branches, and bushes of azaleas are scattered around the property, their bright colours beginning to come alive with these first rays of the sun, and their delicate scents perfuming the serenity of the early morning.

In the branches of the fruit trees, roosting doves awaken and begin their search for food. Seeking out grass seeds, they quietly flutter around the damp dirt ground, keeping a nervous eye out for potential predators. They are soon joined by a small group of magpie robins, also fluttering around looking for their breakfast of insects and worms. The roosters of the area are also awake and sending out their morning call.

From behind the two large doors that form the main entrance to the house, comes the sound of a wooden beam being removed from the door. Seconds later the doors creak open, letting the first light of the day trickle into the front room of the large bungalow. Out steps the Matriarch of the household. She is already bathed, impeccably dressed, wearing an intricately woven sarong kebaya, her hair neatly tied up in a bun: attention to her appearance is an important part of her morning rituals. In her hands she clasps three smouldering joss sticks. Taking a few steps out onto the veranda, her grace in tune with the serenity that comes only with being the first to welcome these early rays of the sun, she raises the joss sticks above her head and looks up to the sky in quiet prayer, inviting Kwan Kong, the God of War, into her home.

Upon placing the burning joss sticks in the copper urn hanging from the veranda ceiling, she enters the front room that spans the entire width of the house, just inside the main door. There are two altars in the room and she proceeds first to the large one on the right. It is dedicated to Kwan Kong, who had just been invited into the house moments earlier. With this warrior god having now assumed his position on his altar, the Matriarch again raises three new joss sticks, this time in homage to him. Next, she proceeds to the altar of the ancestors situated on the left. For a third time she offers up three joss sticks in prayer, invoking the protection of the ancestors for the day ahead. Upon the altar are four tablets, each representing the soul of a single ancestor. Three are from previous generations, but the fourth is far closer to her heart – that of her husband, whom she bade farewell from this earth some five years earlier.

Thus ends her morning prayers for a safe and prosperous day, not only for herself, but also for the entire household of which she is the head. It is a job that belongs solely to the eldest member of the family.

In the rear section of the house, Hood Hin, the second son of the Matriarch, and his wife, Daisy, are beginning their morning. Their two daughters, Connie (three), and Cecilia (eighteen months), are still asleep. Hood Hin bathes himself first in the kamar mandi, the wet bathroom attached to their bedroom. Even in the steamy warmth of the tropics, the water drawn from the bak mandi (a large cube-shaped bathtub) with the ladle is chillingly refreshing as he pours it over his head. While the northwest monsoon is providing plenty of water for the wells at this time of year, bathing is nonetheless a short, simple and manual affair where only the necessary volume is ever used.

As Hood Hin prepares himself for work, Daisy gets ready and wakes their daughters. The bedroom remains dark, though enough morning light is creeping in through the wooden shutters to enable everyone to wash and dress without lighting any of the lamps. It is important to start the day well. Waking up on time, washing, and dressing neatly before presenting oneself to the world outside are considered necessary to ensure a good day ahead.

With all of them ready, the family proceed to the front section of the house where the Matriarch is waiting to greet them. Hood Hin greets his mother first, followed by his wife and their two children. Then, just as the Matriarch had done earlier, Hood Hin and Daisy turn to pay their respects to the ancestors, including Hood Hin's father, at the ancestral altar. And so is greeted the new day. As is every day. The simple ritualised morning prayers and greetings to the gods, the ancestors, to the Matriarch, and to each other, form the foundation on which a successful day can manifest itself.

And so also is greeted what will become the first day in the life of Tan Kim Peng Clarence.

PART ONE

THE CHILDHOOD YEARS

(1941 – 1959)

The stone at Bukit Brown Cemetery containing Clarence's name, Tan Kim Peng, etched in under "Grandsons".

Chapter 1
A Name Etched in Stone

The bicycle was ready to go. Each morning for the past few weeks Hood Hin had made sure that its tires were pumped up and its gears were well oiled. So when the call finally came, he ran out the door, down the stairs, grabbed the bike from under the old wing, and cycled off as fast as his legs could go. Out the driveway, then a sharp right on to Lengkong Tiga Road, the rear wheel almost skidding. Leaving a small cloud of dirt in his wake, he hurtled down the unsealed road, then right onto Changi Road. Kampongs rolled past him in a blur. He sped past a karung guni man pushing a bicycle loaded high with flattened cardboard boxes and made a left down Joo Chiat Road.

A few hundred metres later he braked sharply in front of a terrace house at Joo Chiat Place, jumped off his bike, and ran up the stairs to the main entrance. Panting, he gasped to the lady at the front desk, "Madam Chye Neo must come quickly. Daisy is ready to give birth!"

Madam Chye Neo was the district midwife. Every birth in the area she delivered, or at least knew about. Although Kandang Kerbau Hospital (more commonly known now as KKH) was the main maternity hospital at the time and had been delivering babies since 1924, Daisy had no interest in this modern approach and chose home births with the assistance of Madam Chye Neo, who also delivered her first two children. Some women chose not to go to Kandang Kerbau for superstitious reasons, preferring their own traditional medicinal practices over a Western approach. Daisy simply saw no need for the hospital: to deliver at home was perfectly natural and convenient for her.

Motorised transport was not so commonplace at the time, and people generally walked, cycled or rode in a trishaw to their destinations. With the house on Kembangan Hill being a good two miles away, there was no time for walking so the midwife and her assistant hailed a trishaw from across the street and made their way to the family home. Safe in the knowledge that help was on its way, Hood Hin raced ahead on his bicycle to return to his wife, who was fast becoming more than ready for their newborn's arrival.

Soon thereafter, on Saturday, 25th January 1941, in the room that the family slept in, Clarence made his entrance into this world.

———————

The months leading up to Clarence's birth had been an interesting time for Daisy, and those around her. Though, of course, for them it was just the way things were. Ever since it was apparent that her third child was on the way, much of Daisy's life had been governed by numerous rituals known as pantang. The Malay word for taboo, pantang refers to superstitious behaviours that are said to affect health, business deals, success in exams, and luck in all things. They have been an integral part of people's lives in Singapore and Malaya and the non-observance of them will quite likely bring ill luck upon transgressors.

It is said that once aware of a child in the womb, evil spirits are eager to put an end to a successful birth and will try anything to harm a mother and her child. As a result, an endless number of pantang specific to pregnancy have been handed down through the generations to ensure the safety of both mother and child. To limit the chance of encounters with these primarily outdoor spirits, Daisy had to be particularly careful whenever she left the house, especially at dusk when the spirits are at their most active. In the final months she would have rarely left the house at all. Iron nails are particularly useful in warding them off, so she had been wearing an iron-nail-shaped hairpin to hold her hair in place.

The occasional visit by wild monkeys to the property will have been of concern as well, lest a glance at one of them results in her child being born looking and acting like one. Such *terkenan*, or afflictions, would be a great embarrassment to the family and would surely send tongues wagging about how careless she must have been regarding these *pantang* during her pregnancy. Luckily, no eclipses had been visible in Singapore in the predeeding nine months. The sighting of such an event by the pregnant mother would surely have resulted in a birthmark appearing on her child's face.

Hood Hin and the family's maid would have been caught up in it too, busy pampering Daisy and satisfying her cravings lest the child inside come out grumpy and drooling. In the last days Hood Hin was additionally busy after work, ensuring that all the drawers and cupboards in the house were unlocked, as well as clearing all the blocked drains around the property. Even neighbours and strangers will have played a part, for to reject any requests from a pregnant woman, even one you do not know, would be a grave mistake and leave them with the shame of being responsible for any imperfections in the child. So, should a pregnant woman walk past your house and request some fruit from your tree, better you give it to her.

———————

Selecting a name for a newborn can be an arduous task for any parent, and perhaps even more so for those of Chinese lineage.[1] With Clarence's birth however, it was a simple task for Hood Hin and Daisy. His Chinese name, Tan Kim Peng, had already been determined well before he was born: it had existed on his grandfather's tombstone since his death in 1936. His grandfather had passed away before the grandchildren were

---

1   One common technique was to engage the services of a geomancer who, using details of the time and date of the child's birth, will refer to Chinese astrology to come up with a list of auspcicious names from which the parents can choose. In many cases, the grandparents or other relatives will be given the responsibility of naming the child.

born, so the predefined names of four of his descendants, two grandsons and two granddaughters, had been etched into the tombstone. Therefore, the name Tan Kim Peng was literally cast in stone, waiting for its rightful heir to be born.

———————

It was Clarence's grandfather who was responsible for the house and its surrounding estate that contained rubber plantations and farmland. Obviously a man of wealth, Tan Teck Yam had made his early money as a rice trader. Most likely an immigrant to Singapore, he probably originated from Burma, but no-one remembers for sure.

The estate itself was large. Rectangular in shape, it extended from Changi Road at its southern boundary to Kaki Bukit in the north, a distance of a little over a mile. Its width was around one thousand yards, running from the Kembangan canal on the western border through to Chai Chee on the eastern side, covering an area of roughly 400 acres[2] – around 160 rugby fields.

Rubber was one of the great money-spinners of the time (and would become even more so from 1939 as war began to rage in Europe). So once he purchased the land Tan Teck Yam immediately set about turning most of it into a rubber plantation. Many landowners in the area had done the same.

The workers on the plantation were mostly a mixture of Malays, and Boyanese from the Indonesian island of Bawean. The Boyanese lived in a pondok, or communal lodging house, in the southern section of the estate. Language-wise this was a benefit to the family, both the adults and the kids. While the family's bloodline was very much Chinese, they had been in the region for a couple of generations now, and Malay was now their first language.

---

2   In those days Singapore – and most of the world – was using the imperial measurement system, so everyone was familiar with terms like miles, yards, feet, and acres. It would not be until the 1970s that Singapore, and many other countries, began the transition to the metric system.

A small section of the land, down in the valley near Chai Chee on the eastern side, was rented out to Chinese farmers and their families. They ran a vegetable garden and farmed pigs, ducks, and chickens. Along with the children of these families and the kids from the Boyanese pondok, the grandchildren of Tan Teck Yam and his wife, including Clarence, would have more than enough playmates in the years to come, and the large property was to provide plenty of space for them to run in.

The family could have sourced much of their food from the Chinese farmers, but there was no need. At the back of the homestead, not too far from the house, their own pigpen and pond provided more than enough meat and fish for the entire extended family. As was common on farms all over Malaya, the pond and the pigpen were next to each other, creating their own contained ecosystem. On the surface of the pond water hyacinth grew in abundance, with pretty purple flowers, helping to oxygenate the water for the fish. When boiled with coconut fibre, the hyacinth provided feed for the pigs. Water from the pond was used to wash the pigs and their dirt-floored pens. The ground of the pens had a slight incline so that this cleaning water could flow back to the pond, taking with it leftover food scraps and porcine excrement that provided nutrients and food for the fish living in the pond. The fish in turn kept the mosquito numbers down, and provided food for the family.

The house itself was divided into two sections. The back portion, the old wing, was the original wooden house. Typical of most rural houses of the time in the area, much of the design was focused on ensuring it remained as cool as possible in the tropical heat. The floor was raised off the ground, supported by wooden beams, allowing air to flow underneath. The ceilings were very high, providing another natural mechanism for cooling the place. Household electricity was still more than a decade away so there were no fans. But the natural ventilation provided by the louvered windows was enough to keep the place cool in the day. There were no glass windows, as they would have prevented the flow of air. The interior structure was entirely hardwood, whose dark colour provided further cooling benefits.

It was common in this part of the world for a number of generations to be living under the same roof, and family in the house on Kembangan Hill was no exception. Hence Tan Teck Yam had a second house built in front of the original to accommodate the expected arrival of numerous grandchildren. Similar in shape to the first, the new house was larger and made of brick with cement plastered over the top, then painted blue. Brick and cement were far more modern materials than what had been used for generations past. A small bridge was constructed to provide easy access between the two houses. The two large altars that had originally resided in the large front room of the old wing were moved to the large front room of the new main house. Behind these main rooms of both houses were the bedrooms – all very large, with their own bathrooms, and each able to accommodate one young family. Some of the families, including Hood Hin and Daisy's, had access to two rooms.

The furniture in both sections was primarily made from rosewood and blackwood, with intricately carved designs and complex mother of pearl motifs inlaid into the wood, and a gleaming varnish finish. Aesthetics took precedence over comfort here: as elegant as they were, the firm and neatly fitted red cushions placed on the chairs could do little to remove the discomfort of the solid wood seats.

Most of the extended family – the Matriarch's children and their own young families – lived in the old wing, while the Matriarch herself lived in the main house along with her as-yet-unmarried daughters. In the large front room of the main house, three doors opened out to the veranda. The central one was the grandest with its huge doors, the doors through which Kwan Kong, the God of War, entered each morning. The large veranda encircled the main house. Two sets of stairs then led down from the veranda at the front to the dirt yard. This yard, encircling both houses, together with the fruit trees on its perimeter, provided a buffer between the domestic residence and the tall trees of the rubber plantation.

As both houses were raised a good twelve feet off the ground, the space under them made for perfect storage areas. A treasure of baskets containing paper offerings, earthenware, and all sorts of junk could be found there. The ground under the old house was dirt and it had no walls and was open to the breeze and the rain. The main house had a concrete floor with a wall around it, so the more important and fragile items were stored there. For the kids, these areas would provide great places for chasing and hiding games, and exploring the treasure trove held within.

Over the years, the kitchen and dining room in the original house had become too small for the growing family, so a separate larger one was added at ground level on the western side of the main house when it was built. All of the families ate there, either together or separately, as coincidence and circumstance determined, but the room could seat up to forty people, such as in times of festivals like Chinese New Year.

Hanging on the veranda of the main house, in addition to the copper urn containing the joss sticks, was a large paper lantern with the family name displayed on it. At night a burning candle was placed inside. Like many rural properties around the world, indications of property tenancy required something far simpler than a street name and number. The lamp informed anyone approaching the homestead that this was where the Tan family lived.

Yes, Tan Teck Yam had no doubt been a wealthy man. But over time he, and subsequently the Matriarch, did have a lot of people to support too. When he passed away, Tan Teck Yam left his wife with three sons and four daughters, and a growing brood of grandchildren to look after. As tradition dictated, the sons continued living in their parent's home after marriage and raised their families in the ancestral home, while the married daughters moved out and joined the families of their husbands. Although the sons were working and bringing in their own salaries, Tan Teck Yam's wife, who had assumed the role of the great Matriarch, used the proceeds from the rubber plantation and the rentals from the Chinese farmers to provide for the entire household. For the next 30 years she was the focal point for the family. To the many grandchildren who would come to live in her home, she was known as Mama. To outsiders she was Madam Ong Leong Neo. She was a loving and strong woman who provided for all under her care. She also knew that she alone was the link to the past and that upon her rested the responsibility to uphold, and pass on, the Peranakan Chinese traditions within the household.

———————

After getting married,[3] Hood Hin worked in the civil service as a clerk with the Public Works Department, and Daisy was a homemaker. Being a family of comfortable means, they had the luxury of employing an ama chay. Sometimes called a "black and white" because of the colours of their uniforms in households throughout Malaya, the ama chay was primarily the cook and the maid around the house, and when time permitted, the nanny to the young children. However, as the families within the household grew, looking after all the kids became well beyond the capabilities of a single person, so Daisy and the other mums of the household remained the primary caregivers of their young children.

In a culture where the oldest son was greatly esteemed, Hood Hin would normally have stood to gain very little by being the second oldest boy. However, when his older brother married a second woman

---

3 Hood Hin had been dating Daisy at the time of his father's death. Given the importance associated with the mourning period for someone so close, they had to make a very quick decision: tradition dictated that a couple must wait 12 months after the death of a parent before they could celebrate their nuptials, or get married within one month of the demise. Non-observance of this would surely bring bad luck to their marriage. In fact, such was the bad luck associated with death, that often the bereaved family would not even be invited to anyone else's wedding for the next 12 months. The couple chose the latter.

following the death of his first wife and this new couple decided to move out to their own home, Hood Hin became the most senior man about the house (though, of course, the true boss was always his mother, the Matriarch). While the family inheritance always followed the line of the most senior son, and there was substantial wealth to inherit due to the property, Hood Hin was not in fact the benefactor of the estate. The benefactor was to be Tan Kim Peng Clarence.

Yes, perhaps quite justifiably, tradition had figured out that giving the family inheritance to the immediate son just caused laziness and complacency to develop in the next generation, who, more often than not, would whittle it away. To safeguard this wealth, wisdom dictated that the inheritance skip a generation, as if to keep each alternate generation keen. Which is quite possibly how Hood Hin ended up as a clerk at the Public Works Department instead of becoming a wealthy landowner himself.

So, with his birth as the first son of the alternate generation, Clarence was set to become the benefactor of the estate with its plantations and farms and houses upon the passing away of the Matriarch. However, the immense changes that Singapore was to face in the years ahead would severely deplete any benefits that he might otherwise have looked forward to given this position.

Chapter 2
Being Peranakan

The Singapore that Clarence was born into was very different to the one that we know today. In 1941 it was a British colony, part of British Malaya – the states of what we now know as Peninsula, or West, Malaysia plus the island of Singapore. Since its founding as a free trade zone by the British over a century ago it had grown from a quiet, lowly populated, jungle-clad island, to a major trading hub for the region, attracting merchants from all over the world who traded goods to and from Asia. Bumboats, tongkangs, and sampans weaved amongst the small and large ocean-going ships anchored around the harbour. The smaller ocean-going vessels serviced the regional ports around Malaya and Indonesia, while the larger ones headed all over the world: China, India, the Middle East, Africa, Europe and the United Kingdom, Australia and New Zealand, or across the Pacific to the Americas.

The city centre was focused around the port, with the commercial centre located to the west of the Singapore River, around Raffles Place next to Boat Quay, and the civic centre, with the government buildings, on the opposite bank. As many of the workers at the port and in the commercial centre were Chinese, a bustling and crowded Chinatown had developed just to the west of the godowns. The British and other Western residents lived primarily in less crowded areas just north of the city centre, such as Orchard Road, Tanglin, Bukit Timah and Fort Canning. The rest of Singapore was still pretty much covered in jungle and plantations, with small pockets of development and suburbia, and many small villages, dotted around the island.

Heading east from the city centre, along the southern coast, one would soon cross the mouth of the Kallang River. On the opposite bank, where the Singapore Sports Hub now sits, was Kallang Airport, the island's main civilian airport, conveniently located beside the Kallang Basin where the river emptied into the sea. Its location enabled the airport to accommodate both land-based aircraft and seaplanes that were still flying the civilian and military skies. Moving further east, one soon left behind the bustle of the city and the airport and encountered a more relaxed seaside ambiance. Large bungalows housed wealthy expatriates and Chinese businessmen, who had chosen to move away from the growing city centre to the quieter eastern suburbs, within walking distance of the gentle waves lapping up against the shoreline of Marine Parade.

A short distance from the beach was the suburb of Katong. Living here were a number of Eurasian (those descending from mixed European and Asian parentage) and Peranakan families who had also moved east to avoid the congestion of downtown. It was these two groups who were beginning to make their mark on this part of the island perhaps more than anyone else, with their unique architecture, food, and culture. So it was quite appropriate perhaps that the location of Clarence's birth, at the house of his family on Kembangan Hill, was very near to this part of Singapore.

Your Kong Kong, Emma and Luke, just like your Mama, your Mummy, and therefore 50 percent of yourselves, is culturally defined as a Baba-Nonya, also known as a Straits-born Chinese or a Peranakan.[4] His

---

4   The Malay word "peranakan", literally "locally born", is not entirely specific to the Straits-born Chinese, as it can also be used to refer to people of other heritages who have made this part of the world their home, such as the smaller groups of Indian Peranakan and the Arab Peranakan. So, whereas Chinese Peranakan is more accurate a term for Clarence and the family, I have used Peranakan to refer to their ancestry throughout this book. Furthermore, while the word "peranakan" is more widely used today, during Clarence's youth they were always known as Straits-born Chinese or Baba-Nonya, and you will still hear these terms from time to time. Baba-Nonya are gender titles. A Baba is a Peranakan man and Nonya a Peranakan woman.

blood is Chinese, but his culture is mixed. (Technically, Daisy was half-Eurasian so there is a dilution of the Chinese blood, but the culture in which he was raised was definitely Peranakan.) The Peranakans had been living, and still do, along the Straits of Malacca for generations. They had mingled greatly with the peoples of the land and, consequently, their culture is a mishmash of their Chinese heritage and that of the Malay peoples around the Straits Settlements (Singapore, Malacca, and Penang) that they now called home. Hence the term Straits-born Chinese: Chinese born in the Straits Settlements.[5]

At the time Clarence was born many Peranakans spoke Malay, Chinese, and English fluently. Being able to communicate with the different peoples found around the Straits, and armed with an intimate understanding of each culture, enabled them to act as middlemen in business. These skills also opened up employment in enviable jobs within the British civil service (as was the case for Hood Hin) where English was a pre-requisite. Being generally better off financially than their pure Chinese, Indian, and Malay compatriots explains how many Peranakans were able to afford the short migration from the city centre to the new more affluent eastern suburbs.

Culturally, the Baba-Nonya are as rojak, as mixed up, as the pineapple and vegetable salad that bears that name. They are Chinese, yet they are not. They are Malay, yet they are not. They sit on a line between cultures, a people who exist on the border of both, a bridge between the two. Their food is a blend of Chinese and Malay. So are their clothing and housing. They have even developed their own tongue that is a creole of the two. In their appearance they look as Chinese as those from China, while in their hearts they are people of this land.

They are, perhaps, the ultimate embodiment of the melting pot that Singapore has become.

---

5   It should be pointed out that those Chinese who did not adopt some of the local customs and culture to a great degree, regardless of how many generations they had lived in the region, would probably not identify themselves as Peranakan.

Clarence's first month on this earth is perhaps as good an example as any of this cultural mix that he was born into.

The Malays traditionally showed a great deal of respect for the placenta. Immediately following the birth of a child, they would place the placenta in an earthen jar and bury it outside, almost as if it had a soul of its own. The Peranakans had adopted this practice too so, soon after he was born, the placenta from Clarence's birth was buried under a tree on the grounds of the property on Kembangan Hill.

After the birth, Daisy and her son underwent post-natal confinement, a common practice among both the Malay and Chinese to aid a mother's recovery and build up a newborn's strength before facing the world outside. Mother and child were both confined to their room for an entire month. A period of resting and pampering of the mother during which she spent nearly the entire time in bed, it was, and still is, considered a critical remedy to the trauma her body had just gone through.

Confinement is about recuperation and healing, and a number of traditional remedies are carried out during this period to aid in this. The Peranakans had adopted the Malay practice of wrapping a new mother's stomach, first smeared with oils and herbs, with yards of barut cloth. This is intended to help heal her wounds, bring her figure back in to shape, reduce the chances of physical problems later in life, and to ensure she has enough milk for her baby.

In many homes, the confinement room would not have been the most pleasant place to be. Not only was a mother not allowed to bathe during this period, doors and shutters were closed to prevent exposure to the wind, so there was limited air circulation. And because there was no air-conditioning or electric fans, the tropical heat and humidity would have made the room even more stifling and pungent. However, the rooms in their house on Kembangan Hill were big with high ceilings, and some natural ventilation could enter through the open trellised spaces between the top of the walls and the ceilings. Regular rains of the northeast monsoons kept the temperature a little cooler. To mitigate the smells from the herbs and the lack of bathing, Daisy was sponged down daily, and the baby Clarence received a daily bath. Any lingering smells would have been perfumed by the burning of incense, so the room was probably not the stifling bog of stench that it might have been in smaller homes, especially those in the more tightly packed urban areas. Nevertheless, Hood Hin and his young daughters would have been grateful to have had a separate room to sleep in.

Some families employed the services of a specialist confinement lady to help the new mother during this period. For Daisy however, the Matriarch took on the role, assisted by the ama chay. Her job was to massage the mother's body daily and to wrap her in the barut cloth each morning. She was also responsible for preparing the very specific food required for this period. While the barut cloth practice was Malay, the food was very much Chinese, with extensive use of pork and definitely not halal – a key concern for the predominantly Muslim Malaya. Some of the food was not entirely enticing and eaten only because "this must be good for me". Some of it, like pigs trotters cooked in vinegar and ginger, was actually quite delicious and even had the rest of the family hankering for leftovers.

It would have been a rather dull time for Daisy. Limited human contact, limited light, limited time with her husband and two daughters, and no view of the outside world. While she was not supposed to leave the room during the period, it is quite possible Daisy stepped out from time to time. But never far. And heaven forbid if she had ventured near one of the altars in the main house. Perhaps the only consolation was that the Peranakan tradition followed the one-month Chinese confinement period, versus the forty-four days Malay mothers had to endure. So Daisy and Clarence got a two-week discount.

When the end of the first month finally came around, it was a time for great celebration. Daisy was finally able to bathe herself in a hot herbal bath, the windows and doors of the room were opened, and Clarence was introduced to, and welcomed by, the outside world for the first time. In the Chinese tradition, he had his first haircut on this day, which was more of a shave leaving one small ugly patch of hair on the top of his scalp. The shaved hair was then placed into a young coconut with azalea flowers and floated down the longkang, or canal, that ran along the western boundary of the estate down to the sea. Then, as a formal announcement to the world, a gift of turmeric, glutinous rice, two hardboiled eggs, and some curry was sent out to all the relatives and close friends. This last practice was truly Peranakan: the Chinese similarly sent out food at this time, but traditionally a Chinese rice cake instead.

As Clarence was passed around adoring relatives and close friends during these early days there was little talk of how cute he was or how handsome and strong he looked. This was no indication of disdain toward his physical appearance, however. Evil spirits were always lurking nearby. Should they have heard any careless talk of such positive attributes they would have been enraged with jealousy and attacked the baby boy.

And when out of the blue he was heard babbling and laughing to himself, people knew that he was talking to the friendly spirits who had kept him company during his nine months in the womb. They had been his friends and guardian angels over the last nine months, there to defend him against the evil spirits. Through their shared tongue he was communicating with them, perhaps sharing a few last jokes, good wishes, and farewells as he began to leave their world and became more and more connected to this new one.

———

The day of Clarence's introduction to the world was 25th January 1941. Britain and the countries of Europe were currently locked in a war that had been going on for a little over seventeen months. Just six days earlier, the Australian 8th Division, the first troops from the Australian Imperial Force (now known as the Australian Army), had arrived to join British, Indian, and a smaller number of Malayan troops to prepare for the defence of Singapore against a possible Japanese invasion – an interesting occurrence relating to Clarence's birth: almost fifty years later he would end a military career that would define his working life as Singapore's Defence Adviser to Australia.

Life at this distant colonial outpost for the regular citizen was quite normal – for now anyway. The average person in the city went about his daily activities with no real thought of the possibility that the horrors of war could spread to this part of the world. Of course, the Second Sino-Japanese War was being fought in China with tremendous atrocities being committed against the Chinese civilians, but that was also far away. While there were more foreign troops around than normal, and more arriving over the coming months, there was no concern among the general population, save for some in the local Chinese community, including a number of Peranakans, who provided support to their old country in personnel and material ways.

Yes, life was quite normal on the island at the time of Clarence's birth. However, any hope that war would not reach Singapore were dashed less than eleven months later when, on 8th December 1941, a little more than an hour before their attack on the US Pacific Fleet at Pearl Harbor in Hawaii, the Japanese began their invasion of Malaya.

The Japanese, and three grim years of wartime hardship and atrocities, were on their way.

Chapter 3
Japanese Times

It was four o'clock in the morning when the air-raid siren rang out across the island, its haunting scream undulating across the sky. It took some seconds for Hood Hin to make sense of what was waking him up. Had it been daylight he may have grumbled about it being another crazy drill intended to prepare the population for the real thing, but at this hour there was little doubt that this was the real thing.

The first thing to do was to light the wicker lamp so they all could see. Hood Hin fumbled around for the matches and lamp on his bedside table. Daisy, Connie, and Cecilia were now also stirring, trying to make sense of this disruption. He told the children to hurry and follow their mother. Hood Hin then went to his mother's room to help her.

Daisy cradled the still-sleeping Clarence in her arms, hoping the ongoing sirens would not wake him, and left the room. Her two young daughters followed. They made their way through the main room of the old house, through the front door, then down the stairs and across to the storage area under the new house.

For almost a year now the government had been sending out notices about the possibility of Japanese bombing raids. There had been air raid drills from time to time but not for a few months now. The area under the main house, while not a perfect bomb shelter as it would not have fared well in a direct or close hit, was the best option the family had to protect themselves other than actually digging a hole in the ground. While Kembangan Hill was unlikely to be a target for Japanese aerial raiders, two possible targets were nearby: RAF Kallang (Kallang

Airport), which had become the main fighter airfield on the island, and an ammunition dump at nearby Khaki Bukit. Stray bombs from attacks on those places were not an unreasonable possibility. The British military thought that the Japanese were neither good warriors nor good airmen, so off-target bombings were highly anticipated. How mistaken, on both accounts, they would turn out to be.

Moments later, the rest of the household joined them under the house. All over Singapore people were taking cover. Lower down the hill, the Chinese farmers and the Malay rubber plantation workers hid in the shelters that they had dug beside their homes.

Normally, a drill would last for ten minutes whereupon the all-clear siren would ring. This morning, however, tension hung in the air as 4.20am approached and the air-raid siren showed no sign of abating. As they became more awake, the children grew eager to play with each other, but their anxious parents quietly growled at them to keep still and be quiet. And still the siren wailed. Fear began to mount. Whatever quiet conversation had been going on came to a halt as ears turned their attention to the skies above. Would they soon hear the sound of approaching aircraft?

It would be almost another ten minutes of anxiety before their worst fears were confirmed: this was not a drill. The drone of high altitude bomber aircraft came rumbling over the noise of the siren. At around 4.30am they heard faint bursts of anti-aircraft gunfire accompanied by bombs exploding, and flashes of light in the distance. The sound could have easily been mistaken for thunder from a distant tropical storm, but not tonight, a clear moonlit sky. No, this was not a drill. This was the real thing. War had come to Singapore.

Nervously, the family listened. Although the initial sounds were very faint and distant, fear was clear in the eyes of everyone old enough to comprehend what was happening. The families held each other close, some in quiet prayer.

With the bombing sounding distant, curiosity got to the men folk and, despite the concern of the women and the children, Hood Hin and his brother left the security of the shelter to venture outside. From their vantage point at the top of the hill they had a good view of the clear night sky. High up in the western sky, captured by the searchlights, they could make out the shape of aircraft. Japanese bombers, they guessed. Anti-aircraft fire was lighting up the air around them, trying to shoot them down. Faint flashes from what must have been the bombs exploding, or possibly fires, flickered in the western and northern areas of the island.

It seemed like forever as the bombing continued. At one stage the attack appeared to be getting closer. Were they heading to Kallang Airport or the nearby ammunition dump? They looked at one another, hoping they were wrong, then returned to the relative safety of the makeshift bomb shelter.

The bombing raid lasted for around twenty-five minutes. At 5am the sound of the single tone raider-passed siren called across the sky. Everyone relaxed. It was over – for now. Daisy and the women ushered the children back into the house. There was still over an hour of darkness remaining so it was time to get the kids back to sleep. Hood Hin and his brother hung around and chatted. In these times, aside from the newspapers, radio was the main avenue for news, so Hood Hin quickly ducked into the house to retrieve his wireless. The men then huddled around the battery-powered radio on the steps, some with cigarettes in hand. At first the reports were sketchy. It seemed that the targets had been all military focused – RAF Tengah, RAF Seletar, Sembawang Naval Base, and Keppel Harbour. A couple of bombs had fallen on Raffles Place, the business centre downtown. Stray bombs intended for Keppel Harbour perhaps? Kallang Airport and the Khaki Bukit ammunition dump were not attacked. The eastern districts were untouched. The men heaved a sigh of relief: the attacks seemed to be contained to military targets, yet they were anxious for further details on the full extent of the casualties and damage caused.

More complete reports would not come through until after sunrise. And when they did, the news was bad: sixty-one people killed and over seven hundred injured. The Japanese had been very clever, methodical, and clinical in their attack. An initial wave of seventeen Mitsubishi GM3 bombers had flown over at an altitude of 14,000 feet to draw the searchlights and fire from the anti-aircraft guns, creating a diversion for the real bombers to fly in at only 4,000 feet and unleash their bombs with little resistance. Not a single Japanese aircraft had been shot down.

And so it had begun. Dark days were descending upon Malaya and Singapore. Of course, at not even eleven months old, Clarence was oblivious to what had just happened. But there is no question that this bombing raid marked a turning point in the lives of everyone on the island. It would ultimately set the ground for Singapore's independence, and thus ultimately shape the character and life of Clarence.

———————

At the same time that the Japanese were bombing Singapore they were also landing troops in southern Thailand, on the beaches of Pattani and Songkhla, and in northern Malaya, on the beaches of Kota Bahru. All in preparation for a push south toward Singapore, the jewel of the British crown in the region. They already had control of the French colonies of Indochina (today's Vietnam, Laos, and Cambodia), an asset that came with little resistance after they had set up an alliance with Germany, who had taken over France in Europe. From there the Japanese had a prime location from which to launch their air, naval, and land attacks upon the entire South East Asia region.

Around an hour after the attack on Malaya, Japanese aircraft began inflicting a massive attack on a completely surprised US Pacific Fleet at

Pearl Harbor in Hawaii. Within twenty-four hours they also launched attacks on Hong Kong, Guam, The Philippines, Midway, and Wake Island. These were not isolated attacks; they were all part of a very well-planned and well-orchestrated effort to conquer South East Asia, which required the removal of British and US influence in the region.

What was this all about? Why were the Japanese so eager to attack Singapore and Malaya, the US Pacific fleet, then to move on to Indonesia days later, and even conduct war on parts of Australia? At the time, Japan was committed to a major war in China. With a trade embargo placed on them by the United States, they needed an alternative source of supplies for their war machine, without which their China campaign would have ground to a halt. Singapore and its hinterland of Malaya possessed a significant proportion of the world's rubber and tin. Therefore, seizing these locations from British control, as well as the oil fields of Indonesia from the Dutch, became vital military objectives. Given the American occupation of Philippines at the time, its growing interests throughout the region, and probable support they would provide to British forces, they also needed to weaken the US Pacific Fleet. The Allies (specifically Australia, Britain, United States and the Netherlands) had significant forces in Darwin, Australia, which as far as Japan was concerned, also needed to be neutralised. Aside from these pure military motives, there were also objectives around what was called the Greater East Asia Co-Prosperity Sphere, the idea being to "help" their Asian brothers and sisters by driving out the colonialists and replacing them with a Japanese government focused on emancipating the people of Asia. Their activities in China, however, demonstrated a less altruistic intention.

Singapore was mostly untouched for another eight days. There was another attack on the airbase RAF Tengah in the west on the night of 16th December 1941 by two Mitsubishi Ki-21s aircraft, but the wheels of war in Malaya were mostly rolling far to the north. And the news from up there was disturbing. Just two days after the first air raid, two naval ships, dispatched by the British to deter the Japanese from attacking, were sunk off the coast of Kuantan. The sinking of the HMS *Prince of Wales* and the HMS *Repulse*, with the loss of eight hundred and forty British sailors, was not good news at all and was seen as the first signs of chinks in the invincibility of the British Empire's ability to defend its subjects. As the days went by it became apparent that the Japanese were making significant progress down the peninsula. Uneasiness built among the populace.

Bombings on Singapore recommenced on the night of 29th December, and from then on became a nightly occurrence. From 12th January 1942, as Japanese ascendancy continued to rise, they had the confidence to begin daytime air raids. Things were getting critical for Singapore. The death toll was rising into the thousands, and the ensuing chaos was beginning to reduce the overall security around the island.

Kembangan Hill, while being relatively safe from the bombings, saw a rising atmosphere of nervousness. Stray bombs from raids on RAF Kallang had struck nearby Kampong Katong. Furthermore, while having a secure food supply from the grounds of their property, concerns were mounting over the future availability of other staples like rice, oil, and cooking fuel. Clarence's family started to stock up reserves of these basic items, as did everyone else around the island.

Before long, the Japanese were closing in on Johor. Once they had secured the northern beaches of the Johor Strait, they would be in a position to launch their final assault on Singapore. To slow their advance, the British blew up the Causeway joining the island to the Malaya mainland. This would necessitate that the enemy cross the waters of the Straits of Johor separating Singapore and Johor by at most one mile for much of its length, by boats and rafts. But it would only slow the advance; it would not stop it.

On the evening of 8th February 1942 the land-based attack on Singapore began. For the next seven days the island became a battlefield. British and Allied forces made up of Australian, Indian and local Singapore soldiers were being decimated. Civilian casualties were rising at alarming rates. Distribution of food and water was becoming impeded. The Japanese were inching closer and closer to the city centre and before long had gained control of the all important water reservoirs. Within seven days, there was little choice open to the British commanders holed up in a bunker on Fort Canning near the civic centre of Singapore.

On 15th February 1942 Singapore, the Impregnable Fortress, the Gibraltar of the East, the central trading hub of South East Asia, fell. The British surrendered to Japan. What had been for 124 years the pride of Britain in the Far East, the land of tennis, bridge, and sundowners, had become, in the words of then British Prime Minister Winston Churchill, the "worst disaster and largest capitulation in British history".[6]

More damaging long-term for the British Empire, was that the perception of their invincibility had been shattered forever.

For the Peranakan Chinese, and all Chinese, the Lunar New Year is the most important festival of the year. It is traditionally a time of great joy and celebration, a time for visiting family and friends. Fate could not have delivered a worse blow than to place the surrender on the first day of Chinese New Year. On this day, of all days, one avoids work and negative activity in the belief that doing so would cause bad luck for the new year ahead. The capitulation to the Japanese on this most auspicious day was to set the tone for the horrors of not just the following year, but for the next three and a half.

---

6   Bishop, P. (2005, May 29) *The largest capitulation in our history*. Retrieved from www.telegraph. co.uk/culture/books/3642865/The-largest-capitulation-in-our-history.html

It did not take long for Japanese rule to be realised. Soon after the surrender the family saw defeated British, Australian, and Indian troops being marched along Changi Road, at the southern end of their property, headed for Changi Prison. Prisoners of war. The soldiers looked tired, hungry and deflated. They had been fighting for weeks with very little rest. In some ways perhaps there was a sense of relief in their eyes as they marched, away from the terror of the front line fighting that they had endured since early December. And in some ways they did enjoy a respite as the first few weeks of their internment were not too bad. Food and medicine were provided and they were reasonably well treated. However, any light of hope they may have had were quickly extinguished soon thereafter.

Indicators of harsh times ahead for the civilian population began to percolate throughout the island with the news of atrocities being committed by Japanese soldiers. Before the surrender, the Japanese had massacred more than 150 doctors, nurses, and patients at Alexander Hospital, a grim prelude of what the invaders were capable of. If even the sick, the dying, and their caregivers could be treated in such a way, then what of the others?

As Clarence, now thirteen months old, jovially ran laughing to his mother in the garden under the hot sunshine on that first day of the Chinese New Year, a tear came to the Matriarch's eye. She contemplated how happy this child was because he knew so little. As the head of the family she worried greatly about what the future may hold for him and for all under her roof. Everyone knew how the Chinese had been treated by Japanese soldiers in China and there was no reason to think they would be any different here in Singapore. As a community, the Peranakan Chinese would be indistinguishable from the more recently arrived Chinese in Malaya. So even though their connections to China were a distant memory, the Japanese would not be able to tell the difference. Today of all days she felt the need to pray to the ancestors to ask them to watch over the family. And so she did.

The day following the surrender, Singapore was renamed Syonan-To, meaning "Light of the South". To the Japanese, it was to be a beacon of hope for the new Asia. To rapidly suppress any forms of resistance to this beacon, the first of two main horrors to afflict the local population began.

For many years prior to 1942, tensions had been high between Japan and China. This had culminated in the commencement of the Second Sino-Japanese War in 1937. The Japanese were therefore highly suspicious of the loyalties of the Chinese in Singapore, especially given many Chinese still felt a strong tie to their homeland and had provided material and financial support to their comrades' war effort. The Japanese thus undertook a systematic process of eliminating potential undesirables – the Sook Ching Massacre.[7]

Chinese residents were picked up all over the island and taken to screening centres. They were mostly men aged between eighteen and fifty, though sometimes women and children were screened. Individuals were indiscriminately singled out as anti-Japanese and stamped with a triangular mark on their arms. This stamp was their death sentence. The fortunate ones were given a square stamp[8] or a piece of paper indicating that they had been "examined". This was a pass to life. For those with the triangular stamp, the next steps were swift, efficient, and brutal. Waiting trucks at the screening stations took them to remote locations around the island, where they were executed by firing squads.

One of the locations was Siglap Beach, very near to Kembangan Hill. The family would have surely been able to hear the sickening burst of machine gun fire, not long after trucks full of terrified Chinese eyes had rumbled past the southern end of their property.

---

7   The Chinese term, "sook ching", means "a purge through cleansing". The Japanese term for the process was "kakyoshukusei", which has the even more chilling meaning of "purging of Chinese". The term accurately represented its mission.

8   The square stamp on the body had its complications as it would wear off before too long. To delay this process the recipients avoided washing until they received a paper version.

Everyone was scared. No one was exempt from this process. Hood Hin himself was a prime target. Being a civil servant, therefore an employee of the British, he was most likely one of the undesirables that the Japanese wanted to eliminate. He and the family were fully aware of this as he was taken away to a nearby centre for screening. Before he left, he held Connie, Cecilia, and Clarence close and looked them in the eye. He gently placed his hand on Daisy's newly pregnant tummy, as she and the Matriarch tried to hold back their tears. Kissing them goodbye, he implored them to be strong. To speak of death is a big pantang for the Peranakans. So to imply that Hood Hin and his brother may not return would certainly cast a dark shadow on the men as they walked down the dirt driveway, away from the house.

The women broke down in tears. Daisy ran inside and hid herself in her room. Confused, her three children ran after her. Upon finding their mother overcome with grief, they probably asked her what the matter was. How would one answer such a question?

It would be two long nights before the badly beaten frame of Hood Hin hobbled back up the driveway to the house. For those two nights the family had kept vigil in front of the altars, praying that he would be returned to them. His brothers had thankfully returned earlier with papers indicating they had been cleared. Not Hood Hin, however. He had not been given a triangular stamp, but was taken away in another truck. No one knew where the truck went, and the natural thing was to assume the worst.

For some reason though, he was lucky. Perhaps his humble role as a clerk in the less contentious Public Works Department meant he was not of concern. However, lucky for him simply meant no execution. Instead, he was badly beaten at the YMCA Building that had been turned into the headquarters of the notorious Kempeitai, the Japanese Military Police. But he was alive, and that was the most important thing.

For Daisy, this was not her only brush with tragedy. Her brother was an early victim of the Sook Chin brutality. His crime was being a local Singaporean who had fought for the British Army as a volunteer. While many other local soldiers had taken off their uniforms, put on sarongs, and went back to the kampong to hide their collusion with the British, he had refused. Pride told him to leave his uniform on. The family never knew exactly what happened to him, but he had been sighted boarding a truck bound for Pasir Panjang Beach. He was never seen again.

The Sook Ching Massacre was as swift as it was brutal. On 3rd March 1942 it officially came to an end. No one knows for sure how many were killed. The official Kempeitai records indicate five thousand. Others put the figures much higher at between twenty-five and fifty thousand. Regardless, the massacre had not only achieved the intended purpose of routing out potential resistance to the new occupiers, but also instilled an enduring fear into the local population that gave the Japanese the control they desired.

Although the screening was officially over, it was by no means the end of random beatings and murders by Japanese soldiers on the streets of Singapore. Something as simple as not showing your passport, the papers indicating that you had passed the screening, was enough to trigger a violent response. So the Matriarch was always making sure that no one left home without his or her passport. Even returning home late without informing her was a major source of fear, and those who did were duly scolded.

The Japanese may have been well aware that controlling people's food meant controlling people, and from day one of the occupation, they began rationing such items as rice and sugar, as well as other basic necessities like soap and matchsticks. The food shortages hit everyone, regardless of race. For many, the imminent pangs of hunger would become the most enduring memory of Japanese rule.

There was actually plenty of rice available, all shipped in from Thailand, but much of it was kept in reserve and only made available in adequate quantities to the Japanese soldiers and local sympathisers. To control the distribution of food every family was provided with a ration card stipulating how much of the basics they were allowed. Five kilograms of rice per adult per month, to begin with. It was generally low quality rice too: often filthy, contaminated with stones, dirt, and lice. But such was the hunger there was no luxury to throw it away; after two years the ration was reduced further.

Clarence's family were fortunate, for they were farming a portion of their land. Hunger for them was not a major problem. But they did need rice and other basics, so early every morning Daisy made her way down to the market to pick up their rations. As rice became scarcer, the family was able to grow root crops such as tapioca to supplement their diet. For many in Singapore and Malaya tapioca became such a staple that many creative dishes, still popular today, were borne out of the need to use up the root in various ways.

Most people, however, had to rely entirely on the rations for all their food and essential supplies, especially those living in the city. Those with even a small piece of land would turn it into a garden, but it was rarely enough. Stories of people staving off hunger by eating tree bark, and scavenging in the fields and amongst rubbish were common.

It was the Grow More Food Campaign that was to have the greatest direct effect on Clarence's family. The Japanese figured that Britain would want Malaya back and hence blockade the region to prevent food from getting through. To counter this, Japan wanted Singapore and Malaya to become self-sufficient. Everyone was therefore encouraged to grow their own food, and spare tracts of land all over the island were turned into vegetable gardens. School fields were turned into gardens, and horticulture was added to the school curriculum. Even the hallowed Padang in the city was turned into a garden. And before long it was the turn of the rubber plantations of Siglap, Frankel, and Kembangan.

Tears would surely have welled in the eyes of the Matriarch as she stood stoically on the balcony of the house, with her family around her, and watched as the first trees were felled. British and Australian prisoners-of-war had been brought in by Japanese guards to clear her land of trees and to turn it into a vegetable garden. Memories of her husband working on the plantation grounds came flooding back to her. Perhaps more than anything during the Japanese occupation, it was watching his hard work being destroyed in front of her that would have broken her heart most. How was she to support the family now?

Once the land, including the neighbouring plantations, was cleared, strangers from around the island were brought in to work it. The whole area became one big vegetable garden. Tapioca, sweet potato, yam, and corn were the main crops. They grew easily in the soils of Malaya and Singapore and unlike rice, which would only yield one crop per year, were able to produce up to three or four crops annually.

Contrary to the Japanese intentions, the Grow More Food Campaign was a failure. Socialist-sounding slogans such as "The farmers rank first among mankind" and "Shoulder your hoe and march forward into the field" were not going to turn an urban population into farmers. In 1944, with the tide of the war beginning to turn, the Japanese were growing nervous, and the relatively soft tactics used up until then to coerce the population into farming were not producing enough food. The Japanese reduced rations further and started creating farming communes in Malaya to which groups of Singaporeans were sent. Around 3,000 Eurasians, including many family and friends of Daisy, were sent to Bahau in the state of Negeri Sembilan. But even these communes failed. Like the Peranakans, the Eurasians were an urban people. They had no skills in farming. And they would suffer for it, with between 500 and 700 of them dying, generally due to diet-related issues.

There were other hardships that everyone had to deal with. Schools were disrupted. There was very little work. There was always the fear of encountering Japanese soldiers and being beaten, or even bayoneted or shot, for something as arbitrary as not bowing correctly as they walked past. The shortage of food and basic necessities caused massive inflation, resulting in a black market to bypass the banana currency that the Japanese had introduced. Shoes became hard to come by, so many people walked around barefoot. Dates were converted to the Japanese dating system, with 1943 becoming 2603, and the clocks were changed to Tokyo time, a difference of one hour.

Then there were the Allied POWs at the Changi Prison. No one really knew what was going on there at the time, but news of their suffering would sometimes leak out. The POWs were often used for labour around the island. At first they seemed fine. But over time it became apparent that the food shortages were hitting them badly too. Daisy's brother-in-law was interned at the camp for the duration of the war, and it was three and a half anxious years before they would learn that he was still alive. Clarence remembered in the years after the war how this uncle growled at the children if they left even a few grains of rice uneaten at the end of a meal: such a senseless waste of food. These men were forever scarred by their experiences in the prison.

––––––––––

On 30th October 1944, three-year-old Clarence was outside playing with his cousins when his father picked him up and pointed to the sky. "Look," he urged the boy. Way up high they could clearly make out an aircraft. Clarence peered up curiously and said it must be a small Japanese plane. Realising that this plane was different, Hood Hin said no, this was something bigger and higher than they had ever seen before.

To see an aircraft so high in the skies was unusual. Japanese military aircraft were often flying in and out of nearby Kallang airport, but never so high before. And this plane was bigger. Rumours began to spread. Could this be the British coming back? News had trickled through the population, from people listening to the BBC World Service on illegal radios, that since May 1944 the US air force had added a new powerful bomber aircraft to their arsenal. This B-29 Superfortress was a large four-engine propeller aircraft that could fly higher and faster than most of the Japanese fighters. Could this sighting be the Americans starting reconnaissance of the island? Their speculation was right. A few days later, at dawn on 5th November, 53 Superfortresses dropped bombs in the vicinity of the naval base at Sembawang in the north. They had flown from their bases nearly 3,000km away near Kharagpur, in north-eastern India – which meant a total distance of 6,000km back and forth. It was an incredible achievement for airplanes of that time.

A sense of hope crept back into people's lives. Perhaps a rescue was near at hand? The bombing had been highly accurate and focused on military targets, which added to people's confidence. It was apparent that, in the Superfortress, the Allies had a weapon that the Japanese had no answer to.

As it turned out they would have to be patient for the arrival of freedom. Bombing and mine-laying raids around the harbour did not occur again until January 1945. Only then did they become more regular. Morale rose among the people, unaffected by the weak Japanese propaganda around the very few bombers that the Japanese managed to shoot down.

It was two very significant events around 4,500km to the north east on 6th and 9th August 1945 that finally brought an end to three and a half years of misery – the atomic bombings of Hiroshima and Nagasaki. Five days after the Nagasaki bomb, on 15th August 1945, Japan surrendered to the Allies.

———————

Once again Clarence looked to the skies curiously as his sisters played on the porch of the main house, avoiding the afternoon sun. His attention had been grabbed by an aircraft with British markings flying low over the property. Out the back of it he could see what looked like confetti fluttering down in the afternoon breeze. He excitedly told his sisters and the children ran outside with squeals of excitement, jumping at and chasing after what turned out to be small paper leaflets floating down around them. After missing a few that evaded his outstretched arms, Clarence caught one and looked at it with confusion. At four and a half years old he was not yet able to read. By then Hood Hin and Daisy and the rest of the household had rushed out onto the veranda to see what the commotion was all about. Clarence ran to his father, showed him the pieces of paper, and anxiously asked what it was. Hood Hin took the leaflet and read it. He looked over to the Matriarch and Daisy, tears welling in his eyes. Half suspecting what the content said, the Matriarch whispered, "Is it over?"

Walking over to her and holding her close, Hood Hin said yes. The Japanese had surrendered.

The tearful Matriarch pulled Daisy, who had perhaps suffered more personal loss than anyone else in the family, into their embrace. The confused children milled around the trio, who were soon hugging them, smiling and laughing through their tears.

It was over.

———————

With *The Straits Times* quickly back in production under its own name,[9] the headline of its first post-occupation issue on 7th September 1945 read "Singapore is British Again!" Crowds from all over the island joined the triumphant celebrations surrounding the signing of the Instrument of Surrender by the Japanese at the Municipal Hall (now the National Gallery Singapore) and cheered the returning British and Australian forces marching through the city.

Syonan-To, "Light of the South", was supposed to be a beacon for the new Asia. A light for a region free of colonial chains. They were, however, the darkest days in Singapore's history. It was a period that many of that generation would never forgive the Japanese for, and many would also resent the British for failing to protect them. While there was much jubilation among the population that the British had returned, the colonial masters would not be back for long. The war had sown the seeds for independence.

---

9   Publication of *The Straits Times* stopped during the occupation. The Japanese took over the same offices and published a paper called *The Shonan Times*, which was later renamed to *The Syonan Shimbun*.

Chapter 4
The New Year

As the mid-afternoon sun began its descent, the Matriarch stepped out onto the balcony. The rest of the adults were still enjoying a siesta, so, apart from a few of the children playing quietly in the garden, she could enjoy a few moments alone. She surveyed her land to the south. The once proud rubber plantation built by her husband was gone, replaced by vegetable gardens all the way to Changi Road, and now alive with squatters. Some had been moved here as part of the Grow More Food Campaign, and others had more recently arrived from the city centre to escape the infrastructure hardships there. Unlike her original tenants, the Chinese farmers and Malay rubber tappers whom she had known for years, these new people on her land were strangers. Another reminder of the occupation just over.

It was 1st February 1946, the first day of Chinese New Year. For the Chinese, including the Peranakan Chinese, in the region, this was not just the start of a new year, but a new chapter for a people affected so harshly by the Japanese occupation. As the Matriarch surveyed her land, many of the scars, and not just those apparent on the land before her eyes, were still raw. But at least that chapter was now closed. All the bad luck had been swept away in the past few days. And with the opening of the front door earlier that morning, a new hope and the promise of good luck had entered into the family home on Kembangan Hill.

While the Peranakans had diverged in many ways from their Chinese heritage, Chinese New Year was still very similar in form to that celebrated by Chinese the world over. Preparations on Kembangan Hill had begun almost a week earlier on the twenty-fourth day of the twelfth month of the Lunar Year. On this day, known as Xiao Guo Nian or Little New Year, the household deities, most importantly the Kitchen God Zao Jun, reported to the Jade Emperor, Yu Huang, on the family's activities over the previous year. To please Zao Jun, special food was provided for him at his altar in the kitchen before he left to make his report. With this bribe of glutinous rice and brown sugar the family hoped to ensure that Zao Jun could not make too lengthy a report by gumming up his mouth with the sticky rice and sweetening his words with the sugar. As the deities headed off to present their household reports, celebratory firecrackers were set off in the yard to bid them farewell, much to the children's delight.

Once this celebration had been completed the spring-cleaning of the household began. While the season of spring does not exist in the tropics, its significance was well understood in Singapore. Over the next few days the entire homestead was cleaned inside out. More important than simply tidying the place up, the process ensured that any bad luck was swept away so that good luck could come in freely with the arrival of the New Year. The house was decorated with artificial flowers, and important parts, specifically all entrances including the door and window frames, received a fresh coat of red paint. This colour would scare away any evil deities or bad luck that may be looking to enter the house over this period. Special attention was given to cleaning the kitchen and the altars of both the ancestors and deities, with last year's decorations being replaced with new ones. This was not a time of the year that Clarence and the other children particularly looked forward to, as they knew they would be roped in to help out. The cleaning was all completed by the eve of the New Year, after which all the brooms were put away. Heaven forbid if anyone should pick up a broom accidentally on the first day of the New Year. In doing so they might accidentally sweep away the good luck that had just entered the house.

On the eve of Chinese New Year, the Matriarch, Daisy, the ama chay, and all of Clarence's aunties prepared the food for the Reunion Dinner to be held later that night. Living on a farm meant that many of the important ingredients for the feast were easily available, including pork, a very important meat at this time, which would find its way to the table in numerous forms. For much of the population around the region pork was still hard to come by in these months following the Japanese occupation. The Reunion Dinner is the most important meal of the year. If there was one annual meal that everyone had to be home for, then this was it. All the sons were expected to be at the home of their parents, with their wives and children in tow. With the entire family living under one roof, this order was already in place for the family on Kembangan Hill. (In years to come, as he got older and eager to venture out with friends, Clarence would learn of the nagging associated with ensuring that everyone was back in time for this meal.) The gaiety of the occasion was one that everyone looked forward to, so everyone was generally home in time. It was a great chance to reminisce about the events of the last year and to talk about hopes for the future.

No one was to be left out of the reunion meal, including the ancestors and the deities. So that afternoon a thanksgiving prayer specific to the occasion was first offered to them to ask for the safe passing of the previous year. They were then offered a selection of the foods that the family were to share later that night, along with some fruit tea and flowers, placed upon their respective altars. A separate table was also set up with food offerings for the wandering souls, those spirits who had no home. These were the "Good Brothers" who had died with no family to look after them. Their spirits were believed to be roaming around with no roof to rest under so it was considered a charitable act to feed them at this festive time.

Once the deities and ancestors had completed their meals, the food upon their altars was returned to the kitchen to be re-cooked along with the rest of the Reunion Dinner food. How did the family know that the eating was finished? Simple. Every now and then someone would return to the altars and throw two coins. When two heads turned up, that was the sign that the spirits had all had their fill.

When the food was ready and everyone was home, the great Reunion Dinner feast began. Given the large contingent present they would all have to take their turn in the dining room beside the kitchen: the men folk first, followed by the women and children.

———————

Upon completion of the Reunion Dinner, the final preparations for the arrival of the new year began. With no electric lights, life normally slowed down a lot after dark, so most evenings of the year saw the children in bed quite early. On the eve of Chinese New Year however all the children were allowed to stay up late. In fact, since it was believed that their staying up until midnight would lead to long life for both the children and their parents, the kids were actively encouraged to stay up. It was almost a moral duty. For a five-year-old Clarence and his cousins there was of course no hardship in this as they ran around chasing each other inside and outside the house.

The Chinese New Year Eve festivities ended late in the night with the closing of the main door. This was a very important and significant event. If not performed at the right time then bad luck was sure to flow into the house before the arrival of the New Year. The Matriarch was very particular about this. Therefore the great Chinese Almanac, a book that every family had a copy of, was referred to in order to determine the exact timing at which the door should be closed. After the door was closed no one was allowed to enter through it. Any movement into and out of the house after this time had to be made by the back door.

With this formality completed, it was time to head off to bed to await the arrival of the new year. As the mothers gathered the children into their rooms, the men lit all the lamps around the house and closed all the other doors and windows. This way they could be certain that the evil spirits would not dare to enter the house on this most auspicious night.

Perhaps even more ritualised than the closing of the door was its opening the following morning. Everyone had risen very early on this first morning of Chinese New Year to ensure that they were all washed and dressed in the new clothes bought specifically for the occasion. These clothes were always red, or at least with an obvious red component to it, so as to keep the evil spirits away, especially from the children, who were particularly preyed upon. The new clothes and also new haircuts represented a fresh start. This was the best-dressed day of the year for the family. Everyone's hair was in place, shoes were shining, and not a stitch was out. To be anything less would have been a great disgrace to the gods and the ancestors, and to the Matriarch.

Once everyone was ready, the entire family of the Matriarch, her five children, and twelve grandchildren – including Clarence's new younger brothers, Kim Chuan, (Colin, born in 1943) and Kim Swee (Carlton, a newborn) – gathered in the large front room of the main house. At the auspicious time, once again determined by the almanac, the Matriarch lifted the wooden lock and opened the door, letting the new light of the new year enter, accompanied by the deities of the heavens and earth and good luck.

Following the grand opening they all paid homage to the heads of the household. First, with three joss sticks in hand, everyone prayed at the altar of the deities, then that of the ancestors. The Matriarch first, followed by the men, then the women and children. A procession was then made around the house with incense, using a crucible of burning sandalwood. Symbolic money was then burnt in offering to the ancestors to ensure that they had enough to spend in the other world. Firecrackers were also let off, once again to ensure the evil spirits were scared away during this auspicious day.

The final formality of the morning was for the family to pay their respects to the living head of the household, the Matriarch. For this, she took her place in a special chair in the centre of the main room, and one by one everyone greeted her by kneeling down at her feet, clasping her hands, wishing her "Gong He Fatt Choy", Cantonese for Happy New Year, or "Panjang Panjang Umur", the Malay wish for a long life. Hood Hin first, then the other men, then the women, then the children. For the children, this was an exciting time as they would each get an ang bao, a red envelope containing a gift of money. This was intended as a blessing and a wish for a smooth year ahead. Of course this deeper meaning was no doubt lost on the young Clarence and the other children, as it most likely was on your younger selves, Emma and Luke.

With this formality completed chaos broke out as everyone began wishing each other a happy new year. Hugs and handshakes and ang bao were exchanged amongst the entire family. Clarence, like all the unmarried children, was especially diligent in greeting all the married adults as it meant receiving an ang bao from them too.

And then it was down to the dinning room for breakfast, which included a number of snacks more common around Chinese New Year, such as cookies, pineapple tarts, and love letters.

In years to come, when the family had enough money to buy a car, after breakfast they would bundle into it and drive to the Bukit Brown cemetery to visit the grave of the Matriarch's husband. It was always a special moment for Clarence to see his name, Tan Kim Peng, on his grandfather's headstone. After paying homage to the grave, Hood Hin would take Clarence around the graveyard and tell him the stories of some of the other characters buried there.

After this excursion they headed back home for more food and drink and rest. The first day was very much a family-only day. Visiting others

Clarence and one of his cousins, Kim Cheong, at the graves of
their mutual grandparents, at Bukit Brown Cemetry. Ong Leong
Neo (the Matriarch) is resting on the left, while her husband,
Tan Teck Yam, rests on the right. Between their graves, you can
just make out the stone that contains the names of Clarence and
other family members.

and receiving guests could not happen on the first day of the new year –
that was reserved for the next few days. And no work could be performed
either as to do so would result in one working for the rest of their life.
Many other pantangs were applicable on this first day, such as how it was
bad luck to break something or use a sharp knife.

The Chinese New Year celebration is a fifteen-day affair with each day
having its own significance. The first day, including the Reunion Dinner
on the eve, was by far the most important. It was about the immediate
family (the paternal side), so everyone stayed put at their homes, unless
they were visiting the graves of their ancestors. The second day was about
heading out and visiting the maternal side of the family. So early the next
morning Clarence and his family set off on foot to visit Daisy's parents.
Their cousins headed off to the homes of their respective maternal
grandparents. The Matriarch remained at home, awaiting visits from her
married daughters and their families. Her one unmarried daughter and
the ama chay stayed at home with her, helping to accommodate visitors.

Daisy's family home was not too far from Kembangan Hill, perhaps a kilometre or so. Walking along the unshaded dirt road in the tropical heat, all dressed up, would not have been the most comfortable of experiences. But the kids walked everywhere anyway, so it was not too much of a big deal for them. The anticipation of more ang bao and playing with their maternal cousins, and the occasional crackle of noisy firecrackers along the way added to the children's excitement.

It would have been a beautiful sight seeing families walking the streets all over the island dressed in their new clothes. The Chinese women in their elegant cheongsams, with their men in silk tunics and trousers; the Peranakan women in their equally graceful and beautifully embroidered sarong kebayas, and their men in either the Chinese-styled tunic and trousers or the Western jacket, shirt, tie, and trousers. The sarong kebaya is another classic example of the marriage of the Chinese and Malay cultures. Similar in style to the blouses and sarongs worn by Malay women, both sarong and kebaya are embellished with elaborately embroidered Chinese images, with the kebaya in lighter fabric and often more revealing than their Malay counterparts. While the sarong kebaya was everyday wear for many Peranakan women at the time, those worn at Chinese New Year were far more elegant and elaborate.

Once they arrived at the home of Daisy's parents, Clarence and his siblings, led by their parents, greeted their maternal grandparents sitting on the central chairs, in the same fashion as the previous morning. And sure enough, once they had been handed their ang bao they all eagerly rushed off for a day of playing and eating with another set of cousins, before returning home in the late afternoon.

By the end of the first two days, the lack of sleep and the long days of eating, drinking and playing will have taken their toll on the entire family. So thankfully it was considered bad luck to go visiting on this day. The third day was a day of rest.

Then on the fourth day, the visiting started all over again. Sometimes Clarence and the family would visit others. Sometimes visitors would come to Kembangan Hill. As the ancestral altar in their home contained the tablets of two generations, the house had to be made open to any guests wishing to pay their respects. It was the Matriarch's duty to be around to greet them, so she would always remain at home during these fifteen days. Over the entire period a multitude of uncles and aunts, cousins, friends, and colleagues would come by to visit the ancestors and family on Kembangan Hill. The guests were not just Chinese and Peranakan. Malaya had been a multi-cultural mix for many generations now and it was not uncommon to receive visits from friends and colleagues of other cultures and religions during this time. While the primary purpose of these visits was to pay respects to the ancestors at the altar, it also provided a chance for Clarence and his family to catch up with distant relatives whom they had not seen over the last year, and in some cases to meet ones they had never met before. It was also a chance to indulge in the numerous snacks that Daisy and Clarence's aunties had laboriously prepared earlier: pineapple tarts, love letters, prawn crackers, prawn rolls, and many other traditional biscuits and kueh (traditional Peranakan cakes).

For the Peranakans, aside from days one and two of the Chinese New Year period, only two others were of significant importance. The ninth day was the Birthday of the Jade Emperor, one of the most important gods of the Chinese religious pantheon. For some Hokkien Chinese this day is considered more important than the first. With many Chinese in Singapore being Hokkien, many of the Peranakans in Singapore are also of Hokkien ancestry. Given this connection, the ninth day was important for the family on Kembangan Hill, and special prayers were offered to the Jade Emperor on this day. However, it was not considered by the Peranakans to be more important than the first day.

The final day, the fifteenth, is known as Chap Gor Mei. The significance of it as the Chinese equivalent to Valentine's Day would have been lost on the young Clarence. But it was still a fun and joyous end to the festivities. The family would head down to the Singapore River in the city to watch the floats, while young singles would eye each other up and try to meet potential partners under the full moon, under the watchful eyes of their parents. Of course.

Standing again on the balcony of the last afternoon of Chinese New Year in 1946, the Matriarch's thoughts moved to the future as she shifted her gaze to the children playing happily on the dirt ground just in front of the bungalow. Her eyes teared as a smile appeared on her face. Tears for the hard years, the chapter just closed. A smile for the new year, the hope of new life just beginning.

But there was much work to be done. The Matriarch's most immediate concern was how to support her family with the loss of the income from rubber. Turning to Clarence, who had joined her on the balcony, she put her hand on his shoulder and said, "We need to rebuild this place for your stewardship, my dear boy."

Alas, the building of Singapore would take precedence over that family goal in years to come. With the island back in British hands, the process of getting Singapore back on its feet was already well underway. It would take a good five years before life on the island returned to pre-war levels. But at least there was no longer any fear of violence or starvation.

The period immediately following the surrender had been a tumultuous time. The days between Japan's surrender on 15th August 1945 and the return of the British on 12th September 1945 were fairly lawless, with looting and revenge killings of Japanese collaborators, who were hated by many of the local population. The Japanese were tasked by the British to maintain law and order until the British could get their own house in order and send their own troops and police. But any respect the Japanese had garnered during their occupation had been based purely on fear. With this swept away, all respect for them disappeared immediately and so did their control of the population. When the British troops returned, the Japanese were put to work on civil projects around the island before they were repatriated to Japan, helping to re-build much of what they had destroyed. This irony was not lost on the local population.

The squatters now living on the property had left the city centre as much of the infrastructure had been destroyed there. In some ways they were refugees in their own country. Their presence had given Hood Hin a new job as a landlord collecting rent and managing the upkeep of their altered land. Like many, Hood Hin had not worked during the occupation, so the arrival of the squatters had its benefits. And with no income from the felled rubber trees, the rental was to become an important new revenue stream to support the family. Many essentials were still in short supply as much of the world's production was still getting back on its feet. But things were slowly getting back to normal.

―――――――

In the now famous words of Lee Kuan Yew, independent Singapore's first Prime Minister, at the second of a series of radio talks in 1961 titled "Battle for Merger": "My colleagues and I are of that generation of young men who went through the Second World War and the Japanese occupation and emerged determined that no one – neither the Japanese nor the British – had the right to push and kick us around. We were determined that we could govern ourselves and bring up our children in a country where we can be proud to be a self-respecting people."[10]

10 One recording, at 5 minutes and 5 seconds, can be found here: www.nas.gov.sg/archivesonline/ audiovisual_records/record-details/508e51ca-1164-11e3-83d5-0050568939ad

Chapter 5
Kampong Kid

One lazy morning, Connie (nine), Cecilia (seven), and Clarence (five) left the family room, leaving their younger siblings fast asleep with their parents. They made their way down the stairs and out to the dining room attached to the kitchen. The stray dogs that had made the homestead their home were lying outside the kitchen. The family often fed the leftover food to these dogs, who provided some security for the family by barking at strangers near the premises, much to the consternation of the postman who had learnt to ring the bell at the gate before entering the property. Aside from feeding them, the family never really engaged or played with the dogs, but they never chased them away either.

A number of the younger cousins soon joined the three siblings in the dining room. After breakfast, the kids headed outside to enjoy another day of play. The older girls suggested they play Teng Teng, also known as hopscotch. The younger kids eagerly agreed. Clarence then set about etching the court into the hard clay ground using a stick. Teng Teng was a simple game that even the younger kids could join in. Using small stones as their markers, the kids took turns throwing the stones and hopping through the squares, to the cheers of the other children standing by.

After some time Clarence became bored. Teng Teng, while generally enjoyed by everyone, was more of a girl's game as far as he was concerned. He was looking for something a bit more adventurous. So, he headed off to visit the Boyanese boys in the pondok down the hill at the southern end of the estate.

The Boyanese kids were the children of the labourers who had worked on the family's rubber plantation before the Japanese occupation. After the trees had been cut down there was no more work for them but the Matriarch let them stay on the land. Where were they to go anyway? These men were ethnically Malay, from the small Indonesian island of Bawean about 160km north of Surabaya in east Java. They had migrated to Malaya, and particularly Singapore, to work as labourers and often married into the local Malay population. They tended to stay in these pondoks, which were self-contained communities, where they provided support amongst themselves. When the British returned, the Boyanese men supported their families by doing odd jobs as chauffeurs, gardeners, or general labourers. Hood Hin employed some of them on an ad hoc basis to help around the homestead and the wider estate: fetching water from the wells, cleaning the longkang, or harvesting the coconut from trees left on the estate. It was always odd jobs. No monthly salary. Theirs was a simple village life in the pondok. But they were a satisfied people. Especially the kids, who just wanted to play outside. And now, that was all that Clarence wanted to do too.

As he approached the pondok Clarence noticed that his Boyanese friends were already outside. One of them, Hamid, said they were preparing to catch some birds, and invited Clarence to join them. Whoa, that sounded like a lot more fun than playing Teng Teng. This was the kind of action that Clarence was after.

Catching birds with these guys was a game of skill, patience, and cunning. The boys already had in their possession two lovebirds, one male and one female. This morning they were going to use the "game of love" to capture a second male lovebird. To begin the process the boys gathered some gum from one of the few remaining rubber trees, a cempedak tree and a terap tree, that were dotted around their pondok. They then mixed the three gums together to make a soft, gooey glue. The resulting sticky mixture was rolled over the length of a stick, leaving a portion at one end clear. The female bird, which was already domesticated, was placed on the gum-free end of the stick. The stick, with the female, was then placed up in a nearby tree. One end of the stick had a hook on it, which was used to attach it to the tree, and a separate pole was used to lift the stick up into place. The male bird was placed in a cage at the bottom of the tree from where he sang songs for his love. Had he not been placed in the cage he would have flown to his lover. And therein lay the cunning. Other male birds in the area would hear these two lovers singing to each other and try their hand at competing for the female. The boys then retreated about ten metres, and quietly crouched by some bushes on the ground. Then they watched and waited.

Sure enough, before long a male lovebird started joining in the chorus of love songs. He flew onto the same tree but higher up, as if to evaluate the competition and assess his plan of attack. As he sat there, taking his time to see if the caged male was going to pose a threat to his advances, the boys watched anxiously from below. The free male started to make his move, fluttering and hopping closer, bit by bit, to his potential love. Eventually their prey made his final valiant flight, landing on the gum-covered stick right next to his new love. He was stuck.

Quickly and quietly, Hamid ran to the tree, lowered the stick using the pole, and placed his new captive into a small cage before he had any chance to wrestle himself from the clutches of the gum.

Clarence was impressed. It was his first time bird-catching, and he loved it. Soon thereafter he began mixing his own glue and catching birds as a hobby by himself. He enjoyed it so much that, in time, his dad built an aviary for him to place all his captives in. At three metres square and just over a metre tall, it was a decent size. Over the next few years his hobbies would become more and more adventurous. With these Boyanese boys, the Chinese boys from the pig farm, his cousins, his uncles, his dad and friends at school, he would develop a lifetime passion for the outdoors.

Soon after they had secured their catch Clarence heard his name being called out from a little way back up the hill, in the direction of the homestead. It was Connie. She had been sent down with a message that Ah Soh (referring to the ama chay) needed some mangoes and papayas and their dad had deemed it his job. Clarence dutifully replied that he was on his way. When a request came in from Hood Hin, Daisy, the Matriarch, or even Ah Soh, it was acted on immediately. The homestead was surrounded by all kinds of fruit trees and it was the job of the boys to climb the trees and harvest the order of the day. As the boys enjoyed climbing trees, it was not considered too much of a chore.

Clarence decided to get the mangoes first as the tree was a simple one to climb with lots of branches. The papaya tree was another matter entirely. Like coconuts, the fruit of the papaya tree is found at the top of a tall, skinny, trunk. To get up to the fruit, Clarence placed his hands firmly on the opposite side of the trunk, then, with his feet on the side facing him, began climbing up like a monkey. Once he was within reach of the fruit, he locked himself into position by wrapping his legs around the tree, thus freeing his arms up to pick the ripest papayas. To climb down the tree with fruit in hand is a pretty impossible task, so he called out to Connie to catch them as he dropped them. He then climbed back down, picked up the mangoes, and followed his sister back to the kitchen, where Ah Soh was preparing lunch.

———————

After lunch the children continued to play games around the house. By mid-afternoon dark, cumulonimbus clouds were building in the northeastern sky, which meant that a thunderstorm was not too far off. Getting wet was not much of a concern for the kids; in fact they enjoyed playing around outside in the heavy tropical showers. No one died from the rain and stories of people being killed by direct hits from lightning were rare. More likely than that though was the risk of being hit by a falling branch of a tree that had itself been hit by lightning, which tended to occur more in these rural, tree-clad areas than in the cities where the taller buildings there would often take the brunt of such strikes. So when lightning was spotted, the call would go out for all the kids to come in. With the heavy rain and dark clouds, it became very dark indoors. There were no electric lights in the household at this time; all internal lighting came from the oil lamps that tended only to be lit at night. So during these storms the kids tended to head to the dining room for a drink and a snack, or to play a game of five stones (also known as knuckle bones), or other games on the veranda. More often than not the storms would pass quite quickly, maybe an hour or two, and before too long they would be back outside playing.

Playing outdoors in the dust, and sometimes the mud, and the heat, made for dirty and sweaty young bodies at the end of day. So before dinner the kids would head to a well to wash themselves. There were three wells around the homestead that provided the household with all its water needs. Two, away from the house and down the hill a little, were used for bathing. The third was near the house itself. Water from this one would be transferred to an earthen jar in the kitchen for drinking and cooking. The ground around the wells was cemented to prevent the inevitable muddiness, and each of the bathing wells was surrounded by an atap leaf fence to afford some privacy. It was the children who bathed at these outside wells. The adults opted for the greater privacy of the bak mandi tubs attached to their rooms.

Washing was a simple process. Each of the kids had their own bucket and would use these to draw water that they poured over their body. Bars of soap were kept by the well for bathing. Of course the water was never heated. As strange as it may seem, even in the tropics the well water could at times be surprisingly chilling.

The wells were not only about washing and cooking. The kids loved playing in and around them too. It was the closest they could get to having their own backyard swimming pool. In the tropical climate they provided a great respite from the heat of the day. After heavy rains the wells would fill to the top, and the children could not resist the temptation to jump in. The depth was well over their heads, around thirty or forty feet, so doing so was pretty risky. But with the beach nearby they had all learned how to look after themselves in the water. They all survived.

By the beginning of the 1950s, as Clarence approached ten years old, tap water supplied by the government began to appear around rural Singapore. At first families in the kampongs would share water from a cluster of centrally located taps. It was not until the late 1950s that the family was able to install pipes into the house itself using water from the government supply. Hence Clarence was reliant on the wells for all of his youth.

———————

These were carefree days. Fun days. Days of laughter, joy, mischief, and adventure. The rural setting gave Clarence and the other children the space, freedom, and time to enjoy themselves. Mostly they were free to do what they wished. There was little nagging from parents. It was normal for kids to climb trees, chase each other around and explore the estate without parental supervision. Sure, kids fell, knocked themselves, bruised and cut themselves. But that was life. More often than not such painful encounters would be addressed by a simple pat on the shoulder, and the kid would be off running around again.

As he grew older, Clarence's free time would become even more adventurous. Some days would be spent fishing down at the longkang. There were no fancy rods or bait though, just a line on the end of a bamboo stick hung out over the river bank, using a worm dug from the ground as bait. On other days, particularly during the windier months around August, the children might go kite flying.

For more ambitious fishing trips, Clarence and his brothers would walk with their father down to East Coast Beach to catch larger fish. If low tide was expected, they would grab some roots of the tubar trees growing on the hillside on their way down. With the low tide they could walk out to the coral reef just offshore where the fish were plentiful. Once there, they would squeeze the roots so that its juices fell into the reef, causing the fish to become drowsy. It was then an easy job for the kids to scoop the fish up with their nets. With much less shipping in the Straits of Malacca than there is now, the water was clear so they could easily see their prey. It was a far cry from the coastal waters off East Coast Beach today.

A real treat for Clarence was to join his father hunting and shooting flying foxes and birds at night around the property. The large estate was alive with avian life. "Honey suckles",[11] waterfowls, herons, doves, magpie-robins, sparrows, starlings, golden plovers, snipes – and lovebirds, of course. Some were local birds. Some were migratory, visiting from distant lands, such as the golden plovers and snipes coming in to escape the harsh Siberian winter. Of these, it was the waterfowls and green pigeons, both local Singapore birds, which were most likely to end up on the dinner table.

Sometimes the hunting was part of a seasonal culling exercise, to reduce the number of pests on the property, such as the flying foxes that came at night to eat the rambutan and durian flower nectar, or the civet cats that ate the fruit on the trees. Among the stray dogs hanging around the homestead there was one who would always join them on these pursuits. He was welcome as he made himself useful by finding the prey that fell to the ground after being hit by a pellet from the gun. When Clarence was old enough his dad let him have his first go at using it.

---

11 While there is a bird called the honey sucker (not honey suckle), it is not found in Singapore. It is likely what Clarence and his friends called honey suckles were actually sunbirds.

It was not just guns he learnt to use for shooting. One of Clarence's uncles, who also lived in the homestead with his wife and children, was a master of making catapults. His wife did not let her children play in the dirt so the uncle taught this art to Clarence instead. Together they would head off into the trees and hunt down "honey suckles" with this primitive, yet effective, improvised weapon. Clarence would end up hunting a lot with his brothers and cousins.

It was one activity, however, that he would later look back on with regret. "Such a beautiful small innocent bird. Not a pest. Not a meal. Just a target," he would lament.

Chapter 6
Off to School

At eight in the morning, standing still under the hot sun, the first day of school was all a bit strange to nine-year-old Clarence. Standing to attention, saying prayers, and singing "God Save the King" with the Union Jack, the British flag, flying overhead. He was familiar with the song and the flag. He had heard "God Save the King" regularly on the radio, as well as at the movie theatres where it was always played before the movies started, with an image of the Union Jack fluttering away on the screen. The movie-goers all stood then too. The prayers were strange though. Not similar at all to those the family said in front of the ancestral altar at home. References to Jesus? Mary? The Holy Spirit? Who were they? These were not concepts that would overly occupy the mind of a kampong boy, but it certainly was something different. He was surrounded by strangers too. The other boys around his age looked just as nervous as he was. The older, more confident boys looked somewhat daunting. Then there were the teachers, most of whom were men dressed in long white cassocks.

After the singing, one of the teachers stood on a stage in front of all the gathered boys and spoke at length in English, a language that Clarence was not entirely comfortable with yet, so the words were somewhat lost on him. The thick Irish accent did not help either.

And so began Clarence's first day of school – and the end of the carefree days of running around the estate whenever he chose.

Earlier that morning, Clarence, Cecilia, and Connie had jumped into the car that their father had recently purchased, the first for the family on the hill. Hood Hin dropped the girls off first at Katong Convent, the girls' school run by the Infant Jesus Sisters, before turning back along East Coast Road to Saint Patrick's, a Catholic boys' school, to drop off his young and nervous son. Clarence was dressed in white shirt, white shorts, white socks and white canvass shoes, the staple uniform for many schools throughout the tropical locales of the British Empire.

Clarence had passed Saint Patrick's many times before on the way to East Coast Beach, Marine Parade or Katong. He had often thought how grand and exciting it looked from the outside, especially when he saw students running around playing games in the school yard. That day, it appeared even more so as he stepped in for the first time. It was located on a fifteen-acre plot that still houses the school today. Two grand three-storey brick buildings and a third smaller one held the classrooms, dining halls, and dormitories for many of the teachers and the handful of boarders who came from places like Hong Kong and Christmas Island (which was under the jurisdiction of Singapore at the time). The grounds were beautiful, with a lot more greenery than there is today. Hibiscus, frangipani, and bougainvillea flowered around the property.

On the southern side of the school, where Marine Parade Road now runs, was the beach, with the waters of the Singapore Strait lapping against the boundary of the school. A student in Saint Patrick's could hear the sound of the waves gently kissing the beach outside the classrooms, and smell the fresh sea air. This was an area that Clarence was very familiar with, having fished and played there many times with his father and friends. The gun emplacements built on the sands by the British as a deterrent to a seaborne attack by the Japanese were still present, providing another reminder of the war. Some sections of the beach near the school were home to fishermen who worked the fish farms just off shore. These men lived in small wooden shacks under the shade of the coconut trees that lined the coast, with their long boats pulled up high enough on the beach in front of their huts to ensure they would not be stolen by the high tide.

———————

It was a somewhat odd bunch of people at school in these early post-war years. The war and the Japanese occupation had really disrupted all areas of life around the island. Many schools were closed for much of that time. Saint Patrick's itself was closed and commandeered by the $2^{nd}/13^{th}$ Australian Army General Hospital in the months leading up to the first attacks by the Japanese, in anticipation of casualties from fighting. Then once they captured the island, the Japanese established an administrative centre in the school grounds. When the schools reopened with the return of the British almost four year later, many of the students whose education had been disrupted returned to continue where they had left off. As a result there were now a number of older boys around, some as old as nineteen. As far as Clarence was concerned these were fully grown men. Many of these boys were fairly prominent around school, if not for their size then for their regular appearance during assembly for a six-of-the-best caning. They were always getting into trouble, often for fraternising with the girls up the road at Katong Convent.

This was an era that, looking back with the politically-correct-tinted glasses of today, might be considered very strict schooling. But the boys did not fear it. It was just the way it was. If you followed the rules, did your homework, kept quiet in class, put your hand up, spoke only when spoken to, addressed the teachers appropriately as "Father", "Sister", "Brother", "Sir", or "Madam", then you would be fine. And do not fraternise with the girls at Katong Convent.

Saint Patrick's School was run by the De La Salle Brothers, a Catholic religious order. Also known as the Christian Brothers, they had set up a number of schools around Malaya, as they had in many parts of the world, and Saint Patrick's was one of the newer ones. The property was originally established in the 1930s as a quiet seaside retreat for the Brothers, until it was soon realised that there was a need for a school in the East Coast districts of Singapore to cater for the growing population there and to take some pressure off Saint Joseph's Institution, the original Catholic boys' school downtown near City Hall. While the De La Salle order was originally established in France, the teaching staff at Saint Patrick's were primarily made up of Irish brothers, supplemented with a small number of lay teachers.

One of the teachers, Brother Anthony, was known around the school as The Watchdog. His reputation preceded him. According to the older boys, Brother Anthony kept a cane inside his long white cassock as he wandered around the courtyard during break time. It was said that he would whip out his cane and strike an unsuspecting transgressor on the spot. Again, it was often the older boys who suffered from his wrath, invariably for something like smoking behind one of the blocks.

Such rumours naturally instilled a sense of fear and curiosity in the new boys. They figured out pretty quickly who Brother Anthony was and tried to spy this supposed hidden cane as the Irishman wandered the yard. Clarence and his friends would soon learn, however, that this man-of-the-cloth was friendly enough. As always, play by the rules and there was nothing to fear. These older schools were not entirely passionless places that we might sometimes imagine them to have been. For example, the boys were sent home sometimes when it rained and they had become cold and wet. Even in the tropical heat, the presence of rain could drop the temperature just enough to cause the body of a young boy, in wet clothes from playing outside, to shiver when he returned to the classroom. Yes, the teachers were perhaps at times to be feared, but they were fair.

The regimental life of school was a bit of a change for the young kampong kid. Getting up at 7am was not such a big shock to the system, as rural life was driven by sunlight hours and the sun rose a little before 7am anyway. It was more having to be out the door and in the car by 7.30am, then in the school yard for assembly before heading off to a full morning of sitting in a classroom. Up until then life had been about doing a few chores around the house after breakfast before heading off to play amongst the trees, or to catch fish and swim down at the longkang or beach with his brothers, sisters, cousins and friends living nearby. But like all kids, he got used to the new life quickly. Before long he had struck up friendships with new kids from school, and hanging out with them daily gave him something to look forward to.

His subjects were pretty similar to what students cover at school today. Science, English, mathematics, algebra, mechanics, physics, chemistry, geography, and literature. As it was a Catholic school, there was also bible studies. Rugby, football, basketball, track and field, badminton, cross-country running, and cricket were all available and encouraged as extra-curricula activities. Clarence was never a strong runner, but with the annual cross-country race held around the family estate, his local knowledge enabled him to perform a little better than his legs might otherwise have allowed.

While life became more academic and disciplined, these school days never dampened Clarence's love for the outdoors. If anything they only intensified his passion and his desire to get back outside at the end of the school day and on the weekends. During primary school the students had no after-school sport, so Clarence and his older sisters would head back home in their father's car when classes finished at 1pm. After eating lunch, doing homework, and running a few chores, he still had plenty of time to go kite flying, catapulting, fishing, or run around, somewhere on the estate.

When Clarence began secondary school at the age of twelve, Hood Hin figured his eldest son was big enough to cycle to school and back, so he was no longer dropped off or picked up by car. One benefit of biking to school was that Clarence, and many of his relatives and school friends, had their own bikes. This meant they had even more freedom to roam further away from the homestead to explore the extended neighbourhood by themselves.

———————

Aerial photo taken from the south, of Saint Patrick's School, around 1960. The school is sitting on the beach front, where Marine Parade Road now runs. East Coast Road can be made out running along the top of the picture. The longkang, Siglap Canal, that ran along the western edge of Clarence's estate at Kembangan can be seen running along the right (eastern) border of the school.

As an old boy of Saint Patrick's School, Clarence was invited back in the mid to late 1970s to give a talk to the students. On the left is Brother McNally, the principal of the school from 1975 to 1982.

Heading out with his friends from class one Friday afternoon, Clarence suggested they all meet up the next afternoon to go kite fighting. They all agreed enthusiastically and settled on meeting at Karikal Mahal at 1pm the following day. None of them had watches, but they all had clocks at home and lived in the area so there was not much difficulty of keeping to schedule. This was a time well before mobile phones, when many homes did not even have a landline. So plans for after school and weekend activities were made in advance and face to face, and kept to strictly.

Once outside of the school gates, they all farewelled each other, jumped on their bikes, and weaved through the chaos of cars, bikes, and student pedestrian traffic that always formed there on East Coast Road at this time of day. Clarence and his brothers and cousins headed east for about 500m before taking a left up Frankel Avenue, past the residences of some of the British soldiers staying there. Growing up, Clarence never really had much to do with the Europeans, but these folks would smile and wave to the boys as they passed along the dirt road.

As they rode Clarence recalled how it had been a much less relaxed scene a few years earlier during the riots precipitated by the Maria Hertogh custody battle. During three days in November 1950, Malay and Indian Muslims had targeted Europeans and Eurasians all over the island. Clarence witnessed how, in response to this, the British soldiers and their families around Frankel Estate had taken to travelling around in army trucks, and how some of the soldiers had carried weapons as they walked the neighbourhood, sometimes not even in uniform. Apart from this observation, the riots had not caused too much of a problem for Clarence's family. That did not, however, mean that it was not a major event on the Singapore historical calendar. By the time the riots had been subdued, 18 people had lost their lives: seven Europeans, nine Muslim rioters, and two policemen. It really was a tragic event and one worth reading more details about elsewhere. Among other things, it highlighted the immense cultural and religious difference between the rulers of Malaya at the time, the British, and their subjects.

Shortly after riding through Frankel Estate the boys rode up the hill to the homestead and turned in to their driveway. They then rode around the back of the house, jumped off their bikes, leaned them against the outside rails of the stairs, and ran inside to drop off their bags and get changed. They then headed into the dining room for lunch. Clarence's younger sisters, Carmen and Christina, and a few of the younger cousins were already there eating lunch.

The young kids all yelled with joy as the older children walked in, the youngest of them running and nearly knocking Clarence over as they hugged his legs. Being twelve years old now, Clarence was practically an adult in their eyes and his return from school was always a moment of great jubilation for them. Very quickly however, Ah Soh had them back to their seats to finish their lunch.

Ah Soh greeted the boys and pointed them to the pot of sayur lodeh that was sitting on the stove in the kitchen. They made their way to the pot of light vegetables cooked in a light yellow soup of coconut milk curry. They each grabbed a bowl, placed in them a few rice cakes, spooned in some sayur lodeh, then took their bowls to the dining table. Soon after they sat down, Connie and Cecilia and the cousins who attended Katong Convent arrived home in the car with Hood Hin at the wheel. They too joined them for lunch.

Daisy entered the dining room to greet them and make sure that everyone was filling their stomachs. This was also the best time of day to dish out chores before the children all disappeared for the afternoon. "Peng," Daisy called out to her eldest son, putting him in charge of catching some catfish from the pond. Just outside the kitchen were a couple of large concrete tubs of water that held a selection of live fish, placed there so that they could be easily accessed by Ah Soh, or Daisy, or whoever was cooking a meal. The tub's location meant that fresh fish was always available for breakfast, lunch or dinner, without the women having to go over to the pond to catch some themselves. Furthermore, fish straight from the pond tasted muddy, so a few days in the clear water of these tubs helped clean them out. But the fish did not fly to the tub magically. When this fish supply outside the kitchen ran low, someone had to fish them out of the pond and transport them to the tubs. And invariably that was Clarence's job.

But first he had to do his homework.

So, once he had finished his lunch, Clarence headed back to the family room, took his books out of his bag, then found a spot on the veranda of the old house to do his work. With the sun still high in the sky, this section between the two houses provided the best shade from the heat of the day. Electricity at the house on Kembangan Hill was a few years away yet, so they always tried to get as much homework done during the daylight hours as they could. They could use kerosene lamps once the sun went down, but these were not tremendously bright, so it was easier to do homework by daylight. While certainly not the top of his class, Clarence was an above-average student and generally did not find his homework too challenging, so it was not long before he was able to head off to do his chores.

As he approached the pond, the little piglets in the pen beside it squealed and scrambled to the fence, thinking that Clarence was coming to feed them. Their large mother lay on her side in the shade, her head in the cool mud, oblivious to the ruckus made by her children. Like many other creatures in the tropics, she knew that the hottest part of the day was a time for rest and not for running around like her little piglets were. Clarence leaned over the fence and scratched their heads as he walked past the pen.

The large pond contained a few species of fish: catfish, snakeheads, gourami. Standing against the pig pen were fishing rods, with lines and hooks. The first thing Clarence did was to bait them up with worms he found in the dirt. Then, one by one, he cast the lines into the pond, and planted the butt end of the rod into the dirt so it would stand by itself. Clarence waited for a while, hoping some fish would quickly snare themselves on the line. After some time, he picked up a rod to check if there was any weight on it, which was a clue that a fish had snared itself. Sometimes, though, the hook was simply caught on one of the submerged logs of wood at the bottom of the pond (that had been left there when the pond was first created). Luckily, this time, there was some weight on the line. Clarence reeled it in, winding the string around a wooden stick. As he did so, the line tightened and slackened in turns, suggesting a fish and not a piece of wood. This was confirmed by splashing on the water surface a few moments later.

With the fish on dry land, he removed the hook from its mouth, and placed it into a bucket of water that he had brought along for the job. He knew that the women would expect more than just one fish, so he checked the other lines, and added a couple more fish to the bucket.

There was other ways to catch fish in the pond. If he had no success with the lines, he could sink a big net into the water and wait for the fish to get trapped in it as they swam around. In the dry season, it was even easier – the fish would be forced to hide in the mud as the water would get quite low, making it hard for them to swim around. All Clarence needed to do then was to wade into the mud and catch them by hand, being careful not to get pricked by the catfish barbs.

With his mission complete, he carried the bucket back to the kitchen area, tipped the fish into the tub, then went to find someone to play with. Friday was here. The weekend had arrived. It was time for more adventure.

––––––––

When Saturday afternoon rolled around, it was time for kite fighting with his school friends as planned previously. So, after lunch, Clarence picked up his kite and jumped on his bike. He eagerly rode out the driveway, back down Lengkong Tiga, across Upper Changi Road – first stopping to allow a mad bus driver career his vehicle past – then past his school – where a group of students were playing a game of rugby – and finally another 500m or so up the road to the large grassy patch in front of Karikal Mahal.

Karikal Mahal was a landmark in East Coast at the time. It started life as a beachside residence for a rather wealthy Indian cattle merchant. He had bought the large plot of land just east of the shops of Katong in 1917 and built a mansion with four houses for his numerous wives on it. Around the houses were gardens with fountains, sculptures and an artificial lake. On the shorefront side, the residents could take the stairs from their verandas down to the beach. It was a grand place indeed. Palatial. Then in 1947 the property was bought by a rubber company and turned into a hotel. The hotel was given the name Renaissance Grand Hotel, but many, including Clarence and his friends, continued to use the old name of Karikal Mahal. On the northern side of the property, along East Coast Road, was a large open area of grass that would attract children from all over surrounding kampongs and estates to play football or fly kites. Clarence had flown kites many times during his primary school years, but only in the family estate. Now that he had a bike it was a lot more fun to come down here to play.

As the large grassy field came into sight, Clarence stopped his bike at the junction of Still Road. In those days the southern end of Still Road ended at East Coast Road, with Karikal Mahal sitting on the opposite side.[12] Clarence looked north up Still Road and noticed two of his buddies, Suan and Teck, waving to him not far away. Once they reached him, the three boys rode across East Coast Road and onto the field.

---

12 It was not until the early 1970s, when the government bought the land, that Still Road was extended through the hotel, splitting the property in two. Some of its old buildings still stand in place today on either side of Still Road South.

There were already some other kids playing football on the grass. Clarence and his buddies sometimes joined them. And who knows, perhaps if he had played with them more regularly he may have one day donned the jersey of the Singapore football team, as a number of these regular faces eventually did. Aside from these footballers there were already a few kites in the air, and that was what he and his friends had come for. A battle was about to begin!

The boys rode to the other end of the field where the kite flyers were, jumped off their bikes, and prepared for the fight. The goal of this popular game was to bring down an opponent's kite by cutting its string as it flew high in the air. To do this, the boys had laced the strings of their kites with ground glass. It was quite a process, but such was the pride of, and therefore preparation required for, a champion kite flyer. During the weekends, in their kampongs or the yards of their houses, young boys all over the island prepared their weaponry by pounding the broken glass of a bottle with a mortar until it was very fine. They then mixed this glass powder with a paste made from animal protein or rice. The string, often cotton stolen from their mother's sewing kits, was placed into the mixture and stirred with a stick to coat it with this armoury. Once coated, it was hung between a couple of trees to dry, before the boys wound it around a tin can or stick in preparation for the next fight. It always paid to have a number of armoured strings and kites on standby, just in case you ended up having a bad day on the battlefield.

Kneeling on the ground preparing his weapon, Clarence gave out a short "ouch" and grumbled quietly under his breath. He had cut his finger on the string. He shook his finger, which was bleeding very slightly, then stuck it in his mouth to lick his wound clean. The glass was so fine that such injuries were minor, but it always paid to check for imbedded shards after such an incident, as one does for a splinter or prickle. This was one of the risks of this game, but a minor one for these toughened kampong kids. His friends teased him, suggesting his misfortune was an indicator of his performance in the impending fight. In a world where pantangs abound, they had invented their own.

Clarence looked at the other group of boys who were already flying their kites. He suggested to his friends they duel with the other group instead of among themselves. That's how it was with kite fighting. It was not necessarily a fight between you and your friends. Anyone on the field was fair game. And if you had the biggest, brightest kite, then you were just asking to become the target of others.

In the meantime, more of their school friends had turned up. While these new arrivals prepared their kites, Clarence, Suan, and Teck launched theirs into the air to get a feel for the wind. By this time of day, the afternoon sea breeze was beginning to pick up more, which was ideal for these fights as it ensured the kites fly higher, thus keeping the strings taut. They waited for their buddies to launch their kites. Eyeing up a couple of target kites from the "enemy", they moved in for the attack. Their opponents were only too eager to have some competition and, once they became aware of the attack, war began.

It was a challenging game, trying to break your enemies' string. And it was exciting. The players would manoeuvre their kites close to the enemy's so that the strings touched. Once in contact, they would quickly pull their string down and release it, to create a sawing action intended to cut through the other's string with the glass coating. Hence, the tautness of the strings created by the afternoon sea breeze was very important. Of course, it was naturally a game of risk. In order to cut the opponent's string you risked having yours cut by theirs. But that only added to the excitement.

Yells were heard all over the park as the boys tussled with each other. Sometimes, if you had prepared your string well and luck was on your side, it would be a short battle and you would cut your enemies' line within a few seconds. More often than not, however, long and great struggles would ensue. With a number of fighters joining the cause, the lines would all become entangled.

Cries of success rang out as each battle came to an end with the demise of someone's kite. "Hanyuuuuuuut!" the boys yelled as the loser's kite began its fall to the ground. "Hanyut" was Malay for "floated off" or "gone", and here it meant that someone's string had been cut and their kite was now floating to the ground. Not only did this cry herald the end of a battle, it was also an invitation for all around, particularly those not holding one themselves, to rush to the stricken kite. The first to reach it was entitled to claim it for himself. While the loser of the battle was allowed to join the race and reclaim his kite, it was no longer his by right: by losing the battle he had forfeited his ownership. Whoever grabbed it first became the new rightful owner. However, with so many kite-chasers stampeding for it, and so many hands grabbing at it, the flimsy structure of paper and small sticks often would not survive to see another fight.

The afternoon proceeded. Each boy had brought a bundle of kites and a few reels of string to ensure he was equipped with enough ammunition to survive a number of defeats. At five cents per kite, it was quite an investment for a young boy at that time. Of course, not having a kite did not mean you were totally out of the game as becoming a kite-chaser always gave you a chance at a new kite.

The boys could play this for hours, as long as the wind allowed. As 5.30pm approached, the number of kids on the field began to dwindle. Dinnertime was fast approaching and, for most, being late for dinner was considered extremely disrespectful to the family. With a long ride back uphill, Clarence wound up his strings, took his leave, and headed back home.

———————

Kite fighting was just one of the many pursuits that Clarence played with his peers. It was certainly one of the more aggressive activities and as such was generally only played by boys. Other days saw Clarence swimming or fishing in the longkang running alongside the estate or down at the East Coast beach by the Malay fishing villages, in front of the school or the beachfront bungalows owned by British, European, and American expatriates and rich Singapore businessmen. If they were lucky, or unlucky as the case probably was, they would spy a naked Brit who had a habit of parading himself on his porch overlooking the sea. Some days, they might find themselves chasing each other around the kampongs or perfecting their catapult skills on the birds around the property. And then there were the school-related sports, such as rugby or soccer, which he would head back to school for after lunch.

For more family leisure activities, the family would often jump in the car and head out to Loyang Beach. Daisy's father had a small bungalow there, and during the first week of the school holidays the extended family would all stay there. This beach was far more suited for swimming and picnics than the nearby East Coast Beach, which was a little polluted due to the comings and goings of the Malay fishing boats.

And then there were the movies. There were a few indoor theatres around the island, but Clarence and his family and friends often headed to an open-air night cinema nearby. For ten cents a movie they sat outside on wooden benches and watched the show of the day, sometimes even in the rain. Most of the movies in these rural settings were in either Malay or Chinese. English was not widely spoken by the people in the kampongs, so movies from the West were not so popular. From time to time the cinemas were set up within their estate and these Clarence and the family were able to watch for free. It was their land after all.

Clarence's school years were fun times. Although school had taken away some of the freedom he had enjoyed in his childhood, he was developing an even greater enjoyment of the outdoors. It was not only a chance to simply run around and be a boy, but also as a chance to meet and laugh and engage with others away from the homestead, in the neighbourhoods around the eastern part of Singapore.

———————

After some years the time came to start thinking about what to do once he left school. What to do with his life. He was a good student, but the idea of further study did not attract him. To move into a profession would mean having to qualify for Saint Joseph's Institute, which was one of the top pre-university schools at the time, and a brother school of Saint Patrick's. Entry was tough though, and Clarence was not greatly attracted to the idea of more years of hard study. Nor was he attracted to the idea of a professional life, a life indoors. His maternal grandfather, Daisy's father, had wanted him to go to Australia to study medicine and was prepared to cover the cost of such an education, but he was not interested in that either.

So given he did not want to become a professional and was not interested in further study, he completed his final year of school at the age of eighteen having attained the Overseas Senior Cambridge Exams. Of course, the educational system was British and so were the exams. This qualification would at least open up employment options within the police and the civil service.

Yes, an outdoor life was what he wanted. Exactly what kind of an outdoor life though, he did not know.

Chapter 7
Working on the Docks

It was a wet and muggy January morning in 1959, around 7am on a Monday. Clarence had risen a little earlier to wash up, dress, and have breakfast before heading out the door. He was a little anxious about the day ahead as he walked down the dirt road to the nearby bus stop on Changi Road. He waved down the next bus heading into town, greeted the Indian driver as he got on, and sat near the rear. He did not often travel as far into town as he was going that day, so it would be nice to sit back and take in some of the less familiar sights along the way. The Malay bus conductor followed him to his seat, asked how far he was going, then tore off a ticket for him as Clarence passed over the fare.

The rickety bus, with all its windows open to allow air to flow through and keep its occupants cool from the tropical heat, pulled out of the bus stop and continued west along the main road connecting the east coast to the city centre. Before long, Changi Road became Geylang Road, then Kallang Road after a few more kilometres. Near here, they passed the entrance to the now closed Kallang Aerodrome. A few years earlier, in August 1955, the new Singapore International Airport had opened at Paya Lebar, and all civilian flights to and from Singapore had been moved there. Kallang Airport had served as the island's civilian airport since 1937, but post war aviation was booming. With the advent of higher performance aircraft, including the arrival of the jet era, and the increase in the number of flights, Kallang was no longer viable. Bigger and faster aircraft needed longer runways, larger numbers of aircraft needed more parking space and maintenance facilities, and increasing numbers of passengers needed a bigger terminal building. With the growth in the residential area around the airport there was no room to expand. Consequently a brand new airport had been built.

So, where a few years earlier the bus passengers might have seen a BOAC Constellation or a Malayan Airlines DC-3 parked on the airport apron, all they saw now were a few remaining buildings of the old airport and a new vehicular route for the growing populations of the east coast to access the city. As they are still today, the new road was named Nicoll Highway, and the bridge carrying this road over the mouth of the Kallang and Rochor rivers became Merdeka Bridge – Sir John Fearns Nicoll being the British Governor of the island at the time, and Merdeka being the Malay word for independence, a reference to the political evolution that was currently taking place in Malaya.[13]

Continuing past the old airport the bus soon approached the Kallang Gas Works. Everyone around town worried that the tall tanks of gas found here would one day go up in flames, so many of the local population, Clarence included, referred to the Works as "huay sia", which was Hokkien for "fire city". Given the havoc that potential saboteurs could create here, the facility was guarded by fierce Gurkha soldiers from Nepal. And what a fearsome lot they were. Since their recruitment into the British Army in the early 1800s they had gained a reputation the world over for their courage in the face of the enemy, their fearsomeness in attack, and their loyalty to their commanders. The Gurkhas served in a number of roles, and for different countries, around the world, and in 1949 a Gurkha Contingent had been formed as a part of the Singapore Police Force. It was these men, ex-British

---

13 The original Kallang Airport control tower and passenger terminal building and some of the old aircraft hangers still remain today, located on the opposite side of Nicoll Highway from the Singapore Sports Hub. The Sports Hub itself sits on the area of the old airport's runway.

Army Gurkhas, whom Clarence saw each morning as his bus passed this facility. In the years to come, when he was in the army, he would develop a deep respect for these men.

Taking a left around the gas works it was then on to Crawford Street, crossing the Rochor Canal and following the Rochor River for a short distance before turning right on to Beach Road. As its name suggests, Beach Road ran along what was once a part of the original beach of this part of Singapore. In the very early days of European settlement a walk along this stretch would have taken one in front of large beachfront bungalows and villas with the waves of the Singapore Strait lapping on their doorsteps (one of these villas would eventually evolve into the luxury Raffles Hotel). But that was a long time ago and, following a land reclamation project back in 1843, the waterfront was now a block away. On the reclaimed land stood the Beach Road Market, a police station, a couple of theatres, an army parade ground, and the Britannia Club, where British and Allied soldiers would go to drink and brawl, much to the consternation of the management and posh residents at the Raffles Hotel immediately across the road. Aside from these establishments, much of the land was pretty empty and glimpses could be caught of the Strait stretching from the shore a block away across to Batam Island to the south.

After passing the elegant Raffles Hotel end of Beach Road the bus continued west, now dropping off more people than it was picking up as the civic centre and central business district approached. Along Connaught Drive, with The Padang on the right, its well manicured grass separating that very English of institutions, the Singapore Cricket Club, at one end and its Eurasian response, the Singapore Recreation Club, at the other. It was another world back then. Gin and tonics, cricket, and tennis had returned quickly with the return of the British after the Japanese Times. While these activities took place at many locations over the island, primarily by expatriates and wealthy local businessmen, these two clubs were possibly the most well known among the general population, given their central location. Both were still bastions of male and racial privilege, although the Recreation Club was opening up, having recently opened its doors to non-Eurasians and would very soon allow women to become members. The Cricket Club, on the other hand, would take a little longer to fully open its doors to non-Europeans and later women. These were different times.

On the northern side of The Padang stood City Hall, with its Corinthian colonnades, flanked by the domed Supreme Court on the left and the elegant St Andrew's Cathedral on the right. Stretching along the southern length of Connaught Drive was the newly named Queen Elizabeth Drive, so named a few years earlier in recognition of the coronation of Queen Elizabeth the Second, the ultimate ruler of Britain and her colonies, and thus Singapore. In the evenings families, friends, and couples strolling along this pedestrian area could enjoy the sound of the sea lapping against the sea wall, the freshness of the cooler evening breeze, and the sight of a multitude of ships parked in the anchorage and beyond, while the trees shaded them from the evening sun. Perhaps it was the vistas in this civic centre of the island that shouted most loudly, visually at least, its British colonial influence. This influence, while rapidly waning, was still very much around as Clarence sat in the back of the bus.

After passing Empress Place on the left bank of the Singapore River, the bus made a left turn across Anderson Bridge. This was one of a few short bridges near the mouth of the river that marked the link between the civic centre that they had just driven through and the hustle and bustle of the commercial centre on the other side of the river around Raffles Place and Keppel Harbour.

Already, the lighters and tongkangs (barges used to carry cargo from the boats in the harbour to the godowns along these lower reaches of the Singapore River) were busy at work and hundreds of mainly Chinese coolies could be seen loading and unloading goods from what looked like a melee of a hundred or so of these small vessels crammed into the river basin along Boat Quay. All the boats were rubbing against each other. It was so jammed that even if their tongkang was a hundred feet from the quay, the other boats provided a bridge for these slim, bare-chested workers to walk over with their gunny sacks full of goods on their back, or heads.

Directly on the other side of Anderson Bridge stood the Fullerton Building, where the General Post Office, or GPO as everyone knew it, was located. A tunnel underneath Fullerton Road, upon which the bus then travelled, provided access for international sea mail to be transferred quickly from the GPO to the boats parked at the pier on the other side of the road.

Now skirting the heart of the city's financial district, the bus continued onto Collyer Quay with Raffles Place, and its banks and large business houses, on the right. On the left was Clifford Pier, the main entry and exit point for international passengers arriving and departing by ship. Flying was an expensive endeavour in these days, so ships were still the mode of transport for most people travelling overseas. Passengers and crew from the vessels parked within and outside the inner anchorage would pass through this building, and for many foreigners Clifford Pier was where they first stepped foot on Singapore soil.

Collyer Quay soon turned into Shenton Way, with its main feature on the seaward side being the Telok Ayer Basin, where more lighters were bustling with more workers and more goods being moved between the wharves here and the ships in the inner anchorage. On the right side of the road the Telok Ayer Market was in full swing, and would have been since the wee hours of the morning. The rumble of the bus engine drowned out the squeals of pigs and chickens as they endured their final moments on this mortal coil. The market had been serving the area for over a century now and hence, among the mainly Chinese working there, it was (and still is) known as Lau Pa Sat, Hokkien for "old market".

A short while later, at the end of Shenton Way, the bus turned right on to Keppel Road and down toward Keppel Harbour, the small stretch of water located between the mainland and Pulau Sentosa, or Sentosa Island. When the bus pulled up at the stop outside the offices of the Singapore Harbour Board, near the King's Dock, Clarence alighted.

And so began the first day of his working life.

The wharves were an exciting place. The entire area surrounding Clarence's work place was bustling with shipment activity. The Singapore Strait had always been important as the main shipping channel between the Indian Ocean and the South China Sea. Since its founding as a British colony, Singapore had rapidly grown to be the major hub in the region. Large ocean-going vessels with cargo from far away Europe and the Americas would head to Singapore and offload their goods. These would then be redistributed to the smaller coastal vessels, that would carry them on to other ports in the Asia-Pacific. Of course, cargo was travelling back the other way too. All of it would be moved between Keppel Harbour and the wharves at Tanjong Pagar, Telok Ayer Basin, and Boat Quay, stored temporarily in the godowns, or moved directly out to other waiting ships by the lighters and tongkangs.

So this whole downtown area, on both land and sea, was a hive of activity. The coastal vessels would park within the inner anchorage, that area defined as between the shore and the mole, the artificial breakwater that had been built to provide protection for these smaller vessels from the northeast monsoons. The larger vessels waited outside in the Strait until it was their turn to come in to the deep water anchorage that Keppel Harbour provided, sheltered by the islands of Pulau Brani and Sentosa. Oil storage and bunkering was also a major draw of shipping activity and income for the port, supplying fuel to ships in between their runs. In addition to the shipping activity, trains chugged regularly in from Malaya to the north with their loads of tin and rubber bound for other parts of the world. Most of the goods passing through this port was transhipment cargo: cargo coming in from one overseas port, then moving on to another. Singapore's port was a hub, and a very successful one.

The port's importance to the economy of the British empire had not been not lost on the Japanese. Perhaps that was why, in addition to the airfields around the island, Keppel Harbour was a target for their first bombing raids in December 1941. By knocking out the port's infrastructure they could diminish the island's ability to re-supply itself. Hence the Japanese had devastated the area of Clarence's workplace early on in their assault on Malaya. When the British returned, the place was a complete mess. The dockyards had fallen into disrepair. Sunken ships littered the waters, which made navigating and parking floating ships around the harbour hazardous. Therefore, one of the immediate priorities following the Japanese occupation had been to clean up the port and get it operational again. Food and supplies for the reconstruction of Singapore and Malaya were vital to help the place get back on its feet again, so a functioning port was critical. Labour had also been in short supply following the war. And although more than a decade had passed by the time Clarence turned up at the Singapore Harbour Board, there was still a shortage of workers, hence the docks were a good place to find a job. Which explains to a degree how he ended up on these wharves of Keppel Harbour.

––––––––––

Clarence spent the next three years working on the wharves of Keppel Harbour as an apprentice electrician with the Singapore Harbour Board. He worked alongside a main wireman, who was essentially his mentor, and eventually completed the requisite hours that would enable him to qualify for a Diploma in Electrical Engineering.

The first year was spent working in the workshop, cleaning and repairing electric motors. In the second year, he headed out with his wireman to work on the ships anchored around the harbour. In the third year, he spent much of his time maintaining the ships' gyro compasses, which involved working on the bridge of the ships, taking them out into mid-strait, and testing the accuracy of these instruments. It was a fun time. Clambering over ships parked alongside the wharf, sitting in one of the dry docks, or anchored in the harbour. At times he would work on other equipment around the bustling wharves and in the offices. For one day and two evenings each week he would head off for a day-release course at the newly established Singapore Polytechnic, just next to the Keppel Wharves on Prince Edward Road, to complete the theoretical component for his diploma. He was also making a lot of new friends from different parts of Singapore.

And he was making money too. Not a lot – he was a lowly apprentice after all – at $14.76[14] per week to begin with. But it was enough to survive on, for a young man living at home. His bus fare was 10 cents each way per day, and for 50 cents he could get a substantial lunch of Malay rice or char siew fun, so there was plenty of money left over for a movie with friends on Friday nights. In his second year, he could do overtime, and on a good week he pocketed $20 in cash from the paymaster (although it may at times not have been the most honest of overtime, with his boss occasionally clocking in for him when he was not around).

---

14 The currency of the time was the Malaya and British Borneo dollar.

This was a fun time. He was outdoors, making new friends, making money, and loving it. His workplace was an exciting, bustling place. The whole city centre was. Far different from the kampong and the rural life back at Kembangan Hill. But it would only take a few years before this restless young man would begin to think that even the wharves were not quite exciting enough.

PART TWO

ARMY DAYS

(1959 – 1965)

Chapter 8
The Emergency

Heading home from work one evening, something piqued Clarence's attention as the bus made its way along Beach Road, near Raffles Hotel. Looking out the right window while passing the Beach Road army camp he observed the young recruits of the Singapore Volunteer Corps going through their drills on the parade ground. He had travelled past this place many times since he had started work on the wharves, and this was certainly not the first time that he had noticed these part-time soldiers training so close to the city centre. But on seeing them today, a new idea was sparked in him. His life and work were starting to settle down and he was looking for new challenges. New excitement.

Perhaps he should give this a shot, he wondered to himself as the bus drove past. Doing so would certainly give him a chance to earn some extra money. And maybe even get out into the jungle and play real cowboys and Indians? Approaching twenty now, he had long moved on from the boyhood games of running around the estate with his friends, but the urge to be outdoors was still strong. The chance to run around in the jungle and get some pocket money for it was quite attractive. The volunteer force would be perfect. He was certainly not interested in a full-time army career, but a part-time commitment was something he could handle. And the parade ground was on the way home anyway. Why not give it a go?

So the next evening after work he jumped off the bus outside Raffles Hotel, crossed Beach Road, and signed up for, unbeknown to him at the time, what would be the beginning of thirty-three years of continuous service in the armed forces of Singapore.

Two evenings a week he headed off to the Beach Road Camp after work for foot drills, marching, weapons training, internal security drills, and training in the manning of roadblocks.[15] In the weekends the volunteer force headed to the north of the island to the Mandai jungle, near where the Singapore Zoo and the Night Safari are today, for field training and firing range practice. Then once a year, they headed across the causeway into the jungles around Mersing and Kota Tinggi, in Johor, in the now independent Federation of Malaya, for two weeks of jungle warfare training.

Depending upon their rank, a volunteer could earn anything from $0.75 to $2.50 per hour. All food, accommodation, and transport during training were paid for. So it was a pretty good deal as far as Clarence was concerned. The government paid him a regular soldier's full-time salary during those 14 days in the jungles of Johor, which was comparable to his civilian pay at the time. Apart from having to release him, as was the law, it did not cost the Singapore Harbour Board a penny as the government took over paying wages to the soldiers during their extended time away from their employers.

Another bonus of joining the Singapore Volunteer Corps was that he did not risk being called up as a conscript, which the British had unpopularly introduced five years earlier with the creation of the National Service Ordinance. Life as a volunteer was a lot more relaxed than that of a conscript. The volunteers had a bit more flexibility in terms of commitments to schedule and attendance at training. A volunteer, for example, would not be penalised for missing training.

Running around in the jungle was a great adventure for the young man. It was a perfect addition to the life he was enjoying on the wharves at Keppel Harbour during the working week. He had no intention of becoming a full-time soldier. Mainly because he had never really thought

15 The primary focus of the volunteer force up to this point had been on internal security so the training was more geared in that direction. This was partly because the British were the ones responsible for the external security of the island at the time.

of it. He was simply happy running around outside in his spare time and getting paid for it.

Anyway, the options for a local Singaporean in the army in 1959 really were not that great. While the rest of Malaya had been granted independence two years earlier, Singapore was now a Crown Colony. The island was enjoying full internal self-government, but the British were still ultimately in charge. And more relevant to Clarence's story, they were still in charge of foreign affairs and defence. Two years earlier, in 1957, under pressure from the local leaders of the time, including David Marshall, Singapore's first Chief Minister and a major figure in local politics at the time, the 1st Battalion, Singapore Infantry Regiment (1 SIR) had been established as the island's first unit of local regular soldiers. Aside from a few junior officers, all the Singaporean 1 SIR soldiers were privates and NCOs. The bulk of its officers, and all the senior ones, were British.

Yes, joining the regular army as a full-time soldier was an option for the young Clarence at the time, but he was happy working on the wharves and playing soldier on weekends.

———————

As Clarence and his fellow part-time soldiers from the Singapore Volunteer Corps (SVC) stood at ease on the parade ground of the Beach Road Camp, their army captain, a British expatriate, briefed them on the activities they would be engaging in for the next two weeks. Things were going to be a bit different during this pending exercise. First up, it would be two weeks in the jungles of Johor, with no nice amenities to come back to in the evenings. It would be similar to their weekends around Woodlands, but it would not be some overnight camping trip.

More importantly though, while technically this would be a training exercise, any deployment to the jungles of Johor in 1959 came with the slight chance of an encounter with real enemy combatants. No, this was not going to be some holiday jaunt. This stint had the potential to turn into the real thing. Clarence and his fellow newbie soldiers were heading off on a training exercise, but it was to be a training exercise that would take them into the tail end of the Malayan Emergency, or what was known locally as simply "the Emergency".

Communism was a major political force throughout the world at this time, and South East Asia was far from being an exception. In Malaya, the Malayan Communist Party, or the MCP, had been established in the early 1930s. They were an illegal group and very much disliked by the British authorities, yet they did manage to amass a large membership. When the Japanese began their attacks in December 1941, the British put aside their differences and accepted an MCP offer to join forces against the Japanese. While the MCP were not fans of the British, they disliked the Japanese even more due to their invasion of, and subsequent atrocities in, China that had begun in 1937 (though of course, the discord between these two countries pre-dated this, but that is another story).

The British then proceeded to train the MCP who, once the Japanese had taken over Singapore and Malaya, retreated into the Malayan jungles and began building up a guerrilla resistance force known as the Malayan People's Anti-Japanese Army (MPAJA). From their jungle bases they recruited, armed, and trained an army that grew to over 6,000 soldiers, and made regular harassment raids on the Japanese. Apart from a few British and Allied soldiers who had stayed behind and managed to escape into the jungles themselves, there was very little contact between the two sides until later on in the occupation.

History is littered with examples of alliances between two unlikely bedfellows against a common enemy. The enemy of my enemy is my friend, as the saying goes. However, history is also littered with examples of such alliances going on to create new complexities once that mutual enemy has been defeated. The British and MCP alliance was no exception.

Initially, with the end of WW2 and the return of the British to Malaya, the MPAJA were welcomed with open arms. They participated in the victory parades, and some of their leaders even received recognition from the British Crown. One of them, Chin Peng, for example, received an OBE from the King for his efforts. (Though within a few years this same Chin Peng would become the most wanted person in the British Empire, and unsurprisingly, lose his OBE.)

But the two sides had irreconcilable differences. The MCP wanted independence for Malaya, and they wanted it fast. The British were also open to the idea of eventual independence, but believed it should take time. What's more, the British were certainly not interested in leaving behind a communist Malaya.

Initially the MCP pursued their agenda within the legal framework, but within a couple of years they increased their activity within the unions in order to disrupt the British rebuilding efforts through strikes. Once the British realised what was going on they quickly pounced on the MCP and closed down the trade unions on 12th June 1948. Four days later, three European plantation managers in Perak were murdered. With the subsequent declaration of a state of emergency over the whole of Malaya, thus began the Emergency. It was to last for a little over twelve years. Under this state of emergency, the MCP was officially outlawed. Chin Peng, who was by now the Secretary General of the MCP, then led his comrades back into the cover of the jungles and reformed a variation of the MPAJA into what was eventually known as the Malayan National Liberation Army (MNLA).

The MCP had been clever. When they walked out of the jungle at the end of the Japanese occupation, they had buried large stashes of weapons and ammunition in the jungle, in the expectation that they would one day need them in an armed struggle for independence against the British. That armed struggle had now begun.

From deep within the jungle, a jungle that they knew well from their three and a half years there during Japanese times, they began a guerrilla campaign against the British. Initially targeting only industrial installations and transport links vital to the tin and rubber industries, it would soon be civilians, both British and Malayan, who would become targets. They also began recruiting more fighters, particularly from those kampongs on the fringes of the jungle.

The British response was to begin bombing and artillery campaigns and sending troops into the jungles to seek out the insurgents. If they could not find and kill or arrest them, then at least they could push them deeper and deeper into the jungle and make their efforts less effective. The British cut the insurgents off from their supplies of food, medicine, recruits, and communication with the wider population. Under the direction of what was known as the Briggs Plan, large numbers of the rural population were moved from their kampongs near the jungle's edge to what were termed New Villages. These villages were surrounded by fences, barbed wire, and security guards, denying the communists access to the support they depended upon. Before long, accessing food and supplies for their life in the jungle became tough. So when offers of amnesty and financial rewards for their surrender of weapons were broadcast to insurgents in the jungle, many came out of hiding and turned themselves in.

The last major blow for the communists came with the granting of independence to The Federation of Malaya on 31st August 1957. With this, a primary raison d'être for their insurgency was swept from under the MCP and given to non-communist interests.

Then in July 1960 the Prime Minister of Malaya, Tunku Abdul Rahman, declared the end of the state of emergency. And so came the end of what had been a more brutal and bloody campaign than is often remembered. Over the twelve years, more than 10,000 people had died – 1,346 Malayan troops and police, 519 British and allied military personnel, 6,710 MNLA soldiers, and 2,478 civilians. Nearly 1,000 people were unaccounted for. It was a very serious event in the history of Malaya.

Patrols into the jungle continued for a number of years thereafter as small numbers of hardcore MCP loyalists were suspected to be holed up somewhere in the jungle, mostly up north near the Thai border. And although Malaya was now independent, the military campaign continued to be spearheaded by the British, with the ongoing support of New Zealand and Australia.[16]

Interestingly, in the eyes of many, the Emergency was a war. However, it was never declared as such because any commercial losses encountered as a result of a declared war would not be covered by the insurance companies back in London. The rubber plantations and tin mines did not want that.

So, by the time Clarence first entered the jungles of Johor, the Emergency was in its dying days. The last serious incident had been in 1958, up north at Telok Anson (now called Telok Intan) in the state of Perak. The general acceptance was that any remaining communists had moved north to the Thai border and were no longer causing any significant problems for the civilian population. Johor was now a "white area", the term used to indicate that an area had been cleared of the MNLA. But there was a slight possibility that small communist elements might still be hiding there, so it was considered possible that Clarence and his fellow fresh soldiers could encounter a firefight during their time in the jungle. The British had been cutting back on their troop commitments

---

16 Interestingly, troops from Fiji and Rhodesia, now called Zimbabwe, were also involved (as part of the British Commonwealth forces) for different periods from the early to mid-1950s.

to the Emergency, so they were quite happy to have the less experienced troops from the SVC operate in these white areas. More experienced British, Australian, and New Zealand SAS soldiers remained committed to the more serious work up north. There were still some pursuits of MNLA remnants going on up there.

The British expatriate army captain continued his briefing to his young protégés on the parade ground at Beach Road. He informed Clarence and his buddies that, while Johor was a "white area", their presence as a part of this training exercise would ensure that it stayed that way. From time to time villagers and the jungle dwellers had reported evidence of fresh campsites left by small groups of unknown people. If insurgents were still there then it was important to keep them on the run and give them no chance to re-establish themselves.

Singapore Volunteer Artillery units would also be up there doing their annual training at the same time, lobbing shells in to the area west of Mersing on a regular basis. It would be fairly random firing as they had no idea where the MNLA operatives might be, if they were in fact there at all. Once in the area, the company would split up into smaller patrols and flood the jungle on foot. With the artillery keeping them awake and on guard at night, and Clarence's patrols not letting them rest during the day, the expectation was that any insurgents who might be there would retreat deeper into the jungle and further out of harm's way, head up north to the Thai border, or be flushed out completely.

While it was possible that they could be forced in to a firefight, it was considered highly unlikely. Given their small numbers at this stage of the Emergency, it would be unwise for an MNLA insurgent to open fire on a patrol. First of all, they would most likely be outnumbered. Worse still, doing so would only draw attention to their location and cause the artillery to rain hell fire upon them. No, chances were that if the MNLA spotted Clarence and his company of fellow soldiers first they would move away if they could, or simply sit still amongst the vegetation until the patrol passed by. It was very easy to hide in the jungle.

Following the briefing, they all jumped into the back of the waiting Bedford three-tonner troop trucks and headed off to Mersing on the eastern coast of Malaya for what would be the first of three two-week missions that Clarence would go on as a member of the Singapore Volunteer Corps.

———————

Clarence enjoyed these forays. Being outside and in the jungle was a lot like playing around his kampong back on Kembangan Hill when he was younger. The trees were relatively tall with not much undergrowth in this part of Malaya, so even the vegetation was somewhat familiar to him. There was something exciting about going on these patrols. They were young and keen for an adventure. They never did see the enemy during these camping trips. Even in their own minds they never really expected to. They were just flooding the area, creating a noise to scare any possible communists out.

Clarence happily continued serving with the SVC for three years. Twice a week, after his day on the wharves, he would head down to the Beach Road Camp for drills, then head to the firing range at Bukit Timah in the weekends, and once a year would be driven north to the jungles of Johor. During this period he graduated from being a recruit to a second lieutenant.

For a few years now there had been full-time military career options for local Singaporeans like him with the 1ˢᵗ Singapore Infantry Regiment (1 SIR), but still none of the available options interested him. In 1963, that changed. A new call for local Singaporeans to join the regular army as an officer was advertised.

Now that, to Clarence, could be interesting!

Chapter 9
Becoming a Regular Officer

One evening after work in June 1963, Clarence made his way to the SVC Camp at Beach Road and, upon walking in the main door, found three of his buddies huddled around the notice board just inside the main entrance to the facility. They were intently looking at a poster that had recently been put up. Clarence greeted his buddies and asked what was grabbing their attention. They pointed at what turned out to be an advertisement inviting young men to join the regular army as officer cadets – for local Singapore men to join the army to be trained as officers.

The four young men stood around the poster, analysing every bit of the minimally worded advertisement and discussed it enthusiastically. It certainly sounded like an interesting proposal. Joining the army as a full-timer would be quite a change in lifestyle but the allure of becoming an officer sounded pretty exciting. And the pay seemed pretty good: $200 a month during training, then $240 upon graduation as a second lieutenant. That was far more than any of them were earning now. You could buy a car with that kind of income and still have money left over.

They mulled it over in silence for a while, each considering the potential ramifications of such a decision on their lives. Then they looked at each other and agreed. "Let's do it!"

And that was it. Clarence and three of his buddies applied to join the regular army. After going through the recruitment tests all four were selected, and they signed on as officer cadets. Before he knew it, in early August 1963, Clarence found himself no longer heading down to the wharves for work, but off to army college for training. Now that was to be a shock to the system.

———————

Clarence dropped to the floor at the feet of the senior officer cadet and performed the twenty press-ups he had just been ordered to do. The afternoon was so hot and muggy that small pools of sweat were already forming on the ground around him. His sweat, and that of his fellow cadets. Once finished with the press-ups he ran back up the stairs, up the hill from which he had come down about a minute earlier.

What a shock this had been. One moment he and a group of cadets were walking up these same stairs from the playing fields below the college after kicking a ball around in their spare time, when out of nowhere came a yell from one of the senior cadets. "Run up the stairs from the bottom, then come back and tell me how many steps there are," he had shouted. Clarence had already been up this hill twice now. Fifty-two steps, he had counted both times. And so had his fellow cadets. They had all muttered the same figure under their breath as they passed each other on the hill. So by now he was pretty sure he had the number right.

But the senior cadet was having none of it. Each time they came back down he barked at them in Malay – "Tak boleh kira, budak banda?" *Can't you count, city boy?* – before ordering them to perform yet another twenty press-ups and to run back up the hill and count the steps again.

As Clarence climbed the hill for a third time he caught up with one of his fellow cadets, and they grumbled about the senior lording it over them, while they continued their run up the hill. They had no doubt about how many steps there were. But that was not going to be enough for this punk. He was going to make them run up and down this hill until he was satisfied.

———————

It had been a hell of a first 24 hours at the Short Service Office Cadet Course (SSOCC) at the training complex of the Federation Military College at Sungei Besi, just south of Kuala Lumpur. Clarence and his buddies had taken the train up from Singapore to the station in Kuala Lumpur the previous day. At the station they had met a bunch of other new recruits from other parts of Malaya, then they were transported by truck to this camp that would be their home for the next few months. Upon arriving they were met by a senior officer cadet, and from this point immediately began what was infamously known as the ragging period. "Pick up your bags and follow me," the senior cadet shouted at them as they jumped out of the truck. What a welcoming place, the young men must have thought.

That first night's sleep at the officer training camp had been shattered at 6am by the sound of a bugle. After quickly changing into their physical training fatigues they assembled in the dark on the square, then were sent on a run by their physical training instructor. Back then, no one went jogging for the fun of it, so for many of them this early morning run was a real shock on the system. Then, it was time to wash up and head off for a quick breakfast before heading back to the square for the muster parade. During the parade the senior officer cadets inspected their uniforms and their stature as they stood to attention, shouting at them for any minor transgressions. Transgressions that could lead to demerit points and doing Saturday morning drills alone. Then they headed off for classes, through which many struggled to stay awake. The ceiling fans did little to keep the heat of the day at bay: the monotonous hum of the motors and the whooshing sound of the fan blades rotating through the air, combined with the heat and the early start, did little to help the heavy feeling on their eyelids. In the late afternoon they were given some time to themselves, so some of them had headed down to the fields to kick a ball around. And it was returning from these fields that this one particular senior officer cadet, this "joker" as Clarence would refer to him, had intercepted them and sent them running up and down the stairs in this meaningless exercise.

This menace kept turning up at various points of their day. At dinner time he turned up yelling at them again. Giving them orders on how to sit down at the dinner table, even how to eat. Pick up fork. Secure some food with the fork. Lift fork at right angles to the table up to the level of your mouth. Move fork parallel to the table to your mouth. Place food in mouth. Return fork to table in the reverse motion to what you just did. Chew. Pick up the fork. And the cycle began again. And again. For every mouthful. You even had to continue the cycle if there was no food left on your plate. Then, as if that was not enough to grind you down, just as you were about to put some food in your mouth this guy might ask you a question, to which you had to respond thus missing that mouthful. "What was going on here?" any sane cadet will have asked. But that was how they ate their meals. Eating square, it was called.

Later that evening, just as they thought they might be able to relax for the day, he turned up again. Clarence and his fellow cadets jumped in shock as the senior cadet stormed into their dormitory hall for the evening inspection, barking at them to stand to attention outside their bedrooms, which they shared in pairs. He walked through the dormitory corridor, inspecting each room as he went. Checking that their beds were neatly made, their clothes neatly folded into one-foot square piles, their boots in the right place, and there was no dust or rubbish lying around. The senior was obviously disappointed that the city boys from Singapore had done their quarters up so nice and pretty. He had turned up looking for a reason to yell at them. But Clarence and his buddies had not given him one.

He took a closer look at Clarence's boots and noticed how clean and polished they were, even after a day of running around outside. Then, as if expecting to catch Clarence out on it, he meticulously inspected the mess tins and utensils they used for eating from in the field. They too were spotless. "Hmmm," he mumbled suspiciously. He found the same orderliness for the other soldiers. This could not be. In the morning he had made sure that the new cadets from Singapore were given the dirtiest, rustiest mess tins – and now they were all clean and polished. Like they were new! The senior was beginning to look a little angry now. He was frustrated that these city boys had managed to foil his attempt to have a reason to mock them.

Determined to show that he was boss, the senior then opened a few cupboards and threw the clothes to the floor. He kicked boots and plates and cutlery all over the room and generally made a mess of their quarters. Then he yelled, "Clean it up, cadets", before storming out of the hall.

After he had left, and was safely out of earshot, the grumbling began about their first day as they cleaned up the mess. This senior cadet seemed to have just one volume and mood: loud and grumpy. The Singapore boys muttered that they had probably done more jungle patrols than this young punk had, referring to the weeks that some of them had spent in the jungles of Johor with the SVC. What could this young joker teach them? But they did not grumble for long. They were exhausted. As soon as their rooms were back in shipshape order, they fell asleep once the lights went out.

———————

The first six weeks of the course were hell. Every day was like this first one. For this period they were confined to the camp and had no weekends off. They were woken by the bugle at 6am every morning for physical training before heading to breakfast. Then it was on to muster parade, followed by a day full of classes. These ranged from academic classes in topics such as accounting, the structure of the Malaysian military, and military tactics, to field training outdoors such as weapons training, marching in the drill square, or survival training. Then dinner at 6pm. If there were no evening courses they would then play a bit of sport among themselves. Rugby, soccer, fencing, boxing. Then it was study time from 8pm to 10pm, then lights out. All periods of the day were announced by a bugle call. The lessons themselves were quite civilised. It was during the intervals and their spare time when the miserable ragging would occur – during meal times, while trying to rest in their dormitories, while kicking a ball around outside.

As mad as this all seemed there was a purpose to this ragging. New recruits came from all walks of life and experiences and senses of entitlement. These first six weeks were about pushing all the cadets right down so that they knew they were on the bottom rung of the ladder. So no matter who you were when you came in, socially or academically, you were all leveled to the lowest rung by the end of the six weeks. At the end of it you were a nobody. Just like the guy next to you. Then they began moulding you into an officer.

In addition to these four city boys from Singapore, there were a few cadets from Sarawak in Borneo, and some Malay and Chinese cadets from the Federation itself. As they suffered together during this ragging period, a strong camaraderie developed among the cadets. This challenging ragging period was forging them together, which was partly its intention.

While everyone had a tough time, the Malayan trainers seemed to be harder on these Singapore city boys than they were on the other cadets. Part of the problem for them was that, apart from being considered city boys (though not many of them would have been true city boys and had grown up in kampongs like Clarence), for the last few years the "Sword of Honour", the prize for the top cadet of each class going through, had been won by boys from Singapore. So the Singaporeans had a reputation for being good. It was therefore the job of the senior cadets to break them down and ensure no ego preceded these city boys. What's more, they knew that some of them, like Clarence, had some military experience already, through the SVC, so they wanted him and his buddies to know that counted for nothing.

To be honest though, Clarence and his buddies had been half prepared for this "bullshit". So it was not an entire shock. They had been briefed by their commanders on what to expect before they left Singapore, and were told just to play ball and stick with it. Fresh cadets from the city were always going to get it tougher. The senior cadets needed their little power play and the best way to deal with it was to simply suck it up and put up with it. They could leave it all behind when the course finished. Their commanders had also given them some useful advice. For example, that they each take with them two pairs of boots and an extra set of utensils and mess tins. "Only ever use one pair of boots, and polish up the other pair of boots nice and shiny and keep them hidden in your cupboards along with these untouched mess tins and utensils," Clarence recalls being advised by the commanders. "Only bring them out for room inspection. It will save you a lot of time and hassle." So, with tips like this, they managed to devise ways to get around some of the nonsense that was being dished out to them. The rest they had to just suck it up and let roll over them.

––––––––––

In total, Clarence and his fellow cadets spent six months at the SSOCC at Sungei Besi. It was tough but it prepared them well. Following the ragging period things became more civilised, but they still worked hard. The focus of the course was to train field officers who could be deployed to lead soldiers into battle. Hence they spent more time doing field exercises than doing academic studies in the classroom. Clarence and his three buddies were the first Singaporeans to be sent on this specific SSOCC course. Other Singaporeans from 1 SIR had previously completed the more academically focused two year officer cadet course, but not this shorter version.

When the six-month course was completed Clarence was rewarded by becoming a fully commissioned officer and became known as Second Lieutenant Tan Kim Peng.

Then it was time for one last challenge. After the passing out ceremony he had twenty-four hours to clean up, ship himself out of his dormitory and get himself back to Kembangan Hill in time for the Chinese New Year Reunion Dinner. His parents, Daisy and Hood Hin, and the Matriarch, were expecting him back and heaven forbid if he did not make it back on time, regardless of any new job title and epaulets that he might now be carrying on his shoulders. So, soon after midday on 12th February 1964, Clarence sped south from Sungei Besi along Federal Route Number 1 in his red MG Midget convertible car, making it back home just in time for the big feast.

And back to a Singapore that was, politically, very different to the one he had left six months earlier.

Singapore and Malaya's geopolitical make-up was continuing to evolve. For some time now the leaders of Singapore had been discussing the idea of a merger with the leaders of Malaya as a way to improve the chances of the island's political and economic survival, and as a way to gain independence from the British. (Remember that, when Clarence left for his officer cadet course at the beginning of August 1963, while the Federation of Malaya was an independent nation, Singapore was still a British Crown Colony.)

The idea of a merger was not something that the Federation of Malaya, led by Prime Minister Tunku Abdul Rahman, was one hundred percent in favour of. One of the constitutional premises of the Federation's existence had been a country where the Malays could rule themselves as they had done so before the British had arrived and imported large numbers of foreigners, primarily Chinese and Indians, to perform labouring jobs around the colony. With Singapore separate to the Federation, the Tunku, as he was commonly known, was comfortable that the population balance, and therefore the political balance, would remain with the Malays, who made up the majority of the population there. Singapore had a large Chinese population, and if they were to be included into an independent Malaya, then the Chinese would be in a position to exert a greater political influence in his country. So he was quite happy to have Singapore excluded when they gained independence from the British in 1957. As were the British, who were quite happy to keep Singapore as a Crown Colony for themselves.

But choices in life are never so black and white, and there were a number of benefits regarding merger, both political and economic, that were recognised by both sides.

The Tunku was well aware of the problems that Singapore's government, the People's Action Party (PAP) government, led by Singapore's first Prime Minister, Lee Kuan Yew, were having both inside and outside of their own party, and he was concerned about the potential for communist interests to gain an ascendency on the island. The idea of a communist enclave developing on his doorstep was something the Tunku was very much against. Although the Emergency was technically over, communists were still causing some lesser problems within Malaya, and if communists were to gain power in Singapore, that would surely not help his own situation. One way to mitigate this problem was to dilute any potential communist threat by absorbing Singapore into Malaysia.

In addition to the communist concerns, economically there was much to be gained for both the Federation and Singapore. The Singaporeans had serious concerns about their economic survival. How was Singapore, this tiny island, going to survive without a hinterland? From the perspective of the government, with Dr Goh Keng Swee as its Finance Minister, a merger with Malaya would provide this hinterland and access to resources and a larger common market, and thus secure its economy. From the Federation's perspective, they would stand to gain from Singapore's strategic location as a major trading hub, and not to mention a significant source of revenue through taxes.

The Tunku acquiesced that merger would be the lesser of two evils. On 16th September 1963, while Clarence was training up near the Malayan capital of Kuala Lumpur, Singapore merged with Malaya. The Borneo states of Sabah and Sarawak also joined in the merger.[17]

A new country had been born. Malaysia.

And Singapore, 144 years after the arrival of Sir Stanford Raffles, finally shook off the shackles of colonialism.

———————

Now that he was back in Singapore, it was time to begin the real work of life as a regular soldier. Once the Chinese New Year festivities were over, Second Lieutenant Tan Kim Peng, along with one of his buddies from his SVC days, headed off to the 1 MIR Camp at Holland Road. Now that Singapore was a part of Malaysia, the 1st Singapore Infantry Regiment, 1 SIR, had been renamed to the 1st Malaysian Infantry Regiment, 1 MIR.[18]

After going through a few formalities at the adjutant's office the two newly commissioned officers were ushered into the commanding officer's, the CO's, waiting room. They waited silently for a few minutes before his personal assistant told them that he was ready to meet them. They then marched in, saluted smartly, and introduced themselves to their new boss.

The CO told them to sit down, and proceeded to brief them on their new roles and what he expected of them and the units they were about to lead. These units were expected to be deployed soon, so their priority was to prepare their men.

---

17 The complete story behind the merger of The Federation of Malaya and Singapore is of course far more complex than the summary provided here, and it's well worth exploring elsewhere.

18 Incidentally, in 1962, a second regiment, called 2 SIR (then later 2 MIR), had been raised and their other two buddies from the SVC days were posted there.

Then the CO, a Scotsman, looked at Clarence and asked him if he had an English name. It was a bit of a puzzling question but Clarence replied, "Yes, Sir. Clarence, Sir." And at this moment, Second Lieutenant Tan Kim Peng was "re-christened" Second Lieutenant Clarence Tan.

Clarence's full name on his birth certificate was Tan Kim Peng Clarence. For the Peranakans, having an English name was quite common. Not that they were necessarily Christian, although many were, including Clarence's mother Daisy, who was Methodist. But it was just that they had historically mingled more with the Europeans over the generations so it was common for many to have English names. Many of the British officers struggled to remember and pronounce Chinese names, so if a young officer did not have an English name, the Englishman would just give him one. As for the Malays and Indians who had signed up, their names did not seem to cause as much of a problem, so they got to keep theirs. As far as Clarence was concerned there were no hard feelings or sense of resentment for using his English name instead of the Chinese name he had used for all of the first twenty-two years of his life. There was no sense that there was any British imperialism or arrogance in it (although there probably was some). It was just the way things were. Given the top brass within the military in Singapore were still British he knew it was simply going to make life easier. So he accepted it.

They were an interesting lot, the British officers in the Singapore military at the time. Of course, Clarence had exposure to them through the SVC, but now he was working with them on a full-time basis. Many of the officers that arrived in Singapore, the field officers anyway, were more senior ones. Mainly Captains and above. And many had already seen service in the Middle East as part of the British Middle East Land Forces involved in the Middle East crisis. It was probably considered a bit of a reward to be sent to Singapore and many received promotions upon what was known as "crossing the Suez Canal", which meant taking up positions at British locations east of the Suez Canal, which of course included Singapore. Technically it was a hardship posting, though, aside from the heat and humidity, there never seemed to be too much of a hardship about it, and they all seemed to live a pretty good life. Their families would be posted out with them, which suggests that it was a nicer place to live than the Middle East, where apparently, families tended not to be posted. In Singapore they lived in nice accommodation, with many taking up residences in the black and whites bungalows dotted around the island. Servants, maids, and nannies were common. A real hardship!

Clarence and his fellow young officers had a great deal of respect for their British commanders. Especially the more experienced ones who had seen action in the Middle East. Given that they had real and very recent fighting experience, there was a feeling that these were real soldiers with something to show for themselves. It was a respect that would prove important, as these were the men who would be their ultimate trainers over the next months, and who could also become their unit commanders and potentially lead them in real combat situations. It was a respect that was returned too. These commanders were mindful that any resentment by the local soldiers would cause problems. "If you give an order and they do not move, then you have a problem on your hands, haven't you?" Clarence would say. The field officers respected the fact that in the field they would have to rely on these local soldiers. Many of these British officers would make the effort to mingle with their local charges after work. Some would even go so far as to learn the local languages.

———————

So as a result of this meeting with his new Scottish commanding officer, Clarence received his "new" name, and his first posting within the army. As Second Lieutenant Clarence Tan, he was immediately put in charge of a platoon of twenty-nine men: 1 MIR, 'B' Company, Platoon 5.

These guys were to become his first military family. They were young men, from privates to sergeants. He would train them, administer them, and look after them. These men would be under his command all the time during his deployment to the platoon. This was no nine-to-five responsibility for Clarence. And they really would become like family. Even the families of his men would become included in the fold.

Clarence would get to meet the wives and young children of his men quite regularly. Once a month, he went down to the soldiers' barracks at Queenstown, the location of the living quarters of his men and their families. There, he set up a table and prepared to pay the wives the allowance that was due to them. As the wives came out to receive their money, Clarence took the opportunity to chat with them and their kids and build up a rapport.

Aside from meeting the families of the men, there was another very important reason behind this monthly encounter. Realising some of the money being paid to the men was being spent at coffee shops and street bars or in the messes on the camp, and also because the men were often on deployment so could not get their cash back to support their families, a separate allowance was paid directly to the wives of the married soldiers. The soldiers still received their salary each month, but this "wives allowance" ensured that the wives got the money they needed to run the household and support the entire family.

Some of the wives lived in kampongs up in Malaysia and were unable to make it to this monthly payday in Singapore. For them, Clarence put the money in to a post office bank account on their behalf. That way, the soldier's wife could access it from a post office near her kampong. Given their extensive network set up for mail delivery, the post offices throughout Malaysia also acted as a bank for the poorer and rural people.[19]

19 This system was developed by the British back in the United Kingdom and then deployed to the colonies and copied by many other countries. It is still in use in many places around the world today. Banking systems like these were set up in a time when the big banks tended only to be present in the big city centres and catered to richer clientele ... but that is another story.

In addition to being a sensible system, it was a great way for Clarence to get to know the families of his men, understand their background, and build a strong unit by developing camaraderie and loyalty amongst them all. And being Peranakan helped. Given that three quarters of his men were Malay he had the advantage of not only speaking their language, but also having a good understanding of their culture.

On a personal level, another big change had taken place in Clarence's life. He had finally moved out of the house on Kembangan Hill. While he would return there to visit the family when on leave and over the weekends, his new home was now with the army, and wherever that would take him. For now, in this first command position, his new home was at Ulu Pandan Camp. It was a new experience, but one that he enjoyed greatly, particularly the camaraderie of camp life. The officers enjoyed the privacy of their own rooms, but they ate their meals together every day and spent hours every night talking in the mess. The mess would sometimes get loud and raucous but in general, the local officers were not a heavy drinking lot, unlike their British, New Zealand, and Australian counterparts. For them, they preferred bonding over quiet drinks than wild drunkenness.

Chapter 10
Riot Control

Late in the afternoon of 21st July 1964, Clarence and one of his fellow officers were preparing to head out for a movie when they bumped into the commander of the platoon on duty that day. There was always a platoon on standby, just in case anything requiring the army's immediate response came up. Upon learning that the two of them were planning to head out, their colleague warned them that it might not be such a good idea. Word was coming through that trouble was brewing in town. Things were turning sour at a procession over by the Kallang Gas Works.

The two moviegoers were not concerned. If there was trouble in town then they were sure that the commander and his men could handle it. Clarence and his friend were off duty, and they were going ahead with their plan to catch a movie.

The two of them jumped into Clarence's convertible and headed out of the camp. However, soon they came across a police roadblock. All cars and pedestrians were being stopped and told to return home. As he approached the roadblock, Clarence, showing his military ID, greeted the police officer in a familial way, the way one might when you are in a similar line of work, and asked him what was going on.

"Sir, problems at the procession are escalating and a curfew is going to be called in shortly," replied the policeman. He advised the pair to return to their camp as there was talk that the army may be called in to back up the police.

So they did. On the way back to the camp they took a detour via the married soldiers' quarters at Queenstown to alert their troops there to be on standby. Arriving back at the camp the pair once again ran into the commander of the standby platoon – this time dressed in his combat gear, armed with his rifle, and about to join his men in the back of a three-tonner troop truck. The duty commander told them that the problems were escalating. The government had declared a POPO and called in the army to help the police. A Public Order Preservation Ordinance was an instrument available to the government that allowed them to bring in the army and riots squads to assist the police in the event of extreme civil unrest.

Things were turning serious. The two officers turned back and began preparing for the possibility of being called out for duty.

———————

Leading up to this event, the merger of Singapore into Malaysia had been an uneasy one. A great deal of political tension had been building between the People's Action Party and some members of the United Malays National Organisation (UMNO) around the special positions that was afforded to the Malays as a part of the country's constitution. The PAP, lead by Lee Kuan Yew, had been pushing for the idea of a "Malaysian Malaysia" where all races would be equal, while ultra-pro Malay members of UMNO were strongly against this. The resulting political racial antagonism developed into a pressure cooker building up too much steam. Then on 21st July 1964, during a procession to celebrate the Prophet Mohammad's birthday, that pressure cooker exploded. Exactly what specific act started it is immaterial, but the riots that followed affected everyone around the island.

———————

The first platoon had been sent out in response to reports of a riot that had broken out between Chinese and Malay youth at Kallang Bridge. When that platoon returned to the camp Clarence would learn from his colleagues that the government had a very serious problem on their hands. In order to contain the situation a curfew was declared for that night, from 9.30pm to 6am the following morning. The army involvement was escalated, and before long Clarence received the order to take his men down to help the police man a road block at Pulau Saigon Circus, near Chinatown. The circus itself, which no longer exists, was a vehicular roundabout. There were very few buildings around it, but a number of important roads connected into it, so it was a logical place to set up a roadblock. As a part of the island's internal security planning, each platoon within the Singapore army had already been assigned a designated area to manage in times of trouble. Pulau Saigon Circus was Clarence's area, and he and his platoon had studied this location before, hence it was an area that they were quite familiar with.

During this era, the army and the police worked very closely together. While some of their army training had been focused on fighting in the jungle, a significant proportion had been directed toward internal security. That is, dealing with civil unrest within the country itself. Until the recent merger with Malaya, the British had retained responsibility for defence, so all the local units had much of their training focused on handling internal security. So, while this was a first for Clarence and his platoon, they had certainly been well drilled for the tasks at hand.

It was early evening on 21st July when the platoon had made their way to Pulau Saigon Circus and set themselves up. They put up a tent that would become the headquarters for their operations, and set up the barriers on the road to control the flow of traffic through their checkpoint. With the curfew in place for the night it was their job to manage it. Working with the police, they manned the road blocks and performed street patrols throughout the surrounding neighbourhoods to seek out and deter curfew breakers and looters.

From time to time during that first night, the soldiers would see a set of car lights approaching their roadblock. Now, technically no one was allowed to be out on the streets during the curfew. Any person on the street was taking a great risk. The platoon were all armed and had been approved to open fire if the situation required. If someone was sighted outside during curfew hours they would be ordered to stop where they were and could be arrested for breeching curfew. If they ran, the order was to shoot them. However, the soldiers remained calm in such situations. No evidence of guns being used by the rioters had been heard and, for now anyway, there was a confidence that no one would dare approach a fully armed roadblock brandishing only weapons of knives and parangs. So Clarence allowed these vehicles to approach, while his men kept their guns trained on them in case the occupants got up to any "funny business". As it happened, given the platoon's road block was close to the General Hospital, most of the activity on this first night, and the successive nights, was people seeking medical attention there. Many were pregnant women on their way to the delivery room. It seemed that everyone wanted to give birth at this time.

It was this kind of situation that made manning a roadblock tricky. Even risky. When a car approached, especially in the night, it was a soldier's job to treat it with suspicion. But you can't just open up on them. The last thing you want is for the situation to escalate due to poor judgement by security forces. When that happens you get bigger problems with the potential for accusations that the authorities are favouring one side over the other. Hence the discipline among the troops and their officers was critical.

———————

The morning of 22nd July was quiet as the sun rose over the island. Although Clarence did not see any casualties, on the first day four people had lost their lives and 178 were injured in other parts of the island. There was a hope that overnight the mood of the mobs would have soothed and the young men, who made up the most part of these mobs, would have calmed down. But that was not how it evolved. It was only a matter of hours before things would heat up again and the rioting reignited. Instead of each side sleeping off their anger, they had more likely used the curfew hours to regroup, take stock of their losses, and plan their revenge. There were plenty of reasons for each side to stay up, brooding and planning their vengeance for the following morning.

It was around 10am when rioting started again in various parts of the island. This time, Clarence's area was affected too. At that point word had come through to his command centre that a small group of young men were gathering near the Boat Quay godowns, wielding spears and parangs. Not a good sign. Even though there was no imminent threat of a clash with another mob, it was important to stub out all such gatherings as quickly as possible. Given it was a small group, Clarence and his police counterpart decided that this was not a large enough disturbance to warrant the army going in. So they placed a call to the Hill Street police station to bring the riot squad in.

Within minutes a blaring siren could be heard making its way to the scene of the gathering. The riot squad were a formidable group, and their arrival at any scene sent fear into the hearts of those who got in their way. As soon as the ang chia, or "red vehicle" in Hokkien, roared into view, the bravado of these rioters disappeared and they started running. The men jumping out of the large vehicles were an imposing and scary-looking bunch. They stormed out of their vehicles and, with wicker shields and long batons in hand, immediately ran after the dispersing rioters. From time to time the riot police would return to Clarence's location with some arrested boys and hand them over to his team for safekeeping, then they would head back to the warren of the godowns to arrest more suspects. More often than not an individual riot policeman would return with three or four arrested youth. Such was the fear they instilled, that even a small group of rioters would dare not resist a single riot squad member. At the end of the roundup the suspects were bundled into the ang chia and taken to the police station for processing.

This went on a number of times over the next few days. In most cases, incidents were directly handled by the police, using the riot police when required. This was technically a civilian problem after all. The police had the powers of arrest, not the army. But since the POPO had been declared, the army provided a backup and supporting role, partly due to the sheer number of resources required to contain the riots, and partly due to the fact that, if things got out of control, a more serious deterrent would be required.

With the resumption of rioting on the morning of the second day, the curfew was re-introduced, and remained in place for many more days as the problems dragged on. For much of this time, the role of Clarence and his platoon remained manning the roadblock and supporting the police in their patrols. At times the platoon was called upon to assist the police in their search for wanted persons. In these situations, in what would be known as "cordon and search" missions, the platoon would encircle an area and the police would go from house to house in search of their target. The role of the platoon here was to stop any runners.

The race riots of July 1964 lasted for eleven days. It was long and exhausting work for Clarence and his platoon, and all the other members of the police and army stationed at various locations around the island. Manning the roadblocks, checking the contents of vehicles, conducting patrols around Pearl Hill, the godowns along Boat Quay, and Chinatown, and riot control. These were tiring, but necessary tasks.

Of course the riots took their toll on the civilian population as well. For eleven days the island was a tense place. People were scared. It was hard to get food and supplies due to the curfew. When the curfew had been reinstated on that second morning, many could not get home from work. They were stranded. Buses and taxis were not working like usual as many drivers refused to go to into certain areas. Some Chinese were working in the city but living in the predominantly Malay area of Geylang Serai and had no means of getting home. The distance was walkable, but it was far too risky for them to do so by themselves. So they went to Clarence's tent at his roadblock and asked him for help. Clarence organised for a three-tonner to take them over to Geylang Serai with a military escort. Then at the other end, there were Malay people working in Geylang Serai wanting to get home to Pearl Hill or other locations around the city. So this same three-tonner would pick them up and bring them back. Throughout these "bus trips" Clarence would be in touch with his colleagues dotted around the town, checking that the vehicles were all getting through safely.

In many ways, unrest within a community is more frightening and unsettling than unrest between different countries or a foe like the MCP. In those situations, it is perhaps easier to view the enemy as the transgressor and to demonise them. But for something like this, within the community itself, amongst people who had lived and worked side by side and trusted and cared for each other for so many years, it is perhaps more unsettling and frightening.

The vast majority of the population had no issue with each other. During the curfew, many people from both sides, young and old, risked their own personal safety by approaching roadblocks during curfew to report on trouble brewing within their own community. Not only did they risk being out and about during a curfew, but they quite likely also risked retribution for their actions from the trouble-makers themselves.

Of course, there was always potential for conflict within the police and army as well, as they were all mixed race. But they held their own. Within the military units, including Clarence's platoon of whom two-thirds were Malay, there were no problems – an achievement of which he and all his colleagues were very proud.

It took eleven days for the turmoil to calm down to the point where the curfews could be lifted completely and the police could be stood down, the road blocks removed and the military returned to their barracks. Over that period 23 people lost their lives, and 454 were injured. From Clarence's observation many of the killings seemed to be tit-for-tat. One Chinese woman killed in Geylang Serai. Then a Malay woman killed in Chinatown. Back and forth. Somehow, he figured, the rioters were getting news of these murders. There had also been significant damage to property, particularly around Kallang and Geylang Serai. Windows were smashed, shops ransacked and burned, cars overturned and set on fire.

Following the riots the government set up multi-racial committees around the island to work with the local communities to resolve concerns arising between the different racial groups. Racial diversity was a reality for Singapore and it had to be managed well. In 1997, Racial Harmony Day was launched to commemorate this diversity, and particularly to educate students about other cultures and the importance of interracial tolerance. Its date is 21st July, the day these racial riots began. And your Kong Kong, Emma and Luke, especially hopes that reading this chapter provides you with a deeper appreciation of the significance of Racial Harmony Day.

───────────

With the riots over, life returned to normal for Clarence back in the army camp. For a while anyway. The next thing in his future? After spending the last eight months in Singapore, he and the rest of his 1 MIR colleagues would spend much of the next nine months living in the jungles of Peninsula Malaysia and Borneo.

Oh, and he did get to see his movie in the end – *A Distant Trumpet*, an American movie about soldiers and red Indians.

Chapter 11
Jungle Training
and the September Riots

Indonesia was not so keen on the idea of this new country called Malaysia.[20] In 1963 Indonesia started to demonstrate its dissatisfaction militarily by making minor incursions into Malaysia's side of Borneo. Borneo was, and still is, a massive jungle-clad island, with the new Malaysian states of Sabah and Sarawak in the north, and the far larger Indonesian territory of Kalimantan taking up the rest of the island. With the formation of this new country, Malaysia and Indonesia now shared a long, mountainous, jungle-clad border on Borneo. While all-out war was never declared, the raids along the border did have to be dealt with. The response was spearheaded by the British military, but since the incursions were technically into an independent Malaysia, she of course was very much involved. It was her land, after all.

To enable a rotation of the Malaysian units, the regiments in Singapore also played their part. While 1 MIR already had engaged in some jungle training, more exposure was going to be required before these units would be in a position to take on experienced Indonesian soldiers in the jungles of Borneo.

To prepare for this, a small select group comprising of Clarence, two other officers, and three NCOs was sent across the causeway to Johor to attend the British Jungle Warfare School at Kota Tinggi. Their job was to master the art of jungle warfare, then to train the rest of their 1 MIR colleagues after completing the course.

---

20 See Chapter 13: Confrontation for more on the issue.

The British Jungle Warfare School (JWS) had been set up in the early years of the Emergency to prepare British soldiers for fighting and living in the jungle – living perhaps being the more important lesson. During times of war, death from malnourishment and tropical diseases like malaria often took more lives than bullets and mines in the jungle battlefields. There was no way a British soldier new to the region was going to be able to step off a plane in Singapore or Kuala Lumpur and immediately be an effective fighter in the jungle; neither the rolling hills of the United Kingdom nor the sands of the Middle East would have prepared them for this tough environment. So, upon arrival, all new soldiers were sent off for a course at the JWS in Kota Tinggi before heading off to fight in the jungle against the MCP. Having been running for a few years by now, the school had a strong reputation around the world and even saw soldiers from the American and South Vietnamese armed forces attending its courses.

The six men spent four weeks at the JWS. Again, for Clarence, being in the jungles of Johor was in many ways like being back home running around the kampongs of his childhood. Sure, the jungle he grew up surrounded by was not as untouched as the wild jungles of Malaya, but there was a certain degree of familiarity that he revelled in. Especially here in Johor where it was relatively clean with tall trees and not much undergrowth. The kampong boys like Clarence were at home in this environment. They knew what plants they could eat. They could easily climb trees to pick fruit to supplement their rations or do some scouting. They were already acclimatised to this rugged environment. Some of the Malay kampong boys were real jungle pros, and would even teach Clarence a few tricks. And given that Clarence had also done time in the jungle when he was with the Singapore Volunteer Corps, this time at JWS was in many ways a refresher course.

For a true city boy, it could be a bit tough learning how to live in this environment. It could protect you and consume you at the same time. So it was critical that they all became totally comfortable living in the jungle. How to deal with the creatures that inhabited it: insects, scorpions, snakes, elephants, tigers, boars. How to recognise and deal with diseases. How to set up camp. How to find food in the jungle. What you can eat. What you cannot eat. How to manage your hygiene. How to manage injuries (even small flesh wounds could turn fatal if left untreated in the heat and humidity). How to navigate. How to hide. How to disguise your movement. How to become one with the jungle.

While Clarence and his five other colleagues were training at JWS in Johor, the rest of 1 MIR had piled onto a train and headed further north to the town of Taiping, slightly west of Ipoh. It was in the jungles of northern Peninsula Malaysia where the entire regiment would train and prepare for their deployment to Borneo in a few months. Taiping would be its headquarters. Clarence's 'B' Company itself was then repositioned away from the 1 MIR headquarters to their own forward operating base in a small town called Tapah, about 30km southwest of the old British tropical retreat of Cameron Highlands. Their first few weeks will have been a bit of a dull time for Clarence's platoon. While the other platoons of 'B' Company headed out for patrols in the nearby jungle, they remained in the camp. Without Clarence there to lead them they could not conduct patrols, so they ended up with the rather mundane job of guarding the camp.

As it turned out, they would be stuck on guard duty a little longer than originally planned: Clarence's journey to join them up north was delayed.

Instead of being driven by an army Land Rover, Clarence had opted to drive himself up to the JWS camp at Kota Tinggi at the beginning of the course. It gave him and his buddies some flexibility whenever they had downtime during the jungle training. With the course now over, he and two other Singaporeans squeezed into the car for the drive back to Singapore, their haversacks crammed into the small boot. The plan was to drive back to their camp at Ulu Pandan in Singapore, park the car, hand over their rifles, then jump on the next train to Taiping to rejoin their units.

That was not how things happened though.

After an hour or so of driving, the three men arrived at the causeway connecting Singapore to the rest of Peninsula Malaysia. Once there, they received news that a riot had broken out on the island and that a curfew was about to be put in place. Again. It was just over a month since the end of the last unrest.

Since their regiment was out of Singapore, they decided to head to the camp of 2 MIR to see if they could be of any use to them. With 1 MIR out of town, 2 MIR had been called in to assist with riot control. But these three men from 1 MIR were of no use. They did not have their platoons, so they had no men to take on patrols. The next logical thing to do would have been to head up north to join their own units. But that was not possible either. Trains in and out of the island had all been stopped as part of the riot control measures so there was no transport for them to Taiping. They were advised to head home and enjoy a break until it was all over. Clarence's platoon would have to enjoy their guard duties at Tapah camp for a little longer.

The three men then drove over to their own 1 MIR camp. With the regiment posted up north the camp was pretty much empty. The only people left were the rear party, a handful of non-combatants who had stayed behind to hand over the camp to a new unit. For personal protection, Clarence was issued with a couple of magazines of ammunition for his rifle, then it was time to head back to the house on Kembangan Hill to sit out the disturbances. Since his two friends lived along his route home, he offered to drop them off at their homes.

His two colleagues lived on Mountbatten Road, just past the old Kallang Airport and near the southern coast. Since these two men were married, the army provided them and their families with small bungalows in this area (some of which still stand there today.). Upon arriving at their house, Clarence joined them inside for a small bite and a chat. By the time he was ready to continue the final couple of miles to his home, the curfew had already come into force. His colleagues suggested that he wait out the curfew at their house; they had enough room for him to sleep over. But Clarence would not have it. He was in uniform and was carrying a weapon. He felt it inappropriate for him to stay like this in a family home. He was willing to risk driving during the curfew and figured he would be alright if he was stopped.

So Clarence got back in his car, bade farewell to his colleagues, and began the final short leg home. The afternoon was eerily quiet. No other vehicles were on the road. No one was out walking. Technically he should not be out too. But he figured that he had no choice. As he drove he was not sure what he should be more concerned about – being sighted by the police or being set upon by a group of Malay or Chinese thugs. He made a left to Telok Kurau, and then right to head further east along Changi Road. Turning left on Lengkong Tiga Road, he began the final stretch up the dirt road to the house on the hill.

Suddenly from the corner of his eye he caught some movement. A man was running out from one of the houses in the kampong located at this southern end of his family's estate. Before he knew it, the man was standing in front of him on the road, frantically waving to him. Clarence quickly stopped the car.

One's initial reaction to such an encounter during a time of civil unrest like this would probably have been shock and fear. Clarence became a little less anxious when he realised that the man in front of him was not some riotous lunatic, but one of his childhood friends, Hamid. The boy who had taught him how to catch love birds. Hamid was calling his name, warning him of something, panting from the dash he had just made out to the road to intercept Clarence. As he approached Clarence's car, he gestured at him to turn off the road into his kampong. Naturally Clarence was a little perplexed. When his friend explained the situation, it became quite clear that something bad was happening further up the road. Something that Clarence needed to stay clear of. According to his friend, a group of ten or twenty Malay youth from Kampong Batak, in nearby Eunos on the other side of Kembangan Hill, had come to their kampong to create trouble. They were currently gathered just up the road and it was suspected that they had just killed a Chinese guy. If Clarence were to continue up the road, then he could be next.

Clarence turned left, off the road, and drove into his friend's pondok. He would be safe here. Here everyone knew him and would be able to hide him from this mob if they came through their kampong. Given he had his gun with him, Clarence figured that he might be able to contain a small group if he did encounter problems. But not a group of this potential size. Staying with his old childhood friend in his kampong was the best option.

After parking the car, Clarence and Hamid moved to a concealed location where they could peer up the road without being seen by the mob. Sure enough, it was a decent sized group and they seemed to be milling around looking at something in the ditch running along the side of the road.

Using a nearby public telephone, one of the elders in the kampong had called the police and before too long the siren of a police car could be heard in the distance. Upon hearing this, the group of youth made a run for it, probably heading back to their own kampong in Eunos. As the blaring sirens got closer, Hamid and Clarence were able to make out two police cars turning onto Lengkong Tiga. At that point they felt it was safe to step out from their hiding location and onto the road. Together, they waved the cars down.

The police cars stopped upon seeing them. The police were initially curious as to what an army officer was doing here as they had not been informed of any military units operating in this area. The police inspector asked Clarence what was going on, and Clarence explained the situation, pointing out where the Malay mob had been milling around. "And there may be a body up there," he added.

Clarence still wanted to get home. He got back into his MG and followed the two police cars further up Lengkong Tiga. A few hundred yards up the road the three cars pulled over at the approximate location where the mob had earlier been milling around. The policemen got out of their cars to search the surrounding area for signs of any victims. Clarence also got out of his car to assist them in their search.

After a short time one of the constables called out, "I've found a body in the ditch beside the road." Clarence looked on as the policemen approached the body. Alas, the victim was dead. He had been stabbed in the stomach with a knife and had bled to death. Clarence recognised the man from the kampong on their property.

Realising that he was not in a position to provide any assistance Clarence thanked the inspector for his escort and said that he could make his way home from here. Concerned that some of the mob might still be hiding nearby, the inspector offered two of his men and their car as an escort home. Clarence accepted.

We will never know for sure if Hamid saved his life that day, but he certainly did save him from a very precarious situation.

———————

These riots lasted for over a week. The initial murder of a Malay trishaw driver that had sparked it all had occurred on 2nd September 1964, and the curfew was not lifted until the afternoon of 14th September. The family kept track of events via the radio. They also had a telephone in the house now, so Clarence was able to keep in touch with the colleagues left behind at his camp. He was also privy to updates from his fellow soldiers from 2 MIR as they ended up doing patrols in the vicinity of their property.

From time to time Clarence and his brother Colin would head down to visit the kampong folks around their estate. They were a mixture of Malay and Hainanese Chinese. They had no problems among themselves and were quite upset about the divisions and the violence that had arisen between Malay and Chinese youth in various parts of the island, much of which was happening only a few kilometres away in Eunos and Siglap. In fact, their friends in the nearby kampongs were working together to keep the bad elements out. Early on during the problems the heads of the two communities had devised a system to warn each other of impending trouble. At the first sign of problems, someone would knock on one of the lampposts within the kampong to warn all their neighbours. Chinese and Malay alike. All able-bodied men would then come out of their homes and form a group to confront the potential troublemakers and chase them away. The neighbours all met regularly under the trees in the kampong during the night, during the curfew hours, as they often did during normal times. But as soon as an army patrol came along they would disperse and return into their homes. They were a tight community. And all were willing to fight anyone who threatened their kampong, regardless of race.

By the end of the problems, 13 people had died and over 100 had been injured. It was the second blight on racial harmony within two months that the island had had to deal with.

With the curfew lifted, the trains had restarted plying the tracks between Singapore and the mainland. Clarence soon thereafter received a call from his camp to tell him they were sending a Land Rover over to pick him up. The driver would take him down to the railway station, where he would take the twelve-hour train ride north to reunite with his platoon. The unplanned holiday was over.

Chapter 12
Hunting for Communists

On 15th September 1964, after a long train journey from Singapore to the Tapah Road Railway Station, Clarence rejoined his company and platoon. His men could now look forward to a break from guard duty and more interesting times patrolling the jungle.

The reason for moving the regiment so far north for this jungle training, instead of the much closer jungles of Johor, was twofold. The jungle up in Pahang was thicker than it was down in Johor, and more like what they would encounter in Borneo. So it provided a more realistic training environment for that pending deployment. In addition to this, the MCP was still active up in the north, albeit at a very low level. Johor had been well and truly cleaned up of the communists by now, but they were still known to have a small presence up here in the north. So their training would have the secondary purpose of mitigating the MCP threat. Again, this was to be a training-cum-operational exercise.

Actually, by now it was not just the MCP that was a concern in the area. While the bulk of the Indonesian intrusions into Malaysia were occurring on Borneo, 1 MIR's patrols were also to keep an eye out for any Indonesian soldiers in this part of the country. The Indonesians had also been making some incursions into Johor so it was quite possible that they could be trying to establish a presence in other parts of the Peninsula. Perhaps landing by boat on the east coast at places like Terengganu. Or by parachute, as they had recently into Johor.

Given that the counter-insurgency was primarily a civilian concern and that it was now a relatively minor problem, it was the Malaysian

Police (and not the army) who were spearheading the operations against the MCP. A small contingent of policemen, known as a Police Field Force, were already based at the camp when 'B' Company arrived to help them out. The camp itself was an old abandoned military camp, probably first established by the British in the early days of the Emergency.

Now that he was back with his unit, it was time for Clarence to get straight to work. The first order of duty was a briefing from the police commander regarding a patrol that Clarence was to take his platoon on the following day. Some of the aboriginal people living in the area had reported seeing some movement in the jungle not too far from their location. Pointing out the planned search area on a map, the commander instructed Clarence to take his men into the jungle to investigate further. It was to be a simple scouting operation. If they found nothing after a day or so, then they should return to the camp.

So early the next morning Clarence took his platoon to begin exploring, and training, in the jungle. After being dropped off by a three-tonner around ten minutes from the camp, the team of soldiers from Singapore entered the jungle to begin their search.

Immediately it became evident that the jungle up here in the north was much thicker than what they were accustomed to in Johor and in Mandai in the north of Singapore. They spent the entire day slowly pushing their way through the thick vegetation. It was hard work, and certainly a shock to the system for the fresher members of the platoon.

The men slowly covered the area they were ordered to, searching for any MCP operatives or any indications of their presence. No rewards were coming through. The platoon were making their way through portions of the Titiwangsa Mountain Range, which included a lot more uphill slopes than any of them had ever encountered on foot before. With Singapore's tallest hill, Bukit Timah, standing at just 163m, these men had very little exposure to hill work. However, the pace of their movement was slow due to the thick vegetation, so they were not as exhausted as they might have been otherwise.

There was something even more novel about to spring itself upon the men as the end of the first day began to draw near. Something that would teach them a valuable lesson on a new threat they might face in the hills. A freezing cold night. Who would have thought that it could get cold in the jungles of Malaysia? This was the tropics, right? The thought of cold weather had never crossed the minds of these guys. But when you are at the top of a mountain that is close to 2,000m high, the temperature does drop. Especially when the night falls and the heat of the land disappears into the clear sky. The nighttime temperatures at these elevations in the Titiwangsa Range could drop below 10 degrees Celsius. And so it was, on that first night in the jungle, Clarence and his men experienced a restless sleep, shivering with only their army cotton fatigues to protect them from, as far as they were concerned, the freezing weather. Not surprisingly, the men broke camp earlier that morning and continued their patrol just to keep themselves moving and warm. That first night had been a valuable lesson. They took more clothes with them next time.

The men continued their search for another hour before Clarence called it off and led the team back to their base at the Tapah. On returning to the camp Clarence reported to the police commander that they had seen nothing. The commander was not surprised. The aboriginals had them chasing a lot of "ghosts"– they received many reported sightings that had come to nothing. Maybe the aboriginals saw them. Maybe they didn't. But the security forces had to follow up on all reports. If nothing else, it kept the heat on the MCP knowing the security forces were continually hunting them. And it kept the spirit of the aboriginals on their side by assuring them that the police and army were looking out for them.

For the next month, Clarence and his platoon spent most of their time in the jungle, following up on reported sightings. Chasing ghosts.

But it was good training. The men were getting used to spending longer periods of time in the jungle without their usual creature comforts and this was important. All soldiers experienced in jungle warfare know that while the jungle can be your friend, it can also be your enemy. So they needed to learn to live in it for extended periods of time.

After a month in Tapah, it was time for a new mission. For this one, Clarence and his platoon jumped on an RAF Douglas Dakota C47 airplane, the military version of the well known DC3, and flew north to a small Police Field Force camp called Fort Tapong, near the town of Gerik, just south of the border with Thailand. Flying pretty much directly north over the jungle-clad mountainous spine of the Titiwangsa range, which stretched all the way north into Thailand, was an enlightening experience for the men, giving them an aerial view of the land they had been living in for the last month. One benefit for combatants living in the jungle was the cover it provided from aerial surveillance. During the Japanese occupation spotter aircraft had been unable to detect entire camps that contained hundreds of resistance fighters from the MPAJA due to the thickness of the canopy. It dawned on Clarence and his team as they flew toward Gerik how much harder it was to conduct aerial searches for the MCP given their current low numbers. Hence, the greater importance of putting feet on the ground and conducting patrols.

As they approached their destination airfield, the aircraft made a few low sweeps around the area to give the men an idea of the terrain they were going to be living in for the coming weeks. As they flew, the pilots pointed out the border between Thailand and Malaysia. Some parts were defined by a small river, with Malaysia on the southern bank and Thailand on the northern one, and the exact border line being at the mid-point of the river. Small wooden bridges could be seen connecting the two nations, allowing movement of foot traffic between the two. The rivers were not wide so swimming would have been another option for anyone wanting to cross should they have little to carry.

After completing their scenic tour, the Dakota flew over a saddle between two hilltops and below them appeared a small clearing in the jungle that was to be their destination. The aircraft headed downwind of the clearing, then made a hard right bank and descended into a valley that led back up to the airstrip. Within a few minutes the rubber of its wheels kissed the dirt of the short airstrip. The Dakota was perfect for this role of carrying troops and supplies into very short and rough airstrips.

They had arrived at their home for the next two weeks.

Fort Tapong was deep in the thick of the Malayan jungle. It was called a fort, but it was really just a clearing in the jungle with a wooden fence around it and a police post inside, and the airstrip. About twenty to thirty people were based here.

The British had built a number of these forts around the country during the height of the Emergency. A number of them had small airstrips built alongside and the Dakota was the largest aircraft that could land at many of these strips, so they were generally not long. Fort Tapong was one of the hairiest to land in. Only around 500m in length, even with the Dakota there would not have been much room for error. The jungle-clad limestone hill at one end of it would have become the final resting place for any aircraft that did not manage to stop in time. Apart from when flying over the top of it, the airstrip only came into sight at short finals so the entire approach had to be flown very accurately, following a river then cutting their engines once the strip came into sight as the plane skimmed over a small hill. The pilots only had a few seconds between seeing the airfield and making a decision to continue to land or not. Even the pilots found the strip intimidating and, not surprisingly, there were a couple of accidents there over its operational period.

Fort Tapong was the latest, and last, of the jungle forts to be established. Built in 1959, its remote location was indicative of where the focus of the fight was at the time: right up near the Thai border, where the MCP was making its "final stand". They were still active, at a very low level, in this region on the Malaysian side of the border, but were retreating into Thailand to escape capture. So remote was it, that the airstrip had to be built by hand by the Royal Australian Engineers. There was no way to get any heavy machinery in to help them. All the trees were cut down, all the dirt moved, and the runway prepared by hand. This was the thick of the jungle.

Once on the ground, it was straight to work for Clarence. First was an introduction to the local police commander, followed by a briefing on the upcoming mission. The briefing covered the terrain of the area, where the Thai border was, the suspected location of the enemy and their recent known and suspected activities, and the operating areas of friendly forces. British, Australian, and New Zealand SAS units were also in the area. There were also very strong words about not crossing the border into Thailand.

"You cannot go over this river," the police commander said, gesturing at a map. "That is Thailand on the other side. Cross over and we will have a big problem on our hands and you will be getting a call from the Tunku [Prime Minister of Malaysia] himself," he said. This rule was very strict. If they encountered suspects who fled across the border, they would just have to let them go. "Let Thailand worry about it."

Next the police commander told Clarence that he was going to need some help from the local indigenous people while in the jungle. He instructed Clarence to follow him. There was a very important man he needed to meet. As the two men headed outside, the rest of the platoon were milling around awaiting their next instructions. The commander smiled wryly at Clarence and suggested that it was best that his men stayed where they were for now.

The commander led Clarence a short way along a path through the jungle until they came across the village of the local aboriginal people. This was the first time Clarence had seen such a village. Young children were running around naked and playing with no care in the world. Men wore no more than a loin cloth tied around their waist, with strips hanging loosely down to cover their genitals. Some of them carried spears, and one was carrying a dead boar on his back that he must have just caught. The women, bare breasted, a few carrying young babies on their back, turned to stare at these outsiders. Clarence now understood why the police commander had suggested that his men stay behind. The young soldiers with their raging hormones would have been embarrassed here with these half-dressed women around. It was obvious that the police commander was a familiar face, as they comfortably greeted him as they walked by. Even having had exposure to Western-style dressing for some generations, these people must still have wondered why it was necessary to wear so much clothing in such a hot climate.

These people had been living in the jungle forever. They knew it better than Clarence knew his own neighbourhood back in Singapore. Most importantly for the security forces, they knew how to track the movement of others in the jungle. Call it skill, magic, or witchcraft; their tracking skills were famous. Because of this they had been recruited by the security forces to help them on their excursions into the deeper jungle, to help them follow the trails of the MCP, and to stop them getting lost.

At the centre of the village was an old man sitting down on the ground. He was small, but by no means frail. Had this same man been seen sitting on a street in Singapore he might have been mistaken for a poor beggar. Here, however, he was the king. He was the Chief of the village and the man the police commander wanted Clarence to meet.

After a few pleasantries, all in Malay, Clarence was introduced to the Chief. "What do you want?" the Chief asked.

"I need a tracker," Clarence replied in Malay, which impressed the Chief. Here was a Chinaman who could speak Malay! The Chief called out to one of the young men standing nearby and appointed him to be Clarence's tracker for the platoon's first mission.

The two men then thanked the Chief, bade him farewell, and returned to the fort with their tracker. As they walked back through the jungle, Clarence noticed that their newly assigned tracker seemed a little reticent, and he pointed this out to the police commander. The commander then explained the situation. There was no doubt that the aborigines were on their side. They hated the MCP as much as they did. However, in the jungle they were neighbours. They had been living together side by side with the communists longer than the government forces had. By helping the army and the police they risked getting in trouble with the MCP who had committed many atrocities against these people over the duration of the Emergency. In the early days of the conflict a number of aboriginal villages had been decimated by the MCP after trackers led security units to one of their hideouts. The aboriginals only had spears to defend themselves. The MCP had guns.

There were very few solid structures in a fort like this one at Fort Tapong, so their accommodation here was tents. As he sat down outside his tent on his first evening, Clarence couldn't help but think that he'd never seen a night so dark. His thoughts drifted off to how things had changed for him over the last year. To think, twelve months ago he was working on the wharves in Singapore as an electrician. Just over two months ago he was managing his patrol during the riots near Boat Quay. A month after that he had a week's forced leave at Kembangan Hill during another week of rioting. That all seemed a million miles away now as he now sat in this camp deep in the jungle, beside the gentle flowing waters of the upper reaches of Sungei Perak, or the Perak River.

It seemed impossible to imagine that this beautiful, gentle, world of the jungle and the aboriginal people he had just met could be so punctuated by the violence of the drawn-out campaign against the MCP.

The following morning, the camp was woken by a shriek and a curse from one of the privates. Everyone jumped up out of their beds and ran outside to find out what the commotion was all about. Outside they were greeted by the sight of the young soldier jumping up and down on one foot with no boots on. He had thrown them aside and was cursing them. Something inside had bitten him.

One of the NCOs went over and picked up his boots, turned them upside down and shook them. Out dropped an ugly black scorpion which, upon hitting the ground, danced around with its tail curled up in the air searching for any enemies. The cursing private hadn't been bitten. He had been stung. Nudging the ugly beast on its way the NCO gave the onlookers an impromptu morning lesson on life in the jungle. If you take your boots off, make sure you shake them upside down before you put them back on. Especially in these dry dusty areas like near the airfield. The scorpions were king here. Or maybe the centipedes were. He could not remember. They liked boots as well.

The other soldiers shook their own boots upside down and peered nervously into them before putting them on.

Scorpions, centipedes, snakes, mosquitoes: these were also enemies in the jungles. A bite from a scorpion or a centipede, for all the fear of them, is more of a pain than anything else. It would hurt and swell for a few days, but it won't stop you from moving. And the platoon will definitely not let you whinge about it and slow them up. Snakes, on the other hand, could be nasty and the Malayan jungle was full of them. The Malayan pit viper and the king cobra were the most venomous. Luckily it was very rare for anyone to actually be bitten. But their presence did make one weary. You might be walking along and about to grab a vine, when suddenly you realise that is not a vine hanging down from a tree but a viper. You had to keep awake while moving in the jungle.

Once they finished breakfast Clarence and his platoon set out for their first mission up here near the Thai border. Their job was to head to an area where there had been some reported sightings of MCP operatives and to stake it out for a couple of weeks. While MCP numbers were very low now, and sightings were rare, every now and then some evidence of their presence would be found, so the pressure on them was maintained by having a regular patrol in the area. In knowing that they were still being hunted the MCP were far less likely to try to mount some form of comeback.

So they all crossed by small boats to the jungle on the other side of Sungei Perak, then off they trekked with their tracker in the lead, followed closely by Clarence, then the rest of the platoon.

The jungle was tremendously thick up here in northern Peninsula Malaysia. In addition to the tall trees they had seen from the air, the undergrowth was very thick. Bamboo was a pain. Big bamboo and small bamboo shoots crisscrossing each other made it near impossible to make out any tracks, let alone to make their own. Rattan vines were another hassle. They had hooks and spikes that would latch on to the soldiers' shirts and hats, further slowing them down as they stopped to unhook themselves. It was tough moving. Hats, heads, arms, and even their rifles were getting caught up in the hanging vines and bamboo shoots. When the opportunity availed itself, they would simply follow an elephant trail. Wild elephants moved through here regularly and left a parting in the jungle behind them as they did. Of course, one might think it silly to follow such a path when hunting an enemy who knew the jungle well. But the theory was that the jungle was so thick that even the MCP would also have to make use of the elephant tracks where they could.

There was just one rule regarding following an elephant trail. Don't rest, and definitely don't set up camp on it. If an elephant is a short distance ahead of you on the track and it gets startled for any reason, it is going to turn around on its dainty wee legs and come stampeding back along the very same trail the grand creature had just parted. The very one you are on. And by the time you hear him trumpeting and stampeding back along his trail you won't know which way to run. Or which side of the hammock to get out of.

The men would see elephants from time to time. Big beautiful creatures. Best left alone in the wild. They could work up quite a temper when startled and could run much faster through the jungles than any of these soldiers could. It was quite possible that Malayan tigers were also roaming the jungles where the men were now patrolling, but they were to never encounter any, which was a good thing.

After a full morning of pushing through the jungle, the unit stopped for lunch by a small stream. Being right on the stream's bank would leave them exposed, so they stopped a few metres from the water's edge to give them some cover should any MCP operatives also be in the area. While the rest of the soldiers sat down for a quick bite, four members of the platoon formed a loose perimeter around them, guns in arms, keeping guard for potential attacks from any opportunistic enemy.

Following lunch the tracker led them across the stream to continue their excursion. Not long after crossing the stream, one of his men told Clarence that his arm was bleeding. Clarence looked down to see thick red blood trickling down from under his shirt sleeve that was folded above his elbow. That was weird, he thought. He did not recall scraping his arm. The aboriginal tracker casually walked over, a cigarette in his mouth, to check on the minor commotion. "Leeches," he said. He then rolled Clarence's shirt sleeve higher to investigate. Sure enough, there was a fat, juicy, slimy, black leech sucking away on Clarence's arm. He told Clarence to keep still as he used his cigarette to burn the end of the leech, causing the ugly slug-like creature to detach and fall to the ground.

Then with an air of confidence, the tracker told Clarence that he probably had more on his body. Everyone else would have them too. The leeches probably attached themselves to the men when they sat down for lunch, with a few more latching on as they crossed the stream. So Clarence ordered his men to check themselves, and sure enough they were all covered by leeches.

Leeches were just another ugly reality of life in the jungle. More a nuisance than anything, they would turn up anywhere water was involved. Generally around streams and rivers, though they would also drop from trees onto passing warm-blooded animals, humans included, in the moist environments found throughout the jungle. Quite small to begin with, once they were on their victim they would make their way to its skin, cunningly moving through small gaps in clothing such as boot lace holes or shirt button holes, then sink their teeth into the victim and suck up to ten times their weight in blood. What began as quite small eventually became quite large. In general they were not a problem, other than looking disgusting and causing minor bleeding. The natural instinct was to wipe them off, but that was not the best option as it meant the teeth could be left behind in the skin, possibly leading to infection, which was not something that a soldier wanted to deal with in the jungle. So the recommended approach in the day was to encourage them to let go by either rubbing salt or tobacco on them, or burning them with a lit cigarette.[21] Since all the soldiers smoked back then, burning was what they tended to do.

Once the soldiers had sorted themselves out and were ready to continue on their way, Clarence asked the tracker how long he thought it would take to get to their destination for the day. The tracker, a man

---

21 This practice is no longer recommended due to risks of the leech vomiting bacteria back into the wound. Current recommened practices suggest using a sharp tool, like a knife, to slide the leech off, or simply to leave it be and let it fall off naturally once it has had its fill.

of few words, responded with a simple "not far, maybe two cigarettes". This must be how the jungle folk measured time, Clarence figured. "One cigarette" meant the time that it would take to smoke one cigarette. Clarence was a smoker himself back then. One pack of cigarettes per week was included in their army ration pack, so why not? So he figured that they only had another ten or twenty minutes to go. Not that long.

After thirty minutes they had not yet reached their destination. So he again asked the tracker for a time estimate. The tracker, somewhat bemused by Clarence's repeated question, said they were maybe one more cigarette away.

Clarence was puzzled. That did not make sense. Most people took less than five minutes to smoke a cigarette. So he decided to keep a closer eye on the tracker as he smoked his cigarette. After a few minutes it all became clear to him. After lighting the cigarette, the tracker would take a puff, then stub it out with his fingers and stick it behind his ear while he savoured the smoke. Then five or so minutes later, he would take that same cigarette, light it again, take a couple more puffs, and repeat the process. This guy made a cigarette go a long way.

Sure enough, another thirty minutes later, the tracker stopped, turned to Clarence, pointed at the ground and said, "We stop here." They had arrived at their destination. This patch of jungle was to become their base camp, their home, for the next two weeks.

From this base the platoon would conduct patrols around the general vicinity of the Malaysian border with Thailand during the day, and set up ambushes for the MCP by night. But that would all start tomorrow. What they needed to do now was to set up their camp. Since they would be here for a little while they could afford to spend a bit more time making the spot more liveable than they would if they were just overnighting. So they figured out where they were going to get their water, where they would bathe, where they would wash clothes and mess tins, where they would go to the toilet. While it was still only mid-afternoon, these important activities had to be completed quickly. Light was scarce enough under the cover of the canopy during the daytime, and the dark of the night seemed to come earlier in the thick of the jungle than it did outside. So they only had a couple of hours to get things sorted.

From this base, during their daytime patrols, a small section of four men would head out with the tracker, scouting out for MCP agents, or any signs of their existence. From time to time the tracker would pick up a trail and quicken his pace like a dog picking up a scent. No one knew what sixth sense these men of the jungle had, and Clarence and his men had no idea what clues they were picking up. Whatever it was, whenever the tracker seemed adamant that he had a lead, the best the soldiers could do was to try to keep up with him.

On one patrol, the tracker was certain he had found a recent trail left by the communists, and once again they followed him in his pursuit. They were on a steady walk for more than two hours through the thick jungle when suddenly they came to a swampy area in a small clearing. The tracker stopped. He peered out across the swamp to the other side. Clarence figured he was mad if he thought the MCP would have gone through that. A swamp would only slow them up and leave them exposed. That's if they came this way at all. If there actually was anyone they were pursuing in the first place.

The tracker looked around some more, peering into the waters of the swamp close to where he was standing. Then, he stepped out onto it as if he was walking on water. He then turned to the soldiers to make sure they were watching, and took some more steps out onto the swamp, carefully looking at where he was placing his feet. He then motioned Clarence to move to the edge of the swamp and look down. To his amazement, Clarence saw submerged maybe an inch below the water level a line of narrow wooden planks stretching from the bank out into the swamp toward where the tracker was now standing.

The tracker returned along the plank, not wanting to remain exposed in the clearing for too long, and said quietly to the platoon commander, "MCP are clever."

"Very clever indeed," Clarence agreed.

The tracker was well familiar with this technique and as soon as he saw the swamp he suspected that their prey had used it to escape. The MCP had learned to build bridges below the waterline of swamps where they could not be seen. When they were being chased by the British or Malaysian army, if they were in vicinity of one of these swamps, they would make their way towards it then run across the bridge to the other side of the swamp. The pursuing forces arriving shortly after would find an impassable swamp with no MCP in sight, leaving them wondering where they had gone. No experienced soldier, including an MCP soldier who had been living for years in the jungle, would dare walk through a swamp as it would severely slow them down and leave them very exposed. It seems that the MCP had merely learnt this trick from the aboriginals themselves, who were already using bridges to get across swamps long before these colonialists and communists turned up and disturbed their otherwise peaceful existence. The MCP had just adapted the aboriginal practice and hidden their bridges below the water line.

In the evenings, while based at this new camp, the platoon set about laying ambushes in an attempt to capture unsuspecting MCP soldiers. In general, the jungle was too tough to move through during the night. It was tough enough to move through during the daytime. Even a bright full moon had no chance to penetrate the thick canopy. The British managed some success in moving at night in the jungle, and had provided a degree of training in this to Clarence and his colleagues at the JWS course, but it was generally considered very impractical. Given the darkness of the jungle, torches were required, and of course these just made you a potential target – as good as painting a target on your body and inviting the enemy to shoot you. Thus moving at night was only considered in extreme situations. Because of the difficulty of moving at night, it was suspected that the enemy would move to and from their jungle hideouts just before dusk and just after dawn, if they were to make the most of the light of the day.

So every evening at 5pm, Clarence would send out a section of men to some of the tracks that were known to exist in the area and they would lay low in the bush in wait for any movement. By 6pm it was pitch black and the unit would stay in position, not moving and not speaking. Just watching and listening, in case there were any late stragglers out there. At 7.30pm they would pack up and return to the base camp. Then the same process would happen again at 5am. They would head out and position themselves before first light and wait on the track until around 8am, then return to camp for breakfast.

───────

The platoon spent two weeks on this particular mission in the jungle before returning to the camp at Fort Tapong. In total, including the time further south at Tapah, they would spend around two months in the jungles of Perak. While the MCP were still active in the region, Clarence and his men never did see any of them, though it was evident from some of their patrols that they were present. Were the MCP aware of their presence? Who knows? The jungle was so thick that you might not even know if an enemy camp was located less than a kilometre from yours. Both groups could have been blissfully unaware of the other's existence.

In time to come, Clarence would look back and wonder whether the trackers knew more than they were letting on. The villagers were caught in a precarious position. They wanted to help the British and, later, the Malaysian government to rid the jungle of the MCP. But they also feared the retribution the MCP might pay upon them and their families for doing so. Clarence wondered whether some of the leads that the trackers took them on were in fact wild goose chases and perhaps there was never anything there to begin with. Chasing ghosts. In most cases, if the tracker did not give up themselves, he would have to step in and call the mission off when they seemed to literally be going in circles.

It was also possible that some of the villagers were double agents. Given that they had been living side by side in the jungle for many years, there is no doubt that relationships would have developed between the MCP and the aboriginals. So, it was quite possible that while Clarence was enjoying a cup of tea with some villagers, they could have been hiding some MCP in their longhouses. Who knows?

Having said this, the trackers and the villagers were regarded to be a great ally in the jungle. They taught the men new tricks for living there. Some aboriginals were actually employed more formally by the government and incorporated into the army. They formed a specific division within the army, known as the Malaysian Rangers, originally the Sarawak Rangers, and did away with their traditional clothes to wear full military uniforms.

The communist insurgency was quiet during the times that Clarence was in the jungles of northern Peninsula Malaysia. While the MCP numbers were low and not a major threat, pressure still needed to be kept on them to prevent any resurgence. It was important work that could not be relaxed, as demonstrated by an escalation some years later into what became known as the Communist Insurgency War, or the Second Malayan Emergency, in 1968 and 1969. More than 350 from both sides died during that episode. (Clarence and his Singapore men were not involved in this for reasons that will become obvious later). The entire problem would not formally end until December 1989 with the signing of the Hatyai Peace Accord in Thailand between the MCP and the Malaysian government.

But certainly during the early to mid-1960s, when Clarence and 1 MIR were in the jungles of northern Peninsula Malaya it was very rare to encounter the MCP. Whenever Clarence and his platoon came close, their enemy would escape across the border to Thailand where they lived quite freely. When this happened, there was nothing the soldiers could do. While the police were allowed to conduct activities across the border, the army most definitely could not. The Thais were neutral in this conflict. While they knew that some of the MCP leadership, like Chin Peng, had set up residence in the south of their country, their approach was that as long as he caused them no problems, then they did not wish to get involved. And with no extradition treaty between the two countries at the time, there was no legal avenue open for Malaysia to get its hands on these people.

———————

At the end of the training-cum-operational jungle exercises Clarence and his men had to get themselves from their remote base at Fort Tapong back to civilisation and to link back up with the rest of their regiment at the 1 MIR headquarters at Taiping. And what a memorable trip that would end up being. During their time there they had become friendly with a number of sampan (longboat) owners who lived along the river. The men were in no rush to get back so, instead of flying, they negotiated with the boat owners to give them a ride back via Sungei Perak. They then packed up their camp and jumped into the sampans. After a challenging three weeks of living so deep in the jungle, they were able to sit back against their packs and relax as they glided down the slow meandering river, in and out of the shade of the trees spilling over the river, shooting rapids from time to time for much of that day. In a few years, parts of this river they were travelling on would disappear as some of the valleys it meandered through would be flooded by a new dam built in the early 1970s, impounding Tasik Temenggor, or Lake

Temenggor. Even Fort Tapong would disappear under the waters of that man-made lake. By mid-afternoon they pulled into their destination of a lagoon near Taiping. Having arrived a few hours earlier than expected the soldiers took the opportunity to rest up on the river bank and enjoy a bit of swimming in the river before washing up, changing into more presentable clothing, and being driven the short distance to the army camp in a three-tonner.

On arriving back at 1 MIR headquarters the men were officially on leave. They were free to head off anywhere they wanted for a couple of weeks. Many of Clarence's single men headed off to the beaches of Malaysia for their rest and recreation. As for him, he jumped on a train[22] and headed back to Singapore. Back to see the family at the house on Kembangan Hill.

---

22 Being an officer in the Malayan army meant Clarence got free travel anywhere on the train network. In First Class too!

Chapter 13
Confrontation

After his two weeks of leave, Clarence was on the train again heading across the Causeway and back up north to Taiping to rendezvous with his men and the rest of 1 MIR. Early the following morning they boarded a C130 Hercules transport aircraft bound for the town of Tawau in the state of Sabah, on the island of Borneo. It was a flight that took around four hours and covered roughly 1,900km pretty much due east in this lumbering troop carrier. By the end of the day, Clarence and his colleagues would be in the jungles of East Malaysia, only a few miles from the border with Indonesia.

It was now 1 MIR's turn for deployment to the Confrontation.

The Confrontation, or Konfrontasi in Malay and Indonesian, was a low-level military conflict between Indonesia and Malaysia. For various reasons Indonesia was opposed to the amalgamation of Malaya, Singapore, North Borneo (Sabah), and Sarawak, into this new country called Malaysia. In part they perceived it to be a colonial plot by the British – a way for Britain to retain an element of control in the region, particularly over their commercial assets (like oil fields and rubber plantations) and allow them to maintain a military presence in the region. This was a potential threat to Indonesia who were just on their doorstep, and with whom they shared a 2,000-km land border on the island of Borneo.

The what, how, why, and when leading up to the beginning of the Confrontation is a little complex and a detailed explanation is beyond the scope of this work, so I will keep this explanation of it as concise as I can. An event known as the Brunei Revolt, in December 1962, is often cited as a key moment. While Indonesia denied explicit involvement in this, on 20th January 1963, a month after the Brunei Revolt, Indonesia's Foreign Minister, Subandrio, publically declared that his nation was against the formation of Malaysia and announced a policy of Confrontation against Malaysia. This was not initially a threat of armed conflict or a declaration of war, but more economic and social in nature, since a significant amount of Indonesian trade went through Singapore's port, and reductions in this directly affected Singapore's economy.

However, some months later, on 13th April 1963, an incursion into Sarawak from Indonesia and an attack on a police station at a town called Tebedu, not far from the border, is generally cited as the beginning of the militarisation of the Confrontation. Cross border raids from Indonesia increased over the following months.[23]

In response to these raids British and Commonwealth forces deployed military units into the dense mountainous jungle along the Malaysia side of the porous Borneo border to counter the incursions and attacks from Indonesia. Among them were the British Gurkhas, as well as elite British, Australian and New Zealand Special Air Service (SAS) units.

Given the nature of the infiltrations and the terrain, this Confrontation was being handled at a platoon level. Small units of men were deployed deep into the jungle near the border for weeks, even months at a time. So dense the jungle and formidable the terrain, in many cases, units were inserted by helicopter in to remote locations where the soldiers built their own bases from scratch. From these bases they would begin their patrols deeper into the jungle and closer to the border. Much of their

---

23 It should be noted that many of these, especially the early, infiltrations were actually conducted by irregular communist and nationalist guerilla groups from Sarawak, Brunei, and Sabah, who were also against the British plans for the formation of Malaysia. They were basing themselves on the Indonesian side of the border and in many cases had regular Indonesian troops leading them. As time went on, the infiltrations became predominantly manned by Indonesian troops themselves.

work involved responding to reports of incursions by the local jungle dwellers. Upon sighting the guerrillas or Indonesian soldiers, or coming across evidence of their presence such as freshly deserted campsites, these villagers would report them to a nearby British, Commonwealth, or Malaysian camp, who would then mount a search operation. So thick was the vegetation and large the area that sometimes these searches could take days, or even weeks. Sometimes patrols were the call of the day – navigating through thick jungle looking for signs of enemy presence. Other times they would simply sit in ambush position by a track or a river hoping that the enemy would stumble into their trap. Even when the enemy was sighted and engaged in a firefight, the success rates were often low. The jungle was so dense that a direct line of fire was always difficult, and the infiltrators would quickly make an escape back across the border to Indonesia.

While most of the military action was focused on the island of Borneo, some Indonesian infiltrations did occur directly onto the soil of Peninsula Malaysia.

Alongside the British and Commonwealth forces, the new Malaysian army was very much involved in efforts against the Indonesian infiltrations into both East and West Malaysia. They operated at the same command level as the British and deployed their own troops to the fight. For one of those deployments, the 2nd Royal Malay Regiment (2 RMR) had been based on the jungle-clad island of Sebatik, just south of the town of Tawau in Sabah, for the last six months. They were due for a break. It was now time for Clarence and his colleagues from 1 MIR to relieve them.

———————

After crossing the waters of the South China Sea, the C130 flew across the coast of Borneo just northeast of Brunei. It then made a right turn and continued in a south-easterly direction. Well into its final decent, the aircraft soon crossed the northern reaches of Cowie Bay, at the western end of the Celebes Sea. To the north of the bay lay the mainland of the state of Sabah. To the south, across the Cowie Bay channel, that was around 6km wide at it narrowest point, lay the island of Sebatik.

Sebatik Island, about half the size of Singapore, was one of two islands on which Malaysia and Indonesia shared a border, the other being the massively larger Borneo itself. Bar the open Celebes Sea to the east, Borneo pretty much enveloped Sebatik. The island was split roughly fifty-fifty by a rather unnatural-looking straight line running east-west, with Malaysia possessing the north and Indonesia, the south – one of those bizarre, yet not uncommon, results of territorial divvying up by the Dutch and British colonial powers when they settled their empire borders in 1891.

Before the aircraft prepared for its final approach into Tawau, 20 miles up the bay, Clarence peered out the aircraft's small windows toward the island that was to be their home for the next six months. Apart from the small township of Wallace Bay at the northwestern end, the island seemed to be entirely thick jungle. Directly below them, on the waters of Cowie Bay itself, were a myriad of small fishing boats out catching their fill for the day. Some in Malaysian waters. Some, a little further away, in Indonesian waters.

Upon landing at the Tawau airport, the men marched out of the aircraft to a number of waiting three-tonners, jumped up into the trucks, and were driven down to the docks on the waterfront. There they jumped off the trucks and boarded a small fleet of landing craft that were waiting for them in the harbour. The next hour was spent powering their way west, back up Cowie Bay over which they had flown just moments earlier.

Soon after midday, after more than six hours of noisy and uncomfortable planes, trucks, and boats, the men finally arrived at the quiet town of Wallace Bay.

Wallace Bay was a small town. A village, really. For many years now Sebatik Island had been a source of timber for the North Borneo Timber Company, and Wallace Bay had been home to a small expatriate community that was managing the company's concessions on the Malaysian half of the island. The village had a lumber mill for processing the trees felled on the island, and many of the local people living on Sebatik were involved in the timber industry in one way or another. The wood plant was still operating when the soldiers arrived and large logs, waiting to be processed, were floating just off shore in the bay.

Wallace Bay was also a fortified village. Earlier in the year Indonesian regulars and irregulars had harassed, looted and burned the villages on the island. So, to ensure the safety of the villagers, the Commonwealth forces had relocated them to new dwellings that were especially built for them at Wallace Bay. Aside from the seaward facing side, the entire village was surrounded by a fence of barbed wire. Beyond the fence line was a thousand feet of cleared land, beyond which the jungle proper began. The clearing gave the guards, who were located in a number of bunkers dotted around the clearing, a clear view of any intruders who dared to show themselves on this open land. No one was allowed outside of the fortifications without being cleared. With the mill and processing plant located within the fence line, the expatriate staff and villagers were able to live and work without having to leave the safety of the fortification.

Having the villagers inside the fence benefited the military campaign on Sebatik in a number of ways. It starved the Indonesians of food supplies looted from the villages and removed the opportunity for the Indonesians to coerce the villagers into colluding with them. It also made it safer for the Malaysian soldiers to patrol without worrying about innocent civilians getting caught up in firefights. Just like during the Emergency, it was important to convince the local population that they were here to protect them.

Wallace Bay was the first time Clarence had seen one of these villages. Those established in Malaya during the height of the Emergency had long gone. It was an interesting place. Everyone seemed happy enough. The place was large for the number of people who were there. And after the terrifying raids on their old villages, it surely must have made them feel more secure. But it will not have been home.

Taking over from 2 RMR, Wallace Bay was to be the new operational headquarters for 1 MIR. For some of the men, Wallace Bay was not their final destination for the day. After lunch Clarence's 'B' Company were ferried by a smaller boat to a small camp deep within the jungle, and nearer to the border. This camp was known as Simpang Tiga. 'C' Company were deployed at a different location in the jungle, while 'A' Company remained at Wallace Bay.

As for Clarence himself, he and his platoon did not immediately join the rest of their 'B' company at Simpang Tiga. There was not enough space on the boat for him and his men, so they remained at the fortified village assuming a security role for the first two weeks.

Chapter 14
Into the Field

Simpang Tiga was a two-day walk through the jungle from Wallace Bay. Normally the men would be expected to walk such a distance themselves. But given they were going to be based there for three months there was a lot of extra gear that had to be carried in. So when it did come time for Clarence and his platoon to join the rest of 'B' Company, they too had the luxury of being ferried there by boat.

After travelling around 12km from Wallace Bay they reached the mouth of Sungei Simpang Tiga, or Simpang Tiga River. Just to the south of the river mouth, barely 3km away, the men could see the Indonesian island of Nunukan. A large Indonesian military base was known to be located there – the enemy.

The flat-bottomed boat then turned left and headed inland up the small river for a few kilometres. Dense jungle vegetation surrounded them on both sides, spilling out over the river as if wanting to swallow them up. Before long a makeshift jetty came into view, alongside which their boat docked. They had arrived at the Simpang Tiga base camp.

The camp was a sizeable place that was able to fit a hundred men at times. It was centred around a small hillock that had been cleared specifically for the camp. Semi-permanent in construction, it was certainly not the height of luxury. But given that the troops from 1 MIR would be based there for six months, and before them 2 RMR had been there for six months, something a little better than tents and hammocks strung between trees had been established. Furthermore, this was a conflict zone so the camp was appropriately fortified. At the centre of the camp, on the top of the small hill, was the camp headquarters. At around 20 feet by 20 feet square, and dug around 20 feet into the ground, it was by far the largest structure in the compound. This was where the company commander had his living quarters and where all the conferences were held. Dotted around the headquarters were numerous small dugouts in which the rest of the men lived. Each dugout was home to two men, and these were where Clarence and his colleagues slept, ate, and sheltered from the rain. The dugouts were a trench dug five feet deep into the ground. On the ground surrounding the edge of each one was placed a five-foot wall made of wood and sand bags filled by the dirt dug from the trench. The wall was designed to provide protection from enemy fire. Over the top of the dugout was placed a tarpaulin that provided shelter from the rain. There were perhaps forty to fifty dugouts, positioned around the entirety of the camp, all facing out and intended to provide security for the headquarters in the centre. In the walls of each dugout were small openings through which the soldiers could fire their weapons to ward off any attack on the base. Between the dugouts and the barbed wire fence that marked the external perimeter of the camp was a clear area designed to expose any intruders. Many of the trees that had been felled to make way for the camp had been left lying in this area, providing obstacles that any potential invading party would have to negotiate as they were showered with bullets by the Malaysian soldiers. The perimeter fence, that marked the boundary of the camp, was square and had just two gates for entry and exit. One at one corner for accessing the jetty where the supply boats from Wallace Bay berthed, and the other at the opposite corner providing access for the patrols out into the jungle. Both entry points had a sentry post to control movement in and out of the camp. The camp was quite a set up for one so deep in the jungle, and amazingly the dugouts and the headquarters had all been dug by hand with shovels. And that would have been after having made the clearing in the thick vegetation, also done by hand.

This camp at Simpang Tiga, 3km from the border with Indonesia, performed as 'B' Company's forward operating base. While here the company's three platoons, including Clarence's, performed three different types of operations that they rotated among themselves. One platoon headed out on two-week patrols deeper into the jungle seeking out infiltrations by the Indonesians. The other two platoons remained at Simpang Tiga alternating between nights in ambush and resting. These ambush positions were located nearby and were intended to provide additional protection against attacks on the base.

Of the rotations, remaining at the base camp was the most comfortable. But it certainly was not heavenly. This deep in the jungle meant that there was no fresh food. There was no kitchen or canteen in the camp. Everything they ate was out of combat ration packs. Food was warmed up in the hexamine heaters that they all carried with them, either in or just behind their own dugout – never after six at night as no fires were allowed when it was dark.

Everything here was wet. The jungles of Borneo are not called rainforests for nothing. Their canvas jungles boots, while tough and hardy, got very wet during the day. Each evening when they took them off they were greeted by the sight of their white, soggy feet. Hence, every night they doused their feet in foot powder and placed their boots upside down on poles to dry. For the rest of the evening they wore their simple army-issued canvas shoes around the camp. Even their dugouts would get damp so, when the weather permitted, they would move their simple canvas stretchers outside and sleep under the stars.

———————

Upon arriving at Simpang Tiga Clarence was keen to get on with exploring the jungle and immediately volunteered to take his platoon out on patrol. So the next morning he led his platoon on their first mission: two weeks of hiking patrols in the jungles of Sebatik.

When they had arrived on Sebatik, his counterpart from 2 RMR, whom they were taking over from, had given Clarence and his 1 MIR officer colleagues a briefing on the situation. The Indonesians had been very active in the area during their time there. Pouring over a rudimentary map of the island, their counterpart from 2 RMR pointed out where they had searched over the last few months and where they had encountered the enemy, or evidence of their incursions.

It was known that the Indonesians had a sizeable forward base on their side of Sebatik. It would have been from there that they were launching their sorties into Malaysian territory. To the south of Sebatik was the smaller Indonesian island of Nunukan, the one they had seen from their boat on the journey from Wallace Bay before heading up the Simpang Tiga River. On this island the well-respected KKO (the Korps Komando Operasi or the Indonesian Marine Corps) had a battalion and a very large camp. In fact, it was suspected to be their largest camp in all of Kalimantan, the Indonesian side of Borneo. British patrol boats operating in the Malaysian waters nearby had observed them shuttling soldiers between Nunukan and Sebatik using old WW2 landing craft.

The purpose of patrolling the jungles on Sebatik was to hunt down these intruders and engage them if necessary. They also needed to ascertain where the Indonesians were entering from and whether they were based up on the Malaysian side of the border. It was tough to find them though. They tended to enter at different locations each time and would quickly return to the Indonesia side of the border once they had completed their sorties.

It was similar work to their training in Perak over the previous months, but there were a few big differences: This current enemy was a far more formidable bunch. The Indonesian army were far greater in number than the MCP were by the time that Clarence joined the army. And, perhaps more importantly, they were a far more professional outfit who had a lot of jungle warfare experience.

From the Simpang Tiga camp Clarence led his platoon into the jungle to patrol an area agreed on with the Company Commander. The immediate objective was to position themselves at the starting point of their patrols, so they made their way to this spot and set up a temporary forward camp from which they would conduct their first patrols. Once they found a suitable place to camp, they checked that the area was safe and decided where to place their sentries for the night. Then they prepared their sleeping arrangements and their evening meal. Their patrols in search of enemy infiltrators would begin the following day.

Every morning during this two-week deployment, Clarence and his sergeant studied the map in detail and planned the patrols for the day. In general the maps of the interior of Borneo were very poor, often nothing more than a piece of paper with a few lines for the borders and maybe a few dots indicating the elevations of some of the mountains or a few towns and rivers. Luckily for 1 MIR, the maps of Sebatik were not too bad. Not perfect, but not too bad. It was not a large island and much of it had been traversed by the North Borneo Timber Company, who had generated their own basic maps, although there were no contour lines detailing the terrain on the island. But they did the best they could with the tools they had. Once the two of them had determined the search area for the day, a section of ten men would move out. Sometimes they were led by Clarence, and sometimes by his sergeant. One of them would remain behind at the camp with the remaining men. The goal of these missions was to first find the enemy, and if the enemy were sighted, the section on patrol would inform Clarence and the entire platoon would then make their way out to confront the enemy.

Given the thickness of the vegetation, searching for the enemy was conducted in a very clinical manner. A point man would always lead the section. He was the primary person responsible for monitoring for evidence of the intruders. He surveyed the bush in front and around him. What evidence were they looking for? Regardless of how careful they were, humans and animals always left evidence, however small, of their passage through the jungle. Anything from broken tree branches to trampled leaves, cigarette butts to food wrappers, footprints to abandoned campsites.

The navigator followed the point man. In the jungle, much of the navigation was dead reckoning. It was never an exact science. Below the treetops there was no way to get a fix on a distant hill or other landmarks. Using his compass and protractor, the navigator would determine the heading to an object up ahead, more often than not a tree. Then he would count his steps to gauge the distance they travelled, tying a knot in a length of string he was carrying for every one hundred steps travelled. The point man would often walk a crooked line. His focus was on surveying the vegetation for signs of human movement and not necessarily keeping a straight line. From time to time the navigator would halt the party so that he could take another bearing, before instructing the team to continue forward in a corrected direction. If the navigator messed up completely they might end up unknowingly retracing some of their own tracks, with the point man mistaking their own movement for the trail of the enemy. Or worse still, accidentally walking into Indonesian territory. This was the wild jungle. There were no fences or big red signs lines on the ground, nor signs saying "Border Crossing" to warn the soldiers that they were about to walk into Indonesian territory. What's more, there were no fancy GPS devices in those days. Sometimes they would follow logging tracks used by the vehicles from the North Borneo Timber Company. But they never walked on the roads. Aside from leaving them exposed to attack, the roads were often too muddy. So they made their way through the bush a few metres in from the roads, under the protection of the vegetation.

Behind the navigator the rest of the section would follow. They kept an eye out for evidence of enemy movement, at the ready for any live enemy engagement. The front two men, the point man and the navigator, had very specific roles. They carried weapons with them, but not always in hand. The rest of the platoon were there to back them up should a firefight suddenly erupt.

Patrolling was a tense activity. Their movement was slow and quiet. There was always the very real chance of engagement with the enemy. At any time an enemy unit in ambush could be waiting for them, hidden among the thick vegetation. Perhaps five of them? Perhaps ten? Perhaps twenty? Perhaps more? The enemy could be lying in wait just around the next corner. They could be watching them now.

The section would update the map as they went along to keep a record of what they had covered. The patrols would also keep in touch with Clarence or his sergeant (depending upon who was back at the campsite) via radio as they moved, with each group having a radio operator. And every evening Clarence would report their progress back to the company headquarters at Simpang Tiga.

When the patrolling section returned to the temporary camps in the late afternoon, the tension was not over. It never was. Especially around dusk, the most tense time of the day. The Indonesians had a habit of executing hit-and-run attacks just before sundown. The timing allowed them to perform their task, then make a run back across the border under the cover of darkness. Clarence wanted his team to be ready for these attacks. So every late afternoon before sundown the entire platoon would be on a heightened level of alertness and would position themselves around the perimeter of the camp in anticipation of an attack. These were known as their "stand to" positions. They would wait for an hour. Silently. Making sure that there was no movement. Then they would stand down and sort themselves out for the night's sleep.

During the night, they all took turns to guard the camp. Two sentries at a time, to make sure both stay awake for their one-hour duty. It was an eerily lonely time sitting there, listening to the normal noises of the jungle, listening for human movement. The nights were dark, pitch black. Even the light of a full moon had trouble penetrating the thick jungle canopy high above them. Clarence himself did not partake in sentry duty per se, but he got up from time to time during the night to check on the guards.

Just before dawn the entire platoon woke to take up the "stand to" positions again. Then thirty minutes after sunrise two sentries would remain to keep a look-out while the rest of the platoon stood down, had breakfast and prepared for the day ahead.

Meals were not the most delightful things to look forward to during these missions. But then again they were not much better back at Simpang Tiga either. The soldiers were living off the same ration packs: high energy biscuits or rice with mutton or chicken curry from cans, heated up in the portable stoves they carried. Some of the soldiers were true kampong folks from villages on the edge of the Malayan jungle. These guys were a real asset when it came to meal times, as they could find eggplants, wild tapioca, or leaves that could be used to supplement the flavours of these mundane army rations.

When morning arrived, there was no time to waste. After their quick breakfast and a cup of tea they would change out of their dry clothes and back in to the army fatigues they wore on patrol, which would probably not have fully dried during the night. They only ever took two sets of clothes on these patrols. One for the day and one for the night, plus a poncho to shelter them from the rain. Then they would begin their patrols again, or first move the platoon to a new forward base camp.

The forward base camps were very temporary. Sometimes they would stay two nights, sometimes only one. They were really just staging points for the daytime patrols so they kept hopping around the area they were assigned to search. And it was too risky to stay in one spot for more than a couple of days anyway. It was possible that Indonesian infiltrators would know about their position, which made the small unfortified campsite very vulnerable, especially at night. Sometimes the decision to move camp was based on their surroundings, such as when they overnighted on a hill where there was no water nearby.

An important part of departing a camp site was the disposal of all rubbish. On these patrols the rubbish would be buried in a hole some distance away from the camp. To completely hide the evidence of a camp site was very difficult. The locations of where they sat and slept and stood left impressions in the undergrowth that would take a good week to return to its original state. However, it was the trash that would give away details of how large their group was. A lot of information can be garnered by the presence of rubbish, so it was important that it was buried, and buried away from the campsite.

Water was the one thing they did not carry a lot of at any one time. Given the heat and humidity in the jungle of course there was a continual need to replenish their fluids lost through sweat. But the jungle always provided ample supply. If they could not catch the rain water that regularly drenched them, there were plenty of streams, though it was often not the cleanest of water – generally muddy and never to be trusted. Who knows what dead and rotting creatures the water may have passed through before it entered their lips? Upon filling their canisters at a stream or pond or, in the most desperate cases, a muddy puddle, they would mix in a couple of sterilising tablets to kill off bacteria and pathogens. It made the water taste nasty, but at least it wouldn't kill them.

One luxury of being on patrol was the chance of encountering larger streams from time to time. Not only would this allow them to top up their canisters with more palatable drinking water, it also meant a more luxurious bath. Back at the Simpang Tiga base camp they had access to a stream, but it was not large. And since that was also the source of water for cooking and drinking they had to be more careful with the way they used it. When they encountered larger streams out on patrols, they would take advantage of them and halt the scouting for a while so they could all take a bath and wash their clothes. Taking turns, of course. Only a couple of men went in the water at a time, with the rest positioned around the site, vigilant for any ambush. Such baths were a welcome and refreshing relief from the humidity of the jungle.

———————

At the end of their two weeks of patrolling, Clarence and his men headed back to Simpang Tiga. While life at the base camp was a relative luxury compared to life patrolling, the challenges of jungle living were not completely over. Simpang Tiga was still deep in the jungle. But at least here there was some semblance of permanence. There was not the continual need to pack up every morning and set up a new camp every night. They had the semi-permanent shelter in the dugout to retreat to, to escape the rain and the sun. Life was a little more relaxed at base camp too. There was less of a reason to continually be quiet and alert as they were a little further from the border. And there was a more rigid and permanent defence strategy around the camp, too.

But it was still jungle living. They still survived on army rations. They still used water from a small stream. They still slept under the stars, preferring it to the floor of the dugout. There was still no electricity, bar a "single set" 12-volt battery that they wired up to a torch hung on a branch to provide a little light in the night. When that torch was turned off, it was still pitch black. Yes, life at Simpang Tiga was still a long way from comfortable living.

Being an officer, there were a few perks that made life in the jungle a little more comfortable for Clarence. All the officers were supplied with a "batman" or a personal servant. Back at their home camp at Ulu Pandan in Singapore this soldier would manage all Clarence's personal housekeeping. Polish his boots, send his uniform to the laundry, clean his room, make his bed, tell his platoon when he wanted them to assemble. The batman also came along for deployments, and Clarence's joined him on Sebatik Island. While on the island there were no luxuries like beds to be made nor rooms to be cleaned, it was still nice to have someone trying his best to ensure he had a reasonably dry, if not one hundred percent clean and creased, uniform to put on each morning. Perhaps his batman's most appreciated role in the jungle came at meal times. Taking advantage of his kampong background, this young private would head into the bush surrounding the camp to find additional food, herbs, and spices, to supplement the tedium of the army rations. The batman was a regular soldier and he would join his officer in their two-week stints away from Simpang Tiga. However, he never left the temporary forward base camps but would stay behind and prepare food for Clarence's return. While from the outside such a role may seem like a luxury, it was an important job that freed the officers up to perform their leadership roles.

For their ambush duty, when based back at Simpang Tiga, Clarence would lead his platoon out to a predetermined location near the border a few hours before dusk and position themselves around what was determined to be a likely path along which infiltrators would enter into Malaysia. Much like they had practiced in Perak before heading to Sebatik, the men would position themselves along one side of the designated area, concealed among the vegetation with their guns aimed toward the target area, and wait. And wait. And wait. Not a word spoken for the entire duration, waiting for the enemy to enter their line of sight. The men stayed in position through the night, and did not return to base camp until after daybreak. It was a tedious but necessary task.

———————

1 MIR encountered nothing during the first three months of their deployment to Sebatik Island. It was as if the incursions had all stopped. Or were they missing the enemy? As a test, an intelligence officer based

at Wallace Bay sent a message through for Clarence to place a little bait out for the Indonesians. Taking an envelope with a 1,000 Indonesian rupiah note[24] in it, Clarence took a small section of men with him and nailed the envelope on a tree near the border, in a location where the Indonesians would be able to see it easily if they crossed over to Malaysia. Three days later, Clarence returned to the location. The bait had been taken. The Indonesians were still infiltrating. But what were they doing then? They were not engaging any of the 1 MIR units.

Of a less subtle nature though, from time to time the Indonesians would lob some mortars across the border, resulting in the night sky coming alive with activity. The British had a big gun at Wallace Bay, so they would lob some back in return. It all seemed rather arbitrary firing to Clarence. The Indonesians seemed to be firing aimlessly. Perhaps they simply wanted to let the Malaysian and British forces know that they were still there, and the British response was simply a "Yes, we know you are." Whatever the reason, Clarence and his team were never perturbed and merely lay outside on their makeshift beds, looking up at the night sky, enjoying the free fireworks spectacle.

———————

When President Sukarno gave his "Tahun Vivere Pericoloso" (Year of Living Dangerously) speech in the middle of August of this same year, 1964, there was some speculation within the Malaysian and British military that, come 1st January 1965, he intended to increase his military engagement in this conflict. Could this have been why things had been quiet for the last few months? Was he preparing for something bigger? Just in case, 1 MIR on Sebatik Island were put on high alert in the days leading up to the end of the year.

---

24 How much was 1,000 rupiah worth back in the mid-1960s? Maybe around one US dollar. Inflation was rampant in Indonesia around this time, so it's hard to nail down what its true value will have been. Perhaps enough to buy a couple of meals back in Kalimantan? Or, of more relevance to a soldier, a few packets of cigarettes?

What this meant for Clarence was that, on the evening of 31st December 1964, he found himself not having a drink with friends or family preparing to welcome in the new year, but sitting in ambush with his platoon on the Malaysian side of the border. Awaiting a possible invasion by the Indonesians. He and his colleagues were a little sceptical about how their current position and numbers were going to be effective. "If they are going to try to 'Crush Malaysia' then they are not going to do so in small units of ten or twenty men. They are going to come across en masse," the men speculated. But there had to be a first line of defence, and they were a part of it.

As they had for many ambush missions over the last few months, they waited. And waited. Nothing happened. They waited all night. Then suddenly, at about 7am, just after sunrise on New Year's Day, from across a river on the other side of the border, came a lobby of shells and machine gun fire. Was this it? Clarence thought. He signalled to his unit to hold still. The shells were not landing near to them so there was no imminent need to retreat or take cover. The Indonesians would have had no idea whether there were platoons lying all along the border waiting for a possible attack. There was a chance that this was diversionary fire intended to make the Malaysian forces think something was going on elsewhere. Or it was possibly fire intended to take out their ambush locations prior to a large-scale invasion by Indonesian troops sitting ready on the other side of the border. Either way, Clarence's orders were to hold his troops in position, ready to engage a possible land assault. So they held their positions, silently waiting as the shells whistled overhead and boomed in what seemed to be random locations.

Then after about ten minutes it all stopped. Followed by silence.

Sukarno had been a hard man to read. From the Malaysian side of things it seemed like he spoke a lot of rhetoric. Was he grandstanding in front of a home audience to appease the local factions? What ever it was, Malaysia and her Commonwealth partners were not going to risk anything and were prepared for the possibility that his words were for real and he really did have plans for an all-out assault on this newly independent nation just trying to find its feet. Or he could have wanted to provoke Malaysia into a military retaliation. If so, then it had not worked. The British and Malaysian governments and military were in no mood to escalate this Confrontation into a full-scale war.

Chapter 15
Of Reconnaissance, Pigs and Hovercraft

In early January 1965 an order came through to Simpang Tiga for Clarence to relocate himself back to Wallace Base, and to report for a meeting at the battalion's headquarters with 1 MIR's commanding officer. The luxury of taking the boat back to Wallace Bay was only afforded to groups with large amounts of equipment to move. So Clarence walked.

After two days of walking through the jungle he arrived at the fortified village of Wallace Bay. One might have thought that life back at the battalion headquarters would have been quite civilised and a welcome respite from his three months at Simpang Tiga and the missions around the nearby jungle. Alas, things were not much more grand here. The soldiers still lived in barricaded dugouts in the clear zone between the village and the perimeter fence. And they still lived on army rations. There were civilians around, and that provided a nice change. The kids running around the village laughing and playing reminded Clarence of his childhood days on Kembangan Hill.

The next morning, he went to the office of 1 MIR's commander. Besides the commander, an intelligence officer, whom he had met from time to time at the base camp, was also present. Something is up, he thought. After a few pleasantries the three men got straight to business.

"Second lieutenant," the intelligence officer said to Clarence, "we need to find out more about what the Indonesians were doing." Apart from the recent brief New Year's party, over the last few months the enemy's infiltration activity on Sebatik Island seemed to have dropped right off and they had no idea why. Was the enemy building up for something bigger? Or were they simply pulling back completely? They had no idea. They suspected the enemy were still making incursions into Malaysian territory, and speculated that it was by the same unit led by the same Indonesian lieutenant each time. They wanted to find out more about this unit – who they were, what they were doing. They instructed Clarence to gather a small team of men to operate in a more covert manner right on the border with Indonesia. Perhaps their current platoon approach was too obvious. So they wanted to try a new technique of using a smaller team, one that could move more nimbly and stealthily. The goal of this team would not be to engage the Indonesians, but to seek them out and observe them and find out more about their modus operandi.

Following the meeting, Clarence put together a six-man team: himself, a senior NCO, a corporal, a radio operator, and two other ranks. After a few days of preparation, they embarked on their first mission.

———————

Clarence led his new unit by foot to the border. No one else was to know about their mission, not even their colleagues from 'B' Company, who were still at the Simpang Tiga base camp, so they took a separate route to avoid the camp and the areas they were patrolling.

The Indonesian regulars from the KKO were very experienced jungle fighters, and they knew how to detect the presence of other people. So the soldiers moved more stealthily as they got closer to the border, disturbing the vegetation as little as possible. It was very slow and very tedious. The men travelled in pairs, in close proximity. They spoke sparingly, using mostly eye contact and hand signals to communicate. By the following morning the men had arrived at the point on the border where the infiltrators were suspected to be entering.

Clarence directed his men, still paired up, to a number of locations to gain different vantage points of their area of surveillance. The men sat and watched, concealed amongst the vegetation. They scoured the surroundings with an eagle eye through their binoculars.

During all their previous patrols, Clarence's units had kept in regular radio contact with headquarters. For this operation it was very different. To reduce the chances of revealing themselves, they had to keep all noise to a minimum. Their only radio communication was with the intelligence officer at Wallace Bay. And of this limited radio communication, none of it was voiced. At predetermined times, both sides would turn on their radio units. Clarence would then make a short burst of Morse code signals to indicate that they were alive and proceeding as planned. Base camp would return a similar burst to confirm receipt. Then the radios would be turned off. Each window of communication was only one minute, so if either party missed a scheduled slot, they would have to wait for the next one. These bursts of Morse code were kept to a minimum. All Wallace Bay wanted to know was whether they were alive or not. The intelligence officer knew what their route was.

At nighttime, their sleeping arrangements made their earlier patrols seem like luxury. Then, they had set up basic campsites to make themselves at least a little comfortable. Here, they just slept where they sat, being extra careful not to upset the vegetation too much lest the Indonesians noticed it. They were also careful not to snore! Their brief radio rendezvous with Wallace Bay were kept going every three or four hours during the night, so Clarence and his radio operator regularly woke from their slumber.

Absolutely no evidence of their presence in this part of the jungle was to be left behind. While this was their own territory, they did not want any Indonesian intruders to suspect that the Malaysians had a new type of unit hunting them. Even their rubbish was handled differently. Instead of burying it as they had on previous platoon missions, they carried everything out with them. Whatever went in had to come out. They left nothing behind.

This new unit would perform five similar missions along the border. These missions were short. Three days maximum. Sometimes they made their way in from Wallace Bay entirely by foot, other times they were inserted to another part of the island by an assault boat and walked into their observation point from there. Not only were these missions surveillance exercises, they were also about experimenting with different operational techniques. At the end of each one Clarence hand gestured to his men to retreat. Then, as quietly as they had arrived, they headed back to Wallace Bay for a debrief with the intelligence officer.

During one mission they went by boat to the edge of a mangrove swamp. They had never traversed a mangrove before and they wanted to experiment with it. What a trial that turned out to be. Not long after being dropped off by the boat they realised that they were in for a long hard day. For starters, a mangrove swamp leaves a soldier very exposed, vulnerable to potential enemy attacks. Worse than that was the mud itself. With every step their boots were swallowed up by the deep, wet mud. Sometimes ankle-deep, sometimes thigh-deep. Pulling their legs out to take each step was like pulling a large rubber sucker off the floor, like walking with two kids holding on to your feet. Every single step was an effort. Every. Single. Step. It was exhausting, painfully slow. It took them a whole day to move just one kilometre. By the time the men made it to dry land they were dead beat. When they finally sat down on firm ground and began removing their canvas boots to empty the mud from them, Clarence muttered quietly, "Well, the Indonesians aren't going to move very fast through that either."

Over the five missions along the border Clarence's unit never did witness any KKO soldiers heading into Malaysian territory. But it had not been totally in vain. If anything, it was a useful exercise in perfecting the art of covert surveillance. A skill that would become critical later in his military career.

———————

Life on Sebatik was not entirely about creeping around the jungle looking for the enemy, living in makeshift camps, sleeping on canvas beds, and eating food out of tin cans. There were other interesting activities going on – at Wallace Bay, at least.

In the early 1950s the world's first hovercraft was developed in Britain. When the military were first introduced to it they showed no interest, but after a few years they came around to the idea that it might be of some use. So they decided to have one built to try it out. Tawau was chosen as the base for their operational trials in 1965, the same time Clarence was there. The first tests focused on running logistical support for military missions in the area, including trips across Cowie Harbour to Sebatik Island. It was exciting for the men at Wallace Bay to witness such a new invention being trialed in the area, especially watching it smoothly transition from the sea to the land and back again. It was a noisy beast whose approach could be heard from miles away.

The craft was so new and so different that the British military could not agree on whose responsibility it should be to evaluate its usefulness. Clarence and his colleagues noticed a number of army, navy, and airforce commanders on the bridge of the craft on a trial ride, and joked that the commanders were arguing amongst themselves about who should be in charge. "The airforce guy thinks it's his because it floats above the surface, the navy guy thinks it's his because it operates on the water, and the army guy thinks it's his because it operates over the land," they surmised.[25]

The testing of the hovercraft also attracted the attention of the Americans, who paid a visit to Tawau to see it for themselves. At this stage they were fighting that major war in Vietnam and were interested

25 This is in interesting contrast to a comment made by the inventor of the machine, Christopher Cockerell, regarding his initial demonstrations to the military in the 1950s. He had apparently later joked "the navy said it was a plane not a boat; the air force said it was a boat not a plane; and the army was plain not interested." Story retrieved from https://eandt.theiet.org/content/articles/2017/04/eccentric-engineer-the-story-of-the-hovercraft-and-silly-chap-sir-christopher-cockerell/

to see how this new vehicle could help them in that campaign. In 1966 the hovercraft was first deployed in that conflict and proved itself to be an effective vehicle of war in the rivers and swamps of the Mekong Delta. Of course, the Americans had to have their own name for it, calling it a Patrol Air Cushion Vehicle, or Pac-Vee (from PACV).

There were plenty of other distractions to keep the men occupied between their missions. One evening, a guard in the camp reported hearing some rattling along the fence separating the fortified village from the world outside. The "high-tech" security alarm system – tin cans tied all along the fence – had clanged, it seemed. Initial investigations into the source of this disturbance came to nothing. Then the rattling happened again the following night. On the third night, a lone culprit was spotted fleeing through the felled trees of the no-man's land clearing from the jungle to the fence line.

Having time on his hands, Clarence offered to bring an end to this menace. He grabbed his rifle, and, with a couple of his buddies, headed out into the clearing to intercept the culprit returning to the jungle. Notification was sent out to all operational units in the area that some gunfire may be about to take place. Not wanting to create too much of a commotion in sight of the villagers, the men decided to follow the intruder into the jungle before they dealt with him.

They followed their target a short distance, careful not to make too much noise. If the figure heard them in pursuit, it might bolt or turn around and try to take them on. The intruder then stopped for a moment. Clarence seized the opportunity. He lifted his rifle, aimed, and pulled the trigger. A loud crack sounded as the bullet rapidly exited from the rifle's barrel and exploded into the air.

Then, all hell broke loose. The squeals of the wild pig whom Clarence had just hit filled the jungle. The wounded beast charged wildly in every direction, squealing and grunting in anger as if determined to find the source of its pain. Clarence and his colleagues watched for a while, moving closer to await its final fall. The noise was horrific.

Realising the animal was going to take some time to die, they decided to leave it alone. It was too dangerous to approach in this state. Never approach a wounded animal. Anyway, it was not going to run far. So they left and returned to Wallace Bay a few minutes' walk away.

All the villagers, hearing the shot and the subsequent squeals, had come out to the fence to see what the commotion was all about. The adults knew what they were listening to, while the young kids were jumping up and down asking what the fuss was all about.

Half expecting to have a cup of tea then return to the scene of a dead pig, they were surprised even half an hour later to still being taunted by the beast's grunts and squeals. In the end they decided to get some sleep themselves before returning to retrieve their prize in the morning. Sometime during the night the creature breathed its last.

At first light, Clarence and his buddies returned to the site of their fallen prey. It had not moved far. Judging from the bloodied and flattened vegetation around it, it was clear that the pig had run around and around in a crazed manner for a long time. It was massive and there was no way the four men were going to be able to lug it back to the village. So they called in one of the army trucks. They then returned to Wallace Bay and handed the pig to the villagers as a gift.

Since the villagers were not allowed out beyond the fence of the camp into the jungle, they were no longer able to hunt for themselves and now had their food brought in from the mainland. So the arrival of this animal, fresh from the jungle, was a very welcome gift indeed. It also gave the men of 1 MIR a bit of kudos, a stamp of approval, amongst the villagers. Actions like this went a long way towards keeping the hearts and minds of the people on their side.

Chapter 16
End of the Tour of Duty

1 MIR's deployment to the Sebatik theatre of the Confrontation was for six months. At the end of February 1965, the regiment was pulled back from the jungle of Sebatik Island and returned to a Tawau camp. Clarence and some men stayed back for a couple more days to brief the regiment that was taking over from them.

When Clarence did finally leave Sebatik to join his colleagues at Tawau, some bad news came through to them all.

About a week earlier it had been reported that Indonesian troops had parachuted into the jungle near Kota Tinggi in Johor. With 1 MIR committed in Sabah, 2 MIR had been called in from Singapore to hunt them down. After a week of searching for the Indonesian infiltrators, one of the platoons from 2 MIR was deep in the jungle, camped up one afternoon in preparation for the night. A number of them had decided to take a bath in a stream at the same time. Unbeknownst to them, while they had been spending an exhausting week trying to track down the infiltrators, they were in fact being followed by the very men whom they were seeking. With their guard down, the Indonesians took advantage of the situation to attack the exposed men with machine gun fire and grenades. Nine of the 2 MIR soldiers were killed and five were wounded.

The news was devastating for Clarence and his men. Many of the victims were from Malaya, but their regiment was still very much considered a Singapore one, and many of the victims were familiar to them. It was certainly a reality check. A sombre moment indeed. After patrolling the jungles of Sebatik Island over these last months,

Clarence had been looking forward to a relaxing evening in the officers' mess sharing a long overdue drink, stories, and laughter with his fellow officers, instead of mulling over this tragic news. This was not a night for celebration. That evening Clarence found himself back in his quarters earlier than he had expected.

Clarence and his colleagues from 1 MIR spent one week in Tawau before they returned to Singapore. Leading up to their departure from Borneo, the Malaysian Chief of Defence Force came from Kuala Lumpur to congratulate 1 MIR on their work in the jungles. Clarence had a chance to meet him, as did all the officers. It was possibly later that night that the Chief of Defence Force met with Clarence's commanding officer to discuss issues that would have a significant effect on the course of Clarence's career.

The following morning the regiment was back on a C130 flying over the jungles of Borneo and over the South China Sea, bound for Singapore and a well-earned, two-week holiday.

———

Once again, it was nice to be back home. To see the family. To catch up with friends. To watch a movie. To eat home-cooked food. It was surreal in some ways to be walking around the city and its surroundings, back in civilian clothes. Watching others go by, caught up in their own concerns, made Clarence realise he had made the right choice in joining the army. Civilian life was now starting to look a little boring.

The realities of the Confrontation were very familiar to everyone back in Singapore. While not fully aware of the day-to-day activities of the military on Borneo, the civilians were certainly affected by this low-level conflict. Since as early as September 1963 the island had been the target of small bombs at various locations. The first two had gone off at Katong Park, only a few kilometres from the house on Kembangan Hill. Initially it was thought that these two bombs were deonated by the communists in Singapore. But it later became apparent that the Indonesians were the culprits. Soldiers from the Indonesian KKO, based on Karimun Island on the Indonesian side of the Singapore Strait, had infiltrated Singapore at night, boating to mid-strait during the high tide, then swimming the rest of the way using the currents. Once in Singapore they had prepared homemade bombs to detonate at the park. They then escaped back to Karimun on one of the many fisherman's sampans lying on the beaches by the Malay kampongs at Pasir Panjang.

Periodic bombings would continue to occur over the next two years. Sometimes they came with warnings, such as a flag being placed on them. For the most part, the bombings were not devastating, although the second one at Katong Park had killed two men. For many of the others that followed it seemed that the intention was more to be disruptive than to cause death or injury, as roads and buildings needed to be closed down while the army was brought in to diffuse them. There was some talk that the saboteurs had originally wanted to target the military bases, but were unable to because of tight security. So they had changed their focus to civilian targets instead.

In total there were 29 bombs over this period, although it is not entirely clear whether all of them were attributable to the Indonesians. There was speculation that some were due to communist factions. The last one was the infamous bombing at MacDonald House in the city, on 10th March 1966, in which three were killed and more than three dozen were injured. Only after that bombing would anyone be caught: two soldiers from the KKO on Karimun.

So while the civilians of Singapore were not in the thick of the fight on Borneo, they had been on a heightened level of alert, and the government had been running campaigns and roadshows and pasting posters around the island to warn people what to look out for. So in some way, his countrymen had been sharing in Clarence's "war".

Chapter 17
MSSU and the End of Confrontation

After his two weeks' leave Clarence returned to 1 MIR's HQ camp at Ulu Pandan. On arrival he was immediately called into the Adjutant's office, where the Adjutant informed him of a new posting. He was to report to the Majidee Barracks up in Johor. The Adjutant did not give him any more details. He was simply told to get his things together, and a jeep and driver would be made available shortly.

When you are living out of a haversack there really is not much to pack – especially when it is already packed since you have just walked into the camp. So, after running around the camp to fill out a few forms, Clarence was soon sitting in an army jeep being driven north.

There had been no time to give the family a call, let alone return home to bid them farewell. He had no idea when he would return. Would he see them the following weekend? In a month? In six months? No idea. Farewells played second fiddle in the army. You just went where and when they told you. That's just the way it was. And you did not question it. You were pawns moved around a chessboard. As a young officer you got treated better than a lot of the other pawns, and you were even able to move some of the lower-ranked pawns. But you were still a pawn yourself.

Where was Clarence heading? He was heading for a course that would steer him toward a special force that would ultimately define what he would be known as for the remainder of his army career and beyond. He was to begin training as a commando.

The greater amount of the military response against the Indonesian incursions during the Confrontation was being handled by the British and Commonwealth armed forces, including a significant contribution by the British Gurkhas. Of that, the British SAS, with help from their Australian and New Zealand counterparts, were leading much of the action. Given that it was their country, Malaysia rightfully felt that it was time that she developed a capability akin to the SAS, maybe not to be used immediately, but certainly to be ready should this conflict escalate. They were now ready to put together such a unit. An elite commando unit. The unit was called the MSSU: Malaysian Special Services Unit.

When the Malaysian Chief of Defence Force visited the soldiers of 1 MIR in Tawau, he had asked the commander for one non-Malay officer from the regiment to join this new unit. The colonel had volunteered Second Lieutenant Clarence Tan. Clarence had no idea why he was singled out. He was young – the youngest officer, in fact. He was single, which meant less of an imposition on family life. He was also perhaps one of the fittest. No doubt, the fact that he had led a small surveillance team right on the border with Indonesia was a factor. But Clarence was not the kind of man to dwell on the reasons too much either. "They tell me to go, I go" was his attitude.

———————

The jeep pulled in through the gates of the army camp at Majidee. As the jeep stopped, Clarence could not but help feel his heart sink at the sight of the dilapidated barracks. "Goodness me. This looks grand," he thought.

MSSU was a small unit, and a multi-racial one. Clarence was one of eight officers; the others being six Malays and one Sikh. There were a little more than twenty soldiers of other ranks. A mixture of Malay, Chinese, and Indians, it was a diverse group that assembled at this rundown barrack on this first day. However, they all had a couple of things in common: each one was extremely fit; they were all experienced soldiers, having served in some way in the Confrontation; and nobody knew anything about this new unit.

The complete veil of secrecy was only partially lifted once everyone was gathered. The men were briefed on the new unit that they would form. Exactly what roles they would play was not revealed to them. But of course the men very quickly began to speculate about the nature of the tasks they might be called upon to do.

After the briefing, the men jumped into the back of a three-tonner and were driven off to another camp to begin training. There was some relief that they were not going to be staying in that dilapidated barracks, but what they did not realise was that they were about to begin six weeks of hellish training that would make their initial cadet training at the Federation Military College at Sungei Besi seem like child's play.

Burma Camp was their next destination. Located not far away near Kota Tinggi, Burma Camp was well known as a jungle training school run by the British. It was also the location of the 40 Commando Royal Marines from Britain, so was already set up with all the facilities required for their impending course.

For the next six weeks the men, led by British instructors, went through the most gruelling physical exertion they had ever experienced. It was a course focused heavily on physical fitness. From the moment they got up in the morning to the moment they went to bed in the evening, they carried a pack with two red bricks in it. Every morning they would start the day with a six-mile run. In the middle of the day they would do a nine-mile speed march dressed in full battle gear. In between they would be running along planks, climbing over walls, climbing up rope ladders, crawling through mud under low-lying barbed wire in the camp's obstacle and confidence courses. There were swims across the Straits of Johor from Johor to Singapore, a distance of over a kilometre, in full uniform, boots, and with no safety boat. There was training in live firing, and in commando raiding and patrolling techniques.

It was an incredibly arduous six weeks that elevated the men to a completely new level of fitness that was unique to special forces the world over. At the end of the training Clarence and his colleagues graduated and were formally inducted as commandos. Each of them received the green beret and stiletto – both symbols that many armies around the world gave to their elite special service soldiers.

Upon returning to their barracks at Camp Majidee after the end of the course, the men were pleasantly surprised to find the dilapidated barracks fantastically transformed. They were beginning to get an impression of the importance and priority that the government and the army were giving to this elite group of men. Not only were their buildings vastly upgraded, but their own training grounds had been built, including replicas of the obstacle and confidence courses that they had been using at the British-run Burma Camp. It was evident that the government wanted to create a force that would be able to build itself up and stand on its own.

And it was clear that they wanted this process to begin immediately as, a few days following the completion of their course, Clarence and his colleagues became instructors for the training of 150 new recruits. While they had been training at Burma Camp, the Malaysian Ministry of Defence had been hard at work screening a large pool of volunteers to be trained up as commandos.

So, having only just come off the same course themselves, Clarence and his new commando colleagues spent the subsequent six weeks doing the course again, this time, as instructors, at the Malaysian army's brand new training facilities in the MSSU camp at Majidee. The recruits came from a variety of backgrounds. Some were from the Royal Malay Regiments. Some were from the Singapore-based 1 MIR and 2 MIR. Some were from the Reece unit, the armoured unit of tank operators, so had been sitting in tanks for the last few years. Since the recruits were trained soldiers, the main focus was to get them all up to the same high level of physical fitness. Their role was the same as for any commando unit around the world: conducting long-range unsupported reconnaissance patrols, ambushes, and short sharp covert raids on enemy targets. In line with this, if enemy combatants were to make incursions into Malaysia, as the Indonesians had done a number of times over the last year, their job would be to seek them out.

Following this initiation course the men spent the next few months participating in ongoing training and exercises. All through this training the men were never made aware that there was indeed a specific reason behind it all, but among themselves they had figured that something must be up. Could there be plans for a commando force to return to Sebatik Island? Or some other location? Or was it all simply preparation for hypothetical scenarios, in case the Confrontation was to escalate?

If there was something in the planning, the men never did find out what it was. Problems were brewing within Indonesia that would put whatever missions they may have been training for on hold.

———————

In the Indonesian capital of Jakarta, a coup d'état was attempted on the night of 30th September 1965. In the process, members of the armed forces, known as the Thirtieth of September Movement, assassinated six Indonesian Army generals. Their venture was short-lived. By the end of 1st October their attempt to seize power had been thwarted. Indonesia then entered into a period of major traumatic internal upheaval. As a direct result of the coup, President Sukarno's grip on power began to slip. With the confusion resulting from the killing of the six top-ranking generals, Sukarno allowed Major General Suharto to take control of the military. Over the subsequent 18 months, taking advantage of the developing political problems, Suharto positioned himself to eventually replace Sukarno as the President in March 1968.

While the 30th September attempted coup did not mark the end of the Confrontation, it was certainly the most significant turning point. Following it, the cross-border activity by the Indonesians into Malaysian territory lessened, although they did not stop completely. At a political level Suharto was more conciliatory towards Malaysia than Sukarno had been, and as the former's grip on power in Indonesia increased, so too did Indonesia and Malaysia come closer to signing a peace deal.

In May 1966 the governments of Indonesia and Malaysia declared that the Confrontation was over, and they formally signed a peace treaty in August that same year.

The overall casualty figures of the Confrontation were relatively low, compared to what an all-out war would probably have resulted in. Since the beginning of the conflict in 1963, 114 soldiers had been killed on the British Commonwealth and Malaysian side. Of these, 29 were from Malaysian military and police units. On the Indonesian side, 590 fighters were estimated to have died. Thirty-six civilians, mostly indigenous people living in the jungles of Borneo, were also killed.

Clarence, and his new MSSU unit, were never called up for missions against the Indonesians. They didn't stop training for the possibility, however. Developments in Indonesia were unpredictable following the coup attempt, and while Suharto was increasing in influence and indicating a desire to end hostilities, technically Sukarno remained the President until March 1967.

———————

It had been less than two years since the now 25-year-old Clarence was commissioned as a Second Lieutenant. During this time he had been a busy man. He had been called upon to lead his platoon in the July 1964 racial riots in Singapore. He had been deployed in the jungles of

Taiping hunting the MCP communists. He had spent six months in the jungles of Sebatik Island against the Indonesians. And he had spent six months training with MSSU. During this entire time he had only once fired his weapon in anger. And that was to kill a pig. Even during the most serious of his deployments, while on Sebatik, he and his unit never came under attack. It was never clear why this was the case. Clarence had always made sure his platoon was very diligent and disciplined with their patrols. Perhaps these patrols had disallowed the Indonesians the chance to stage any attack as they knew the patrols would cut off their retreats. Perhaps. Who knows?

Life had taken many turns for Clarence over the last five years, as it had for everyone in Singapore and the new Malaysia. Now back in Johor with his MSSU family, and with the Confrontation winding down, another major turn of events was underway. Just a few weeks earlier, on 9th August 1965, the state of Singapore had separated from Malaysia.

Singapore was now a newly independent nation.

And Clarence, along with his other Singapore colleagues at MSSU, were now technically soldiers working for a foreign army.

PART THREE

AN
INDEPENDENT
SINGAPORE

(1965 – Today)

Chapter 18
Return to Singapore

The merger of Singapore into Malaysia had failed. From the beginning of the merger, on 31ˢᵗ August 1963, there had been a deep suspicion between the political players in Singapore and the central government in Kuala Lumpur. The main sticking point continued to be a section of the Malaysian constitution, titled Article 153, that enshrined the "special position" of the Malay and other indigenous peoples in the country. A form of affirmative action, it was intended as a way to address the economic imbalances that they were facing. As a people they were by far the largest grouping numerically, but the Malays and the other indigenous peoples controlled a very low percentage of the economy as compared to the Chinese, Indians, and foreign interests. Much of this imbalance had been as a result of British preference to employ, and import, Chinese and Indian labour into their civil service and industry. After more than 100 years of British rule, the Malays had been pushed to the edges of the economy. The intention of Article 153 was to address this imbalance.

The Chinese and the Indians, and the smaller grouping of Eurasians, were of course disadvantaged by this piece of legislation that formed the bedrock of the society in which they lived. As far as they were concerned, they were also people of the land and felt that this was where they belonged. Their ancestry may not have been as deep-rooted in the land as the Malays, but many had been born here, and had built families here. They called this land their home. A Malaysia for all Malaysians was what they wanted. They did not want to be disadvantaged for the "sins of their fathers", or more accurately, the "sins of someone else's fathers".

The federal government in Kuala Lumpur and UMNO[26] were not comfortable with the idea of a "Malaysian Malaysia", that political battle cry put forward by Lee Kwan Yew and the People's Action Party. Even moderates were concerned that the Malays were not ready to compete on an equal footing. Politically, things had been ugly since the merger over this issue, and the Tunku did not want to risk the situation escalating, with the potential for further unrest. He had never really wanted Singapore in the first place, for the very reasons with which he was now struggling. But at the time of the merger he felt that Singapore would fall to the communists and that would have been a worse problem. The communists were now largely contained. For everyone's benefit, he felt that Singapore must leave the Federation.

It is important to stress that the problems were not just communal, as there were also significant economic disagreements. While the original agreement had been for a common market throughout the Federation, soon after the merger measures were put in place that disadvantaged the Singapore economy over the other states of Malaysia. Naturally this led to bickering between Singapore and the central government.

The ultimate outcome was that on 9th August 1965, at 10am, less than two years after telling his people that merger with Malaysia was their future, Lee Kwan Yew declared to a stunned nation and press that Singapore was now an independent country. At the same time, the Tunku addressed the Federal parliament with the same message.

———————

There was not much time for the leaders of the new nation of Singapore to sit around and romanticise about the uniqueness of their situation. They had a nation, not just to run, but to form.

One of the most immediate issues for the government was internal security and defence: internal security to handle general criminal

---

26 The United Malay National Organisation, a major political party in Malaysia.

activities and civil disobedience, and defence against the uncertainty of whether other countries might take advantage of this tiny new nation. Without sorting out these two pillars of internal security and defence there might be no civil society to run in the first place.

But it was going to take time for the Singapore army to sort itself out. When Singapore became independent the 1st and 2nd Battalion Singapore Infantry Regiment had around 1,000 men each. 700 Malaysian soldiers had been placed into 1 and 2 SIR by the Malaysian government, while 300 Singaporean soldiers, including Clarence, had been posted to other Malaysian units.[27] A timeline for their return to their homeland had yet to be determined. Furthermore, there were no senior officers to lead the army. No one had been in the military long enough to build up the experience to become anything more than a Captain, so that was the highest-ranking Singaporean officer at the time.

"It was hardly enough to be called an army," Clarence would later say.

In addition, soon after independence, upon the request of the Malaysians, the Singapore government committed 2 SIR to Borneo as a part of the Confrontation. Trust that Singapore was still on the same side had to be demonstrated. So the presence of Singaporean soldiers in Singapore for the later part of 1965 and the early part of 1966 was even more depleted.

Concerns did not end there. The Malaysian army still had a presence in Singapore for some time after independence in the form of the 5th Battalion Royal Malay Regiment (5 RMR). Also, the two SIRs remained under the command of the 4th Malaysian Infantry Brigade (4 MIB).

This was a very critical time for Singapore. The uncertainties of this new situation and the depleted number of soldiers created a situation of risk. There was however one major ball in their court. The British army was still in town and this helped provide a level of security during this period of transition.

---

27 The 1st and 2nd Battalion Malaysian Infantry Regiments, 1 MIR and 2 MIR, would eventually revert to being called the 1st and 2nd Battalion Singapore Infantry Regiments, 1 SIR and 2 SIR.

So Singapore, for now, was at the mercy of other armies. There were possibly more foreign troops on its soil than there were of their own. They needed to get what troops they had back home as soon as possible, including Clarence. But that would take some time given the operational intertwinement that the two now separated armies (of Singapore and Malaysia) shared.

It would be five months after the separation before Second Lieutenant Clarence Tan returned to Singapore. During that time, along with his Malaysian colleagues, he continued to train with the MSSU unit at Majidee Camp in Johor Bahru.

In January 1966, he returned home.

———————

Clarence was sitting in the officer's mess, quietly eating his lunch and idling his time, at the 1 SIR barracks at Ulu Pandan. It was 1st February 1966 and he was still fresh back in Singapore. So fresh that he had not yet been assigned to a unit. So he really did not have much to do. The field officer for the day, a British major with 1 SIR, came looking for him. He told Clarence that problems had surfaced at the army training depot at Shenton Way. Around 500 new recruits had assembled to take their attestation, or oath of allegiance, there and during the proceedings, a misunderstanding in some instructions handed down the chain of command had left the Malay recruits feeling they were being discriminated against. A bit of taunting from the Chinese and other recruits broke out, and before long rioting began. The commander for the standby platoon was a newly commissioned officer, fresh from the Federation Military College in Kuala Lumpur, and had no experience with riot control. Since Clarence had some experience, the major ordered him to take over the platoon and head down to Shenton Way. So, Clarence changed into his uniform and left the barracks.

By the time Clarence reached the training depot, the riot squad, with their red trucks, were already there and throwing tear gas bombs into the melee of young men. Since they had it under control there was no need for the army to intervene, so Clarence returned with his men to their barracks.

On returning to the camp, Clarence went back into the mess to continue the lunch he had only half completed. As he walked in, one of the cooks told him that a phone call had come in for him. So Clarence made his way over to the phone on the wall. Perhaps the situation had got out of hand and he was going to be needed again? He picked up the phone and introduced himself.

Immediately, from the other end of the phone, came a loud, grumpy, and gruff voice. It was the commander of 4 MIB, demanding to know if he was the officer who took the platoon down to the riot. Clarence confirmed that he was.

"What the hell were you doing, going down there? You are still under the command of the Malaysian Armed Forces and you were not deployed. Why did you go down?" rumbled the irate brigadier. As the head of 4 MIB in Singapore, the man on the other end of the phone was still technically the head of the 1 SIR and 2 SIR. The biggest boss this junior officer had aside from the Minister of Defence himself.

Clarence explained how he ended up taking a platoon down to assist with the riots.

"Well, that was a mistake. Consider yourself under house arrest," the wild brigadier boomed, slamming down the phone.

Clarence hung up the phone, stunned. He was under house arrest. By the hand of a foreign army.

Later that afternoon, 1 SIR's commanding officer and adjutant returned to the camp. Clarence immediately brought his situation to their attention and the regimental commander then called the brigadier to explain the misunderstanding.

The brigadier's issue had not been specifically with Clarence, but with the fact that a military unit had gone down in the first place. The British major had made a mistake. This was an internal security issue, and no order had been given from the very top to involve the army in riot control. So the 4 MIB commander had a right to be angry. In fact, it may not have only been him who had an issue. It was possible that the Minister had called the brigadier to ask why a platoon had been sent down.

There was much confusion and uncertainty as Singapore transitioned to an independent army. Who was in command of whom? Who owned which equipment? Who was allowed to occupy which barracks? The fact that six months after independence a senior Malaysian officer was still issuing commands in an independent Singapore, and able to place a Singapore officer under house arrest, goes to show the complex nature of the transition. It would take time for things to change. But change they did.

———————

A few days following that incident Clarence was ordered to report to Jurong Town Primary School, in the west of the island. Upon arriving at the school he was put through some interviews. He was not told what it was about. No introductions were made. It all seemed a bit strange. Upon exiting the interview he was intercepted by an old colleague from his Singapore Volunteer Corps days who seemed to know more about what was going on. He explained that the Ministry of Interior and Defence were embarking on the process of developing Singapore's army. Over the next few months the Ministry wanted to build up a small core group of 40 or so officers who would become the foundation upon which a more expansive Singapore army was to be built. Being one of the more experienced officers, Clarence would be a part of this group.

Later that same day, Clarence was called back to Jurong Town Primary School. This time he was put through a series of exercises. He spent the next hour being a guinea pig, put through a raft of physical fitness tests. Sit-ups, press-ups, standing broad jumps, and a three-mile run. Once again it was all a bit strange. He was not told the requirements nor the standards to be met. He was simply told to do as many as he could, as fast as he could. It later transpired that he was setting the benchmark for the first batch of new recruits into the Singapore army.

Chapter 19
The Beginnings of an Army

In February 1966, the 60 men, including Clarence, who assembled at Jurong Primary School were drawn from a variety of backgrounds and formed an interesting group. Some were officers and senior NCOs from 1 SIR and 2 SIR. Many, like Clarence, had experience in the field. A few were fresh out of army school, having just graduated from officer training at the Federation Military College up near Kuala Lumpur. Some were from the Singapore Volunteer Corps and so came from other occupations, such as school teachers. A few were police officers. They varied in age, from early twenties to forties. This group of men would go on to form the core on which the Singapore army would be built. Their role? To be trained and to subsequently train the recruits enlisted in the months and years ahead.

And there was no time to waste. There was work to be done. An army needed to be started. With a group of foreigners brought in from a variety of countries acting as their advisors and instructors, they immediately embarked on a new training course to become the first instructors of the Singapore Armed Forces.

But what a shambles the early days of that course turned out to be.

It did not take long for Clarence and his regular buddies to get a feeling that things were not right. For these experienced soldiers, the training they were being put through in these initial days seemed all wrong. They were getting up early in the mornings to do calisthenics, followed by training in the most elementary of military subjects. How to load a rifle. How to judge distances for firing weapons. Individual field craft, or how to look after yourself in the field. Camouflage techniques. Running through a basic obstacle course, components of which fell apart as one officer ran through it, sending him off to hospital. All the training was very basic and unnecessary. New recruit material. It was downright boring.

The men started grumbling among themselves. What was going on? Why were they being taught all this basic stuff? While they may have been a bit young and cocky, they did have a point. They knew it all. Not only were they trained soldiers, they were operationally experienced. Many of them had just returned from deployments to the jungles of Borneo and Johor against the Indonesians. Many had even been deployed against the communists up north in Malaysia in the early 1960s, and been deployed to the streets during the riots in 1964. They had seen live action. They had even lost colleagues to the Indonesians. Not only had they learned all this stuff before, they had applied and adapted it to the jungles of Peninsula Malaysia and Borneo. This basic training was an insult.

Still, they went through the motions. But they very quickly became unmotivated. As boredom set in they began to take it less and less seriously. Being a bunch of mostly young lads, it was not long before the jokers came to the fore.

From their time in Borneo, Clarence and his buddies had learnt that dressing yourself up in camouflage using the foliage around you was not a good idea. Making the camouflage involved breaking off vegetation, and doing that left obvious evidence that you had passed by. Any dead plants, or remains of leaves or branches left lying around, or broken twigs left hanging on trees, were a sure indication to the enemy of your presence. What's more, there was no need for it. The jungle was so dense that you could walk past an elephant a few metres away and never notice it. Camouflage is okay if you are a sniper or doing an ambush in a less densely forested area. But walking trees do cause the enemy to wonder.

To overcome their sense of futility with this exercise, some of them decided to have some fun. Some dressed themselves over-the-top in foliage so that they really did look like walking trees as they emerged from the jungle's edge, while one of Clarence's Sikh colleagues plucked a single strand of lalang, a long grass that was plentiful in the area, and simply stuck it in his turban. "I'm done," he said, standing up and parading in front of the other men. "Bet you can't see me." The men broke out in laughter at the sight of the turbaned man walking around in the open with a single blade of grass swaying above his head.

During another exercise, one designed to teach them how to give commands to execute live fire in the field, some of the men once again were so bored that they started fooling around. When a section commander spots the enemy, one of their jobs might be to direct fire from their unit. To do this, they will call out what is called a Fire Control Order. An FCO is essentially a set of instructions concerning where to direct the fire: how far away the target is, at what bearing, and what it is. Once issued, the men will fire their rifles accordingly. It was a skill that had been drilled into them many times before and, if they had not issued FCOs themselves in live action already, they had certainly performed it many a time in exercises. Now, of course, their foreign trainers had no understanding of the Malay language[28], and the Singapore soldiers used this to their advantage. During this exercise, some of the men gave their FCOs in Malay, but instead of using the standard orders they began yelling out profanities. The result being that, instead of the fire being directed accordingly, the men began rolling around in the grass in fits of laughter, with their trainers being totally confused by what was going on.

The fun continued.

The men figured that some of their instructors, being new to the region, were not too familiar with the torrential rains that regularly visited tropical Singapore and played upon this. "Rain, rain!" cried one

---

28 All army field commands were and are still issued in Malay in the Singapore army.

of the captains as a shower began to fall on them while performing an exercise at the top of a hill. The captain, a cheeky guy who often pulled pranks, motioned to the other men to get up from their positions and follow him down the hill. "Rain, rain," they cried in unison as they ran down the hill. Naturally the instructor in charge of the exercise was somewhat bemused. He did not understand what was going on at all. The sight of these soldiers running down the hill toward him, in total disregard for the exercise, seemed like chaos. As the captain ran past, he shouted to the instructor that in Singapore they did not train in the rain. The men would wait for the rain to stop, after which they would get back to the exercise.

What was the instructor to do? Perhaps this was some cultural thing he was not aware of. He let the men run to take shelter from the rain, feeling somewhat bewildered. And wet.

This was what happened in the first few weeks of their training. The men were bored and this was what bored men do: they play games.

As for the trainers, it was all very confusing to them. They had never encountered such behaviour before. They did not say much about these antics to the trainees themselves. They did not castigate them. But it was clear that the trainees were not motivated and were not taking it seriously.

———————

It was only a matter of time before the instructors' concern made its way up the chain of command. In fact, some of the more senior officers within the group of trainees had also reported their discontent to their superiors. So before long, two and half weeks after the course had started, Dr Goh Keng Swee, the Minister of Interior and Defence, made his way down to the training camp to set everything straight. Key members of the military establishment also joined the meeting that included all the trainees and their instructors.

Dr Goh started the meeting by presenting the case for the importance of what they were doing. He explained why they were conducting the training, and why it was important that the men took it seriously. He pointed out that, militarily, the fledgling island nation was weak. In its current state it would be unable to look after itself in the event of an internal coup or an external attack. Sure, the British, Australians, and New Zealanders were still around, and their presence would certainly deter any acts of aggression against the small island nation. But this would not last. It was Singapore's duty to build up her forces. Having a strong army was critical to the government's nation-building agenda. And this group of men assembled in front of Dr Goh were to be the foundation upon which the army was to be built. They were to be the pioneers, and they needed to behave accordingly.

Following this talk by Dr Goh, led by the more senior officers, the trainees communicated their feelings to the Minister. Given their level of experience they felt they were not being given due respect in the training. Most of them had been in the army for a number of years, and already had significant active experience. They had recently observed the first anniversary of their nine friends from 2 SIR who had lost their lives in Johor. What's more, the Singaporeans were already highly trained. Some had trained in staff colleges. Some had been on tactical courses in the UK. Some junior officers had just completed the officer cadet course in Malaysia. Some had been through specialist training, such as Clarence with the commando unit at MSSU. The men were already well versed in the art of war. They were not fresh recruits, but it was like they were being put through basic training again. They felt that what they were going through was all a waste of time and money.

And it was not just in the training where the problems lay. Administration and communication was messy. And the food was atrocious. Inconsumable for the most part. Horrid, stinky, frozen fish from Russian trawlers (so bad that Clarence would not eat fish for many years following those early days in the Singapore army). That might have sounded petty, but bad food leads to unhappy soldiers. And that is never a good thing. They were not asking for gourmet cuisine. Just simple, edible fare.

The meeting that had begun as a tense affair became more relaxed and open, and the men grew more comfortable in airing their grievances. The Minister and his staff listened – they realised that the men needed to be heard if the programme was to work. And they recgonised that there were going to be teething problems. After some time the meeting was drawn to a close. The Minister acknowledged some things needed to be changed, and gave the trainees two weeks' leave to give them time to find the best way forward.

After their two-week break, Clarence and his fellow trainees returned to the camp to restart the training. Since the meeting with Dr Goh, it had been decided that the process would be more effective if they took advantage of the existing skills within the army and built on them. Training should become far more collaborative. After all, the focus of this course was on grooming them to become effective instructors for new recruits.

As they continued with their training, the men began working together with their instructors to develop new course material that would be used to teach future soldiers. Clarence and his colleagues were assigned to different areas based on their existing skills. Being the one with the most demolition experience, Clarence was "arrowed" to be the demolitions expert, so he helped to put together the training material for that course. Given his significant exposure to amphibious training during his time with the MSSU, he also helped out in that area. Others worked on areas like jungle training, survival, and so forth.

The training continued far more smoothly with this more collaborative approach. We might say that the men had more ownership of the process. Everyone was happy now, though they did retain some of their initial regimes such as the early morning calisthenics. And now they were eating half-decent food.

While the training was smoother now, some residual scepticism remained concerning what some of these instructors could teach them. But the men did learn a thing or two.

One example was moving in the jungle at night. While some of the men, Clarence included, had done a little night training with the British, it was general considered impractical. The general feeling was that the best thing to do at nighttime in the jungle was to set up camp and prepare for the following day. Or at most, set up ambushes. However, their instructors wanted to experiment with night maneuvers because, if it could be made to work, it could be a very useful tactic. By moving stealthily under the cover of darkness, you could outflank an enemy, or surround them completely without their knowledge. So they wanted to introduce night movements to the training. Clarence and his colleagues were not so sure about this idea. The jungle was hard enough to penetrate during daylight. But they agreed to give it a go.

So one dark night they set off into the jungle around the central catchment area of the island, near MacRitchie Reservoir, to an area known as the Woodcutters' Track, armed with a roll of white tape. The instructions were for the leader of the unit to roll out the tape as he moved and the others were to follow by holding the tape. The last soldier was responsible for rolling it up. There was no way you could leave something so obvious behind during a real operation, so it was most important that the last man did his job.

In general, the exercise worked out. While the trainees first laughed at the idea of walking through the jungle at night with a role of white tape, they did later find it to be quite effective. And some time later, Clarence would learn that the US Rangers also embarked on night maneuvers in the jungle, although they used different techniques, and were doing so six hundred nautical miles north in the jungles of Vietnam.

While there were still times when the men questioned parts of the training, the whole process had improved greatly since the big powwow with the Minister. The First Instructors Preparatory Course, as the course would come to be known, continued for a little under three months.

———————

While Clarence and his colleagues had been going through their course, the government had been in the process of advertising for and recruiting the first group of completely new officer cadets to be inducted into the Singapore army since independence. By the end of March 1966, a large number of young men from all over the island had applied for the advertised positions. This was encouraging, especially given the Chinese aversion to joining the army. The economy at the time was tough. Most Singaporeans were still living in squalid conditions in the city slums or simple kampongs, and much of the work available for young men from these communities was tough manual labour or hawking of goods around the streets. Joining the army provided an opportunity for a stable government salary. A base monthly salary of $270 for an officer cadet, with additional top-ups depending on education level, was a nice draw card. An officer cadet with an honours degree could look forward to a total package of $600 per month, with allowances thrown in. This was good money in tough times. The brochure sent out to potential candidates such as school leavers, graduates, and civil servants included the image of a young Singapore army officer driving a red MG Midget convertible sports car. The idea that a kampong kid or city slum dweller could one day afford his own sports car must have been very enticing. The photo reflected a true story: the car belonged to Clarence, and the officer behind the wheel was the man himself. Clarence had been roped in for a bit of marketing for the fledgling army – and it must have worked, as nearly 3,000 young men applied.

Of these applicants, around 300 recruits were selected and reported for enlistment, to form the first batch of officer cadets. On 1st June 1966, just two weeks after they had graduated from their own instructor course, Clarence and his fellow instructors began training this first batch of officer cadets, at the newly created Singapore Armed Forces Training Institute, SAFTI. Clarence was appointed as a section instructor, as well as the officer-in-charge of demolitions training.

That would be his job for the next 13 months: moulding a team of officers and NCOs to join him and his fellow pioneers in leading this tiny but growing army. Clarence would not get to see his charges graduate, though. The Ministry of Interior and Defence had other plans for him. With one week to go, Clarence was sent off to the United States with a younger colleague to embark on US Ranger and Airborne training.

Unbeknownst to him at the time, this was to be another defining moment in his career.

Chapter 20
US Ranger and Airborne Courses

The US Ranger course is one of the most respected courses that an American soldier can attend. Only the best and the fittest are accepted into it. Participants can come from any division of the US army: infantry, armour, cavalry. It is an extremely prestigious course, and is specifically designed to harden the participants up for the toughest of operational engagements. Some say that ten weeks on the course is equivalent to six months in an operational environment. As tough as it was to get into the course, it is even tougher to stay in. Clarence and his colleague learnt this the only way you can.

For the next ten weeks the Singaporeans, with their mostly American course mates, were pushed to their limits. On a day-to-day basis, they had no idea where they were going next, what they would be doing, or when their next meal would be. They went to bed late and got up at 5am every morning; sleep was a luxury. At times they went for days with no sleep at all. It was intense.

The course was split into three phases and at each phase the soldiers' performance was evaluated. There was no room for sympathy. If you didn't make the grade, you were out. Even on day one, people dropped out. The Benning Phase, so named because of its location at the Fort Benning Army Camp in the state of Georgia, was up first. The trainees were put through physical, mental, and leadership assessment and combat exercises. Here, even the fittest were made to question themselves. Then they moved on to the Mountain Phase where they learnt the art of mountain warfare. Rock climbing, mountain climbing, river crossing, and hill work. Next was the Florida Phase, where they trained in the everglades of Florida and never saw dry land for days. To finish it all off, the final exercise involved a patrol through the night, culminating with a raid on a camp in the early hours of the morning and being told at 6am that they had two hours to get back to base. If they got through the camp gate in time, they passed. If not, they failed.

Of the 200 men who started the course with Clarence, less than a hundred made it to final graduation. For the American soldiers, failing was not the end. They had the luxury of being able to re-take the course if they dropped out along the way. This was not an option for the two officers from Singapore. They had to pass. The Singapore government had paid good money for them to be there, so they were more heavily motivated to pass the first time. This was in contrast to some participants from other South East Asian nations like Thailand, South Vietnam (which was a distinct country at this time), Malaysia, and Laos. These countries were all on the American Military Assistance Program, so they got their training for free.

Clarence and his colleague were successful in passing the course on their first try.

———

With the completion of the US Ranger course, the two men immediately moved on to another one at Fort Benning: the US Army Airborne School, colloquially known as Jump School. There they learnt about military parachuting.

Clarence had already made one parachute jump in Singapore before he joined this course. While there was no parachute training in the army in these early days, there was a civilian parachute club on the island. Clarence was friendly with a British major who was into recreational jumping and, figuring that it was the kind of thing that Clarence would be into, he invited him along for a jump. Following two nights of training, Clarence made his first jump out of a small Cessna C172 3,000 feet above Sembawang, in the north of the island. He loved it. But jumping at the US Army Airborne School took it to the next level.

The US Army Airborne School is the US army's basic paratrooper school. It pumps through thousands of jumpers every year. And, just as it is today, the course was an intensive one, split up into three weeks: Ground Week, Tower Week, and Jump Week. During Ground Week, Clarence and his fellow course-mates spent their time learning about their parachutes and how they worked, practising how to exit from aircraft, and how to execute the PLF (Parachute Landing Fall, a technique designed to reduce the chances of injuring themselves during landing). There was also a heavy physical fitness component, culminating in the standard Army Physical Fitness Test.

During Tower Week, the men got their first exposure to height when they jumped from a 34-foot tower in a mock-up parachute harness that hung from a zip line, an exercise intended to introduce them to the unique feeling of jumping from an aircraft, then swinging around below the parachute when it opens (apparently, 34 feet is the point at which people begin to feel uncomfortable about how high they are off the ground). Later in the week they did more realistic practise jumps from a 250-foot tower. In this exercise, the men donned a real harness attached to a real parachute that was already opened around the circumference of a large ring above them. The parachute, attached to the ring, and the paratrooper, were hoisted to the top of the 250-foot tower, from which they were subsequently released, and floated back down under the canopy. In reality, this was their first descent in an open parachute. This ingenious invention gave the trainees real exposure to the final moments of their jumps, without having to go up in the aircraft. During this second week they also learnt what could go wrong and how to get themselves out of trouble – how to fix entanglements, extricate themselves from power lines and trees, and how to deploy their reserve chute (in case the main chute fails). By the end of these two weeks, they had been drilled so much, to the point that muscle memory took over from their fears, that they were ready for the real thing.

On the Monday morning of Jump Week, Clarence and his classmates filed into the back of a Fairchild C119 aircraft at their training base of Fort Benning, Georgina, and flew up to a height of 1,250 feet above the airfield. Even though it was not his first jump, this one did seem a bit scarier. As with many high-adrenaline activities, often the exhilaration of the first time overshadows one's fear, and it's not until the second and third time that fear really kicks in. Reinforced by the previous two week's focus on what could go wrong, Clarence's heart raced as he stood on the open rear door of the aircraft. He then jumped into the nothingness below.

The immediate sensation was that of the wind snatching him and rapidly pulling him away from the aircraft. After what seemed a long time, but was barely seconds, there came an abrupt, but reassuring, tug on his shoulder, and the roar of the wind that had first greeted him as he exited the aircraft faded into absolute silence. He looked up and checked that his large green, round chute was open. Thank goodness for that. After ensuring the lines were not entangled, he surveyed the silent world around him. The airfield waited below, as did the canopies of those who had jumped before him. But there was no opportunity to contemplate this situation for too long. They were only jumping from 1,250 feet, after all. The ground was fast approaching.

While initially floating down, under the canopy, to the spectator, and even the jumper, everything looks and feels rather graceful, and the rate of descent appears to be quite mild. It is not until the last few hundred feet that the true rate of descent becomes apparent. An experience that can be terrifying for the first-time jumpers. The landing speed with one of these army parachutes is on average around 7 metres per second (25 kilometres per hour). And Mother Earth ain't no bouncy castle.

The only tool an army jumper has to cushion their impact upon kissing the ground is their body. As he approached the final 200 feet, Clarence placed his feet and knees together, bent his legs slightly, held on firmly to his guidelines, tucked in his elbows and chin, and crumpled sideways to the ground. Feet first, followed by the side of his left calf, left thigh, left hip, then the left side of his back. He then rolled on to his back and looked up to the sky. It was done.

Army jumping had none of the elegance displayed by the sport and show jumpers that many of us may know today. Army chutes are functional. They will keep you alive but, and even more so with the military parachutes back then, there was no way to slow your rate of descent in the final moments and step out into a short run, like the show folks do. Try to land standing up in an army chute, and you will break something. So, they had to fall right. That's why they had the PLF drilled into them.

Clarence did a total of five jumps with the US Airborne – two with no gear, two in full combat gear, and one at night. The night jump provided the perfect example of how important it was to perfect the PLF. In the dark of the night the men were unable to see the ground approaching, so it was simply a matter of holding the correct body position and waiting, and letting the body instinctively fall to the ground at the moment of impact. At the end of the course he was awarded with his parachute wings.

Following the parachute course, the two men returned to Singapore with the very prestigious US Ranger and US Airborne badges sewn onto their uniforms. Clarence was also returning with a third alteration to his uniform. His epaulets were now carrying three pips. While he was away, he had been promoted to captain.

Chapter 21
Busy Times

One of the most important roles of any government is to create an environment that stimulates the creation and retention of jobs for its citizenry. For a new country like Singapore in the mid-1960s, that meant attracting foreign investment to develop the industries that would employ its citizens to produce goods for export. This was even more important for Singapore given it had (and still has) no natural resources. Before putting money into a venture, a foreign investor wants to have a high degree of confidence that their investment will deliver returns, or profits. They also want to be sure that the country they are investing in will be stable and not susceptible to internal or external problems that would put their investments at risk. To enable this stability, it is also the government's role to maintain a police force and an army that will ensure internal and external security. Hence, as alluded to earlier, the leaders of Singapore in those very early days were adamant that, while building the economy was a major priority, it would have to go hand in hand with the building up of its security capabilities.

While the British still had bases in the country and their presence would be enough to ensure the security of Singapore and allay any fears of investors, discussions in the UK political circles were arising regarding a withdrawal of all their defence forces "east of the Suez Canal". It was not until early 1968 that an actual withdrawal date, December 1971, was announced, but the writing was on the wall. Singapore was obliged to accelerate the process of building their own forces.

One of the initial ideas had been to develop a force focused around a core regular army and a large territorial, or volunteer, force that could be called upon when necessary. This led to the establishment of the People's Defence Force, essentially an independent Singapore's version of the Singapore Volunteer Corps (the SVC, where Clarence had begun his army days). Before long it was realised that, with this approach, a country the size of Singapore, with barely 2 million citizens at the time, would be challenged to put together a sizeable force that could be a deterrent to potential aggressors. Furthermore, while there had been some success in recruiting the first batch of officer cadets, being an enlisted soldier was still not a popular occupation. It was quickly noticed that they were having problems attracting young Chinese to the volunteer and regular forces. "As good iron should not be turned into nails, so too good men should not be turned into soldiers" was a popular Chinese saying. A survey of young Singapore men on their preferred career options found that being a soldier was viewed as the least popular out of the ten careers on offer – one of which was apparently a thief! An alternative approach was required.

A new approach was officially implemented with the passing of the National Service (Amendment) Bill in March 1967. With the introduction of this legislation, all male citizens and permanent residents who were 18 years old were liable to render two years service in the army. After this service, the trained soldiers would return to civil society, but could be called up for up to 40 days of training each year to ensure that their skills and fitness were kept up to scratch. This approach enabled the regular army to be supplemented by a much bigger citizen army, known as National Servicemen and Reservists.

On 17th August 1967, the first batch of National Servicemen enlisted in the army and began their full-time compulsory military training. The 900 young men were to be trained by Clarence's instructor colleagues, assisted by the very green officers whom they had just trained and who had only been commissioned as second lieutenants two months earlier. In all a total of 9,000 18-year-old men had registered following the passing of the Bill, though the majority were not deployed to the full-time army, but part-time roles in the People's Defence Force, the Vigilante Corps, and the Special Constabulary.

Clarence was still training in the US when this first batch of National Servicemen started. When he did return, the training of the new recruits was well under way, so he was posted back to SAFTI as a platoon commander for a second intake of regular officers who had just come in. Three months after that, he was posted out of SAFTI to command a company of new National Servicemen at 2 SIR. One of the original battalions of the Singapore army, 2 SIR, along with his original 1 SIR, was no longer the solely regular regiment he had come to know.

This second batch of National Service recruits, standing in front of Clarence on their first day under his command, generally came from the poorer families which made up much of Singapore's population then. Some came from rough backgrounds and would have had run-ins with the law. The island was a melting pot of cultures and languages and many of the men spoke no English and there was no single language that united them all. To identify the language that each soldier spoke, their names tags were colour coded: The English-educated wore green tags; the Chinese, who spoke a variety of dialects, orange; the Indians, who predominantly spoke Tamil, yellow; and the Malays, blue. Then there were the ones with the purple name tags, who spoke a less common dialect. They were known as the NFEs: No Formal Education.

In an attempt to create a common language, English tutors were brought in for a few hours a week to work with the non-English speakers. The officers and NCOs were generally bilingual, so they were assigned to different units to ensure that at least someone of seniority was nearby to communicate with their charges. To some degree Clarence saw no point in these attempts. For soldiers it was simply a matter of following orders: "Go left, they go left. Go right, they go right." They did not need to understand tactics. All they needed to know was how to follow simple orders. Having said that, having a common language among the soldiers would probably go a long way toward building camaraderie.

Clarence commanded this company through their basic training, before they were sent off for more advanced mission-focused courses and exercises. Then he was posted back to SAFTI to train a new set of section leaders, who were the NCOs who would go on to lead small groups of men in the field during battle.

With the wheels of the fledgling army training programme running a bit more smoothly, and the army rapidly growing in size with the regular induction of new national servicemen, it was time to look at upgrading the standard of the leadership. Most senior officers, like Clarence, were still holding at most the rank of captain. With a bigger army, they required not only section, platoon, and regimental commanders, but also battalion commanders.

So upon the graduation of his section leader course, the next posting for Clarence was to SAFTI's School of Advanced Training for Officers, SATO, where he became a student again. Upon completing this he became the company commander of the Officer Cadet Training School, after which he attended a Command and Staff Course, before being posted to the 4th Singapore Infantry Regiment as the battalion commander.

These were busy times.

Deployment-wise, the early years after independence were relatively quiet for Clarence compared to the years immediately preceding independence. However there was one incident in 1969 that did raise concerns in Singapore and resulted in Clarence and his colleagues being deployed with their units around the city. From Singapore's perspective it was relatively minor. Up north in Malaysia it was a very big issue. Three days after the 10th May 1969 National Election in Malaysia, riots between the Chinese and Malays broke out in Kuala Lumpur following celebratory electoral parades, and spread across the city and surrounding areas.

While certainly not as chaotic as in Kuala Lumpur, some violence did spill over to Singapore and the army and the police were deployed onto the streets for the first time in five years. As he had in July 1964, Clarence headed down to the Central Police Station, with the company of trainee section leaders (who he was training at SAFTI at the time), to man roadblocks and patrol the streets of Chinatown. There was no curfew imposed this time round. The violence had not escalated majorly in Singapore, so it became more of a training exercise for the new soldiers, while also letting potential hooligans know that the authorities were watching the area. In general, life went on as per normal for everyone, save for the presence of soldiers and policemen on the streets.

During their deployment to Chinatown, Clarence's company encountered no signs of trouble. Early on there had been clashes in other parts of the island, but in general the disturbances in Singapore were relatively minor. By the time tensions died down, four people had been killed in Singapore, with 80 injured.[29]

After this two-week deployment-cum-training exercise, Clarence's company returned to their barracks at SAFTI and continued with their section leader course.

---

29 A much higher fatality and injury rate was experienced in Kuala Lumpur and Malaysia itself.

Life was not all about work for Clarence during this period. He was also enjoying life outside of the army, and big changes were taking place in his personal life as well. Changes that would ultimately have direct connections to you, Emma and Luke.

Every Sunday at SAFTI an open house was held for the families of the trainees to come visit. As families mingled with their sons, it was a chance for the officers to meet the families of the boys as well. So, Clarence would take the opportunity to make the rounds of the family groups on the parade ground, introducing himself and learning a bit about the lives of his men. It was during one of these open houses that the 26-year-old single officer first set his eyes on a certain young woman, who happened to be the sister of one of the men in the section he was commanding then.

He did not catch the young lady's name at the time, nor did he have a phone number for her, but he knew he wanted to get to know her better. It was hardly appropriate for him to ask one of his men for his sister's details so, being the resourceful man that he was, he asked a mutual friend for her name, then diligently made his way through the telephone directory looking for her family's phone number. Judy was quite impressed with the effort Clarence had gone to when she fielded a call from him a few days later.

And they began dating. Though there was not much real dating, with most of their contact with each other being over the phone. At the time, Clarence was spending most of his weekends on exercises, so there were few opportunities for the two of them to spend time together. But they persevered and a few years later, in 1968, they got married.

Then about a year later, their first child was born – Tan Lye Hock Melvin Conrad. Your uncle, Ku Ku Mel.

Chapter 22
Commando

The Singapore armed forces had come a long way by the end of 1968. From the meagre two, severely depleted, regiments it had "inherited" in the August of 1965, the subsequent three years had seen it grow to include four infantry battalions, an artillery battalion, and an armour battalion. It had also seen the establishment of a naval volunteer force and an air defence command, the precursors to the current navy and airforce.

When the Singapore army was created, the initial focus was purely on its defensive capabilities, to defend against possible aggressors into its territory. A defensive approach determines the types of weapons and units an army builds up. For example, minefields and fixed position coastal gun emplacements would be considered defensive weapons and strategies intended to discourage an aggressor from crossing your borders. A long-range strategic bomber aircraft, on the other hand, would be considered an offensive capability, as it enables the army to proactively deploy weapons more directly into enemy territory.

It was probably never a stated policy that the armed forces were to be defence-focused only. Perhaps it was simply the more natural way for an army to develop? Clarence recalled a comment by Dr Goh Keng Swee, some years later, regarding the early stages in the development of the army: "If you have a house and no fierce dog guarding it, then any thief can come and steal from you. Singapore needed a guard dog first." Hence the initial task had been to build up the infantry and artillery. These were the guard dogs.

As a long-term strategy however, a purely defence-focused force would not be enough. The SAF, like any armed force, needed to develop a more serious and complete long-term military strategy capable of responding to whatever threats the future might throw its way. In line with this, the country would need to develop a force that could operate covertly behind enemy lines.

In early 1969, a new project began to get under way. Behind closed doors at the Ministry of Interior and Defence, a small group of people started quietly conducting a study on the feasibility of a new type of military capability that would involve a unit of elite soldiers trained in the art of unconventional warfare – operating in a guerrilla manner in small units, and executing hit-and-run, hit-and-return, and hit-and-hide operations. This was not work for infantrymen; this required a dedicated raiding unit: a commando unit.

———————

While in the initial years it was not public knowledge that a commando unit would ultimately be established, Clarence and his colleagues had a hunch that it might be part of the bigger master plan. His training with the US Rangers and US Airborne in 1967 had been the first clue. Another clue was that the newly graduated officers from the Officer Cadet Course had the option to tick "Commando" from a list of preferred career choices on a form they completed, even though such a unit did not yet exist. So there was much speculation that there was something in the works.

When the time did come to move forward with the establishment of a commando unit, the first step was to figure out how to get such a unit off the ground. And there was arguably only one person in the Singapore army at that time with the requisite experience to handle such a task. This one man had been through US Ranger and Airborne training, he had spent a significant amount of time training with the Malaysian equivalent, the MSSU, and he had led exploratory "covert" exercises in combat in the jungles of Sebatik Island.

Major Clarence Tan, now 28, was the logical man to assist in its development.

Sure enough, along with another SAFTI staff officer, Clarence was selected to work on a project to prepare and present a paper to the Ministry of Interior and Defence in support of starting up a commando unit. His colleague was appointed the officer-in-charge for this project and became the primary lead for researching and putting together the requisite white paper.

Given his existing commitment as the commanding officer of the 4 SIR, Clarence's initial involvement was in a support and consultative role. So, at the end of each day, after performing his duties at 4 SIR, the two men would sit for hours discussing and developing plans. Clarence's input was based on his operational experience, while his colleague researched how other armies around the world were operating their equivalent units.

They explored everything. How many men would be needed? What kind of men did they need? What incentives and rewards would be needed? How would they market it? What doctrine did they want to inculcate among their soldiers? What training would be required? The two young officers had been given a huge task. In today's world, this task would probably be assigned to highly educated business graduates. But this was how it was in these early days of Singapore – ordinary people were doing extraordinary things.

The men spent a few months working on the project. On 1st December 1969, soon after they had submitted their white paper to the Ministry, the commando unit was officially formed.

It was hardly an impressive beginning. A small office in a quiet corner of SAFTI was to be the unit's first home. And while four officers had been formally posted to the unit from day one, this first home was initially occupied by just one man (who was therefore the acting commanding officer for a few weeks). The other three were finishing off existing commitments – one was on a course a few buildings away at SAFTI's School of Advanced Training for Officers, while two had been sent overseas to attend commando and paratrooper courses. Clarence himself was not a part of this initial four. While he was still very much involved with the new unit's development at a management level, he remained at 4 SIR for a while longer before ultimately being posted to the commando unit as its first commanding officer.

The first priority for Clarence and his four colleagues was to build up a sizeable force. But recruitment was going to be a tough job. How were they going to make it attractive for people to join? This was not a job that could be undertaken by newbies off the street, so their target audience was restricted to existing soldiers in the Singapore army, which immediately narrowed down the pool of people from whom they could recruit. At the same time, the armour divisions were also recruiting, and they had some impressive toys to show off. They could bring tanks along to their recruitment drives, even to recruitment roadshows in the civilian heartlands. "Come and drive a tank," they said. "Have a look inside one." Armour had videos too, which were a very new thing in those days, and quite an attraction in themselves. What kind of draw cards did the new commandos have to show off? A few foreign weapons. Some camouflage gear. An explosion might attract some attention, but one could hardly go around blowing things up at a recruitment drive.

There were also no major perks or incentives they could offer. The unit's only real selling point was that this job would offer adventure and excitement. "Come and join us if you want an adventurous kind of life."

Commando   233

Recruitment began in earnest when the two officers who had been training overseas returned. But it was a slow and hard slog. They had to do it themselves with no support from the higher echelons nor anyone from the Ministry of Interior and Defence. The only avenue they had was to walk into the existing camps around Singapore, put up posters, and hold talks. Given that this was essentially a poaching exercise, the commanding officers of the existing units were not happy to have these outsiders come into their camps, trying to steal officers and NCOs from under their noses. But at least the COs were not allowed to stop the recruiters from having a go. During these talks, they spoke of a life of adventure, excitement, and the opportunity for overseas training. Apart from a few foreign weapons that regular soldiers would not have seen before, they had minimal props to show off. It was mostly about trying to sell the idea verbally.

Over time they did manage to get the message across, and a few soldiers began to figure out that something exciting was going on. Even some senior officers began to express an interest in joining. Eventually the interest turned into a trickle of applications.

In all, they managed to recruit a core group of 30 officers and NCOs to form their first batch of commandos. It was still a small group though, and more men were needed.

Then, some luck came Clarence's way.

One morning at SAFTI, Clarence noticed a company of new soldiers milling around outside some barracks. About one hundred men had just arrived in the camp and jumped out of some three-tonner transports. On learning that these men, in their brand new uniforms, were fresh recruits, Clarence had an idea. He figured that no unit owned them yet. So, he hurried over to the SAFTI director's office and sought approval to take them under his wing, and to see if he could make commandos of them. The director said yes, and in fact seemed quite happy with the idea.

So just like that, Clarence had his first company of regular commandos. However, they weren't trained yet. The first thing he did was to put them through basic training. Not all of them made the grade, and some were transferred to other units. But a good number made the cut. At the recommendation of a US advisor, this group of survivors were then sent straight off to the US Ranger and Airborne courses. This would be the fastest way to train them up, was the advice. Throw them in the deep end. So off they all went.

Being a brand new unit, another big task for Clarence and his colleagues was putting together the training and exercise syllabus for the commandos. One of the advisors called in to provide assistance felt strongly that marksmanship must be a key focus. "You must be able to shoot. One shot, one hit," he would say. Needless to say, the men spent a lot of time at the shooting range.

Clarence's specialty area, demolitions, was another important focus. A key skill for a commando is to be able to infiltrate an enemy position to sabotage and disable their equipment, whether that be large guns, ammunition stores, aircraft sitting on an airfield, or ships in port. Given that regular bombs and explosives would be too heavy and cumbersome to carry on such missions, the training was focused on improvised demolitions. Lighter options such as plastic explosives were not commonplace at this time. The men would still need to carry detonators and explosive charges with them, but they learnt how to use what they found in the field to make an effective weapon.

Unarmed combat was an interesting area of their training. Given the stealthy nature of their work, they needed to learn how to quickly and quietly disable an enemy combatant with their bare hands, before that enemy had time to reach for their weapon or arouse the attention of others nearby. So the men worked on this intensely, and did so for the entirety of their time with the unit. At the time, the South Koreans were renowned for their expertise in martial arts – they had an entire unit focused solely on the skill. So two instructors from there were engaged to train the Singaporeans: one from their special forces and another from their famous White Horse division. These men introduced the Singaporeans to a military style of Tae Kwan Do in which fighting with rifles and bayonets was included with unarmed techniques. The South Koreans were heavily involved in the Vietnam War as allies of America, and one of these instructors would relate to them his experiences of real-life hand-to-hand combat in that war.

Understanding how to use a variety of foreign weapons, those likely to be used by an enemy, was another important skill the new commandos needed to learn. Operating behind enemy lines very likely meant the soldiers needed to use weapons picked up along the way. While most rifles and guns are fired in a similar manner, it paid to have some familiarity with different types of weapons, as during battle split-second responses could mean the difference between life and death. Hence, the men were introduced to a variety of foreign arms.

The commandos had to be good at all things: even signals and communications, Morse code, and first aid. They needed to become a self-reliant group of men. This was not about becoming a jack of all trades and master of none, but becoming masters of all trades. Although, in reality, they tended to focus the training so that each man became a true expert in two skill sets: Jack of all trades and master of two. The diverse nature of the skills meant that much of the training had to be conducted by the other army units who were specialists in the specific tasks. Some of this could be conducted in Singapore. Training for operating the 81 and 106RG mortars, for example, was conducted by the regular mortar unit. Some training had to be conducted overseas. Men were sent in batches to places like the US for Ranger and Airborne, as well as Pathfinder courses, or to the UK for Basic Marine Commando and Airborne courses. Others were sent for advanced specialist courses such as Parachute Rigger and Special Forces training.

It was an adventurous and exciting start for the new recruits. The SAF Commando Unit was most certainly living up to its promise of adventure. And they were seeing the world. This was not a time when people travelled overseas a great deal so this perk was pretty special.

———————

Given that they were to be a covert force, a lot of their training exercises involved the commandos being discretely inserted into the exercises of other divisions, such as the infantry or artillery. This was good training for both sides. For the commandos, it provided opportunities to hone their stealthiness by conducting raids on "enemy" positions. For the other divisions, it provided reminders that, in addition to the more obvious combatants in front of them, an enemy might also be conducting covert operations behind their own lines. To keep the element of surprise, often the commandos were included in the exercises without the express knowledge of the other divisions.

Clarence and his men especially enjoyed this part of their training. Much of the enjoyment came from the challenge of trying to outwit their opponents. With the fruits of their success being a chance to surprise their targeted division in sometimes – what was for them – humourous ways, their drive to succeed was real. Though in doing so, they made a lot of enemies among their colleagues from other divisions of the army. But that was their job.

Once a year the infantry brigades would conduct a large combined exercise. During one such exercise the commandos were tasked with conducting a raid on one of the battalion headquarters. The exercise took place on the island of Pulau Tekong, off the north eastern tip of Singapore, and the 2nd Singapore Infantry Brigade had set up their headquarters in one of the buildings there. On the way to the target, Clarence and a small patrol of his men had to pass through a swamp. Now, a swamp might not be a piece of terrain that a commander would normally send an infantry regiment through. Chances are that a large group like that would just get bogged down by it, putting them at great risk of being slaughtered in the water. But it could prove a very useful avenue for a small commando unit looking for a discrete route, under the cover of darkness, to approach a target. It also turns out to be a great location to stock up on some unusual ammunition. Clarence and his men crossed the swamp, and then managed to slip unnoticed past the brigade headquarter's security. Then came time for the assault on the building itself. Upon storming the office, instead of simply yelling out "we've got you", Clarence and his men threw mud bombs all over the place, using mud they had picked up in the swamp. On the walls, on the desks, on the paperwork, and at the people themselves. Naturally, the brigade commander was not very happy. But the commandos had done their job.

And then there was the commanding officer of 3 SIB who was so proud of the below-ground headquarters that he had ordered dug out using excavators at the beginning of another exercise. The temptation to undermine his efforts was too great for Clarence's chaps. During that exercise, the "enemy" officers and NCOs operating in that subterranean bunker were seen running out onto open ground to escape the smoke from the smoke-grenades thrown inside by the raiding commandos.

Yes, Clarence and his men had a lot of fun during these exercises. They certainly got up to a lot of mischief and made a lot of "enemies".

By 1973, the recruitment of soldiers into the commandos was not as fast as Clarence and his colleagues wanted. Their policy to recruit only from within the army was impeding their growth. They needed a boost. So

Dr Goh Keng Swee and the Ministry of Defence[30] stepped in, making a policy decision to allow the commandos to start taking in National Servicemen. To enable them to get these fresh recruits up to the fitness and skill levels they required more quickly, the commandos became the first unit in the Singapore army to independently handle their own basic military training. Up until then all new recruits, regardless of which division they would eventually serve with, underwent the same basic training course. Given the nature of their job, commandos needed to be trained to a more rigorous and exacting standard. So if they were going to take in men straight from civilian life then it was key that they had control over this training from the very beginning. In fact, Clarence and his colleagues also gained control of the recruitment and selection of their new recruits, further ensuring that they had the right men for the job. While it was not as ideal as having a unit that was made up completely of regulars, at least they had these NSmen for two and a half years, which was plenty of time to train them up and mould them.

With the advent of recruitment via the National Service route, the numbers in the unit began to grow significantly.

The advisor assigned to help the commandos in the early days of their formation was an interesting guy, and a key ally for the commandos in these early days. A hard and strict man who pushed them accordingly, he was an older guy who had seen fighting, and had been toughened by it. And he was a man that Clarence would come to respect immensely. Not the type of advisor who would sit back and watch his soldiers training from a distance, he was always with them in the thick of action. Up the hills, in the jungles, and everywhere else around Singapore. Wherever their training took them, he followed.

---

30 In 1970 the Ministry of Interior and Defence was split into the Ministry of Home Affairs and the Ministry of Defence.

On one particular exercise, Clarence and some of the unit were conducting a night-time raid against an artillery rapier missile of Air Defence Command at Bukit Batok, at the western end of Pierce Reservoir, near the centre of the island. During the exercise, one of his NCOs told Clarence he saw something out of the ordinary in the distance, moving toward them. A ghost perhaps? Many of the men, especially the Chinese, believed quite firmly in the wandering souls of the dead, and it was not unusual for them to claim sighting ghosts deep in the dark jungle nights during training exercises. Especially when they heard unexplained noises whistling through the bush. Being Peranakan, Clarence had been exposed to such folklore so did not rule it out entirely. He knew that ghosts did love to hang out around trees, and the jungles were full of those. Hence his sergeant's comment certainly made him a little anxious.

The sergeant pointed in the direction of the sighting. When Clarence saw the figure in white robes approaching them, he also thought they were looking at a ghost. It appeared to be carrying something. The patrol stopped and watched the figure approach, ready to bolt if indeed it was a ghost about to terrify them out of their wits.

Clarence called out to the apparition. It replied, in a gruff, authoritative voice: "Is that you, Major Tan?" Goodness me, he thought. It was their advisor.

Although relieved that there was nothing supernatural, Clarence was still surprised. The instructor had taken ill the previous day and was supposed to be lying in a hospital bed, not joining a commando unit on exercises in the tropical heat of the Singapore jungle. They were not at all expecting to see him here. It turned out that he had gotten bored in the hospital, and felt it more important that he was out in the field watching his students train than to be lying in bed. So he had simply walked out of his ward and came to find them. Against the advice, and possibly knowledge, of his doctors. He had not even changed out of his white hospital patient's gown.

Upon linking up with the patrol, the instructor asked Clarence to supply him with one of his best NCOs. Someone that Clarence would trust with his own life. Clarence gestured at one of his men. The instructor looked at the soldier, said, "Right, sergeant. A very simple job for you. You stay by my side. If I fall down you give me one of these injections," and passed him a box of syringes that he had brought with him from the hospital. "Right, back to work, gentlemen. You have a rapier missile to destroy, right?"

And so they got back to work, with their self-discharged advisor in his hospital robes, supervising them until the end of the exercise. This would have been no Sunday stroll in the park. Bukit Batok was higher then than it is now, and the men were climbing up and down and around the hill, through the thick vegetation of the jungle. Yes, Clarence had a lot of respect for this man. He pushed them hard, but he gave as much as he asked for.

———

The unit continued to slowly grow, with a continual application of changes along the way. One of these changes, which for many eyes might be viewed as a seemingly minor one, initially created a bit of a stir from an interesting desk. This was in 1971, and they had just changed their headdress from a brimmed jungle hat to a beret. Clarence was a little shocked when he got a call from the Prime Minister's Office, asking him to explain his decision. The issue was not with the choice of a beret itself. It was to do with the colour Clarence had chosen: Red. You see, most commandos around the world at the time wore green berets, so Clarence's choice of red was a departure from that tradition. But the commando's commanding officer had his reasons, which he explained over the phone to the Principal Private Secretary to Prime Minister Lee Kuan Yew. At the time, the People's Defence Force, the volunteer unit in post-independence Singapore, wore green berets. So did the School Cadet

Corps. An elite commando unit could hardly wear the same colour as other units. They needed to be distinguishable. These other units could have been asked to change, but that would be a big effort. And even if they did, it would take a generation before people would recognise, and respect, green as the commando colours alone. Red was therefore chosen as the next best alternative. This colour had been adopted by other special forces and paratroopers around the world, including the British SAS at one time (though they subsequently changed to beige). And since the Singapore commandos had a significant airborne component, Clarence decided it appropriate to move forward with the red beret. His explanation was accepted by the Prime Minister, and the red beret remains to this day.

Chapter 23
Laju Hostage Crisis

All was quiet on the evening of Friday, 1st February 1974, at the family home on Changi airbase, in the eastern part of the island. Clarence, Judy, and their two kids had been living in the army-supplied black-and-white bungalow for a few years now. As the commanding officer of the commandos, and now a Lieutenant Colonel, such a luxury was part of Clarence's remuneration package. Judy and Clarence were sitting in their living room watching television as four-year-old Melvin and two-year-old Marjorie lay fast asleep in their shared room. The quiet of the camp outside, with portions of jungle flanking some of its perimeter and waves gently lapping the shoreline of Changi Beach nearby, belied the barrage of activity that was just about to come Clarence's way.

The family home at Changi, near Hendon Camp, where the commandos were based.

A little after 9pm the telephone in the main hallway of the house rang. Half expecting it to be a call from her mother, Judy got up from the comfort of her chair and picked up the handset. A moment later she returned to the living room and told Clarence that it was a work call for him. That's a little strange, he thought. Perhaps the caller was another officer on the base. When he answered the phone, however, he was startled to find himself speaking to someone from the office of the Minister of Defence.

"Come immediately to the Minister's office for an urgent meeting. And bring a junior officer along," said the voice at the other end of the line. This was certainly something out of the ordinary. A late Friday night meeting at the Ministry of Defence. What was even more surprising, he was being called directly by the Minister's office and not by a senior military colleague. So, with urgency, he complied.

Saying farewell to his wife, he left the bungalow and walked to the officer's mess in search of a junior officer to take with him. But there was no one around. The junior officers tended to still be single, and were probably out on the town somewhere. It was, after all, the Friday night of a long weekend. Of course, the duty officer was around, but he could not be relieved from his post. The officer told Clarence that one of his second lieutenants had just left for home in Geylang about 30 minutes before, and he could try getting hold of him. So Clarence called the lieutenant, who confirmed he had no plans for the evening. "Stay where you are. I'll pick you up," Clarence told him.

The two commando officers arrived at their destination close to midnight and were immediately led to the office where the Minister, the Permanent Secretary of Defence, and a couple of other ministry staff were already waiting for them. There were no other senior uniformed officers present. They must have came to Clarence directly. It was perhaps an indicator of the urgency of the situation that Minister Goh Keng Swee had called in an operations guy like Clarence, versus the likes of the Army Chief of Staff (who would most likely have been informed of the meeting regardless).

"Lieutenant Colonel, have you heard about the bombing on Bukom?" the Minister said. "And the subsequent hostage situation? What do you know about it?"

"I've heard about it on the radio," Clarence responded, adding that there were a few rumours floating around among the army officers. Other than that he did not know much about the situation. He understood it to be a police operation, and he expected it to stay that way, so it was not on his radar. The Permanent Secretary then filled Clarence and his colleague more fully in on the situation.

––––––––

The previous day, four foreign men had made their way to Pulau Bukom, just south of the main Singapore island, and placed plastic explosive charges against four oil tanks, successfully detonating three of them. In their escape, they had taken over a boat that was used to ferry passengers to and from the island. The ferry's name was Laju. The alarm was raised quickly, and police boats were immediately deployed to intercept the Laju. After a short game of cat and mouse out on the water, a cordon of police boats had been formed around the boat in the eastern anchorage, not far off the coast from Clifford Pier. Soon after a bottle was thrown into the sea from the Laju, and the message contained inside removed any doubts that the police and the government might have had about the seriousness of the situation they had on their hands. The note said:

> We are the Japanese Red Army and Popular Front for the Liberation of Palestine.
>
> Just now, we exploded the Pulau Bukom's tank for the solidarity with Vietnamese revolutionary people. And for making the revolutional situtation after considering the situation of today's oil crisis.

Now we want to negotiation with you. Call at once, Japanese Ambassador! Hostages are in our hand. And we have big explosives with us.

If you let us carryed to the airport we promise you never kill them. But if you try to attack us, we explode ourselves. We want to escape to another country.[31]

The hijackers were from two separate, but related groups – two from the Japanese Red Army, JRA, and two from the Popular Front for the Liberation of Palestine, PFLP. And most threateningly, unless they were given safe passage to a friendly country, they would blow themselves up and kill the hostages in the process.

This was now a serious situation with two very serious militant groups. The Japanese Red Army was a Japanese communist group that had been founded in Lebanon in 1971, with the goal of overthrowing the Japanese government and the Emperor, and starting a worldwide revolution. The Popular Front for the Liberation of Palestine was a secular Palestinian Marxist-Leninist and revolutionary socialist organisation founded in 1967, and had carried out a number of airliner hijackings in the recent years. Both groups had very close ties to each other, and had conspired together for a massacre at Lod Airport (now called Ben Gurion International Airport) in Israel in May 1972. In that shocking event, JRA operatives had killed 24 and injured 80 passengers arriving off a flight. These were two very serious groups, and both with a bloody history. They were not to be trifled with.

———————

It was just over 24 hours since the hijack started, and negotiations were still taking place out on the water. The hijackers were communicating with the police negotiators who were on a boat nearby. Minister Goh

---

31 Text reproduced according to MINDEF records.

confirmed to Clarence that this was a police operation, and that the army was not involved. But, while a negotiated outcome was preferred from the government's perspective, he was concerned that negotiations were taking some time. If they continued to drag, it was possible that the military would be called in, and he wanted to be prepared.

"Can the commandos take over the boat?" the Minister asked Clarence directly.

"Yes," Clarence replied, with no idea how. One could not say no to the Minister. The Minister then asked him what he could do. Clarence thought fast. He had never faced nor trained for such a situation before, but he had to come up with some ideas. Firing upon or blowing up the ship were out of the question – there were hostages on board. The Permanent Secretary asked if going in with divers would be an option. Clarence said the commandos had no combat divers, but that a couple of his men were recreational divers, so they could devise a way for them to approach and board the boat from underwater. As the discussions continued, it became apparent that the commandos would need some time to formulate a suitable plan. So, Minister Goh closed the meeting, instructing Clarence to jump on a helicopter in the morning to fly around, assess the situation, and "come up with some ideas". It had been an interesting and certainly memorable midnight meeting.

The following morning, after just a few hours' sleep, Clarence and his second lieutenant headed down to the helicopter squadron, which was also based at Changi, and went to scope out the situation on the water. They kept their distance as they circled above, so as not to disrupt the negotiations or cause concern among the hijackers. From their elevated vantage point they could make out the Laju sitting in the middle of a ring of marine police boats, with one other boat floating a little closer. A number of Singaporeans were on board that one, negotiating directly with the hijackers. After an hour of flying around and considering their options, they returned to Changi to begin planning.

The biggest challenge for Clarence was assembling a team at such short notice. Most of his men were away for the long weekend, and this was a time well before mobile phones, so it was hard getting in touch, but he eventually got enough men together. For the next few days, while the negotiations continued out on the water, Clarence spent his time at the Marine Police headquarters at Kallang, with his team positioned nearby, rehearsing their options and awaiting orders to go in.

The orders never came through. A breakthrough in the negotiations came on 6th February, seven days after the saga had started. And Clarence's role was about to change from preparing for an assault mission on the hijackers, to providing a security detail to these very same men.

In response to the hijackers' demand for safe passage to a "friendly" country, the government had approached a number of countries in the Middle East in the hope that someone would accept them. Even the North Korean government had been approached. No one wanted the four men. There was also a secondary problem around securing an aircraft to ferry them to their destination. Then, on 6th February, members of the PFLP (in conjunction with members of the JRA and an organisation called the Sons of Occupied Territories) occupied the Japanese Embassy in Kuwait, taking a number of diplomats hostage, in support of their comrades on the Laju. The hijackers in Kuwait demanded that "the Japanese Government send a Japanese airplane to Singapore immediately in order to carry our four heroes to Kuwait".[32] This forced the Japanese government to release a Japan Airlines DC-8 airliner for the flight. Now, as far as the Laju hijackers were concerned, the Japanese government could not be trusted. The Japanese themselves were very keen to get their hands on the two JRA members, and this would be their only chance. So, the hijackers on the Laju demanded that Singapore provided some of their own people as escorts, to guarantee their safety while en route to Kuwait.

32 De Onis, Juan. "Guerrillas in Kuwait Seize Tokyo Envoy And Embassy Staff." *The New York Times*, 7 February 1974, p. 1.

So, along with three of his fellow commandos, Clarence joined a team of Singaporeans onboard the flight to Kuwait. The team ultimately comprised of 13 men, including S. R. Nathan (then Director of Security and Intelligence in the Ministry of Defence),[33] an Arabic speaker (to act as a translator), and Tee Tua Ba (the man tasked with the tough job of actually negotiating with the hijackers over the previous seven days).

———————

It was late in the evening on 7th February when the Laju hijackers and their hostages came ashore at Kallang. Clarence and the commandos joined them in the van, and they headed to the airport at Paya Lebar, escorted by police patrol cars and motorcycle outriders. Being late at night, the roads were empty and quiet.

Clarence's first impressions of these hijackers, as he sat with them in the van, was how ordinary they looked. They were also quite relaxed. Perhaps the negotiations of the last week had given them a great deal of trust in their Singapore escorts. One thing he found particularly interesting was that, apart from their weapons, all the four men possessed were the clothes on their backs. Clarence wondered whether they had entered this mission with the expectation that they were going to die.

Upon arriving at Paya Lebar International Airport, they entered by the more discreet VIP complex, so as to avoid raising any commotion in the main terminal. The Japan Airlines DC-8 was sitting on the tarmac waiting for them. Before boarding and take-off, a few things needed to be sorted out.

First, it was agreed earlier that the hostages were to be released and the hijackers were to hand over their weapons at the airport terminal just prior to boarding. Clarence was present for this process, and there was a brief moment of tension as the hijackers became a little hesitant. No doubt they realised that they were putting their lives entirely in the hands

———————

33 S. R. Nathan would later become the sixth president of Singapore from 1999 to 2011.

of the Singapore government and its agents. But with the reassurance of the man who had been the lead negotiator throughout the saga they handed over their weapons. After what must have been seven harrowing days for them, the hostages were finally freed.

The next thing to do was to vet the Japanese officials and crew who were to join them on the flight. It was quite possible that Japanese security personnel were masquerading as Japan Airlines crew, with the intention of turning the tables once the aircraft was in the air, and it was Clarence's job to reduce the likelihood of this happening. As a first step, he checked with the Singapore Airlines flight operations department as to the minimum number of crew members the DC-8 could operate with. Then, armed with this information, upon boarding the aircraft he discovered that there seemed to be a few too many pilots on the flight deck. So a couple were immediately ejected. Then he inspected and interviewed all of the cabin crew individually. His assessment was that the Japanese had stacked the crew with military personnel. In the end, only two male flight attendants, and a minimum flight-deck crew, were left on board.

With the security check completed, the four hijackers and their Singapore escorts boarded the aircraft. The hijackers were escorted to the rear cabin of the airliner, while the Japanese officials and Japan Airlines' crew were instructed to remain in the front cabin. The Singaporeans positioned themselves in the middle, separating the two groups. They were not to engage with each other during the flight.

Then, in the early hours of 8th February, the aircraft taxied out to the runway, and began its takeoff roll for the nine-hour flight to Kuwait.

———————

The flight itself was a bit of a non-event. "Boring," Clarence said. He and his colleagues kept their eyes on the hijackers and the Japanese throughout. While the four Singapore commandos were dressed in dark suits and ties, their clipped haircuts and fit physiques made it pretty obvious that they were from the military. The hijackers and Japanese would have guessed that they were armed. So, no one got up to any funny business. The hijackers caught up on lost sleep and even engaged in casual conversation with the non-military members of the Singapore team.

It was not until they approached Kuwait that the tensions rose somewhat. A problem surfaced: the Kuwait air traffic controller informed the pilot that their flight had been refused permission to land. This was unexpected as the Singaporeans assumed everything had been sorted out in advance. The DC-8 was at the end of its range and was running low on fuel, so diverting to an alternate airport was not going to be an option. Nathan instructed the crew to inform the tower that their fuel was low and that Kuwait had to let them land. After the plane circled for a short while, the tower informed them that the government had acquiesced and approved them for landing. Soon thereafter, as the sun rose over the desert nation, the airliner thumped onto the runway of Kuwait International Airport.

Once the airliner stopped, in a remote part of the airport, it was immediately surrounded by tanks, armoured vehicles, and soldiers from the Kuwaiti army. The place looked like a war zone. The controller then relayed the message that no one was allowed to get off the aircraft, and that the doors should remain closed. So the group had to sit and wait, uncertain about what was happening outside. A number of hours passed before a long stretch limousine turned up, escorted by police cars with flashing lights and sirens. Nathan was then instructed to leave the aircraft to speak to an official in the car, who turned out to be the Kuwaiti Minister of Defence.

As everyone else waited in the plane, discussions between the Minister and Nathan dragged on. It seemed that the Kuwaitis were quite angry about being involved in this issue. Kuwait had always taken a position in support of the Palestinians, and this had kept them largely out of the problems created by the militant groups. While a number of incidents and hijackings had ended in Kuwait, the Japanese Embassy incident was the first time a hostage situation had started on their home turf. They were not happy.

Things did not really move forward until the Japanese Ambassador to Teheran turned up at the airfield to negotiate with the Kuwaiti officials. Nathan sat in the back seat of the limo listening in for much of the conversation, and would return to the aircraft from time to time to update Clarence and the rest of the Singapore team on the proceedings. The Kuwaitis wanted to end the Japanese Embassy hijack, and to get the hijackers out of their country, so they wanted the PFLP hijackers from the embassy to join their four comrades from the Laju hijacking and fly off to some other country. The Japanese, on the other hand, wanted to guarantee the safety of its diplomatic staff, its Japanese citizens onboard the aircraft, and the DC-8 airliner itself. A country that would accept the group of hijackers also had to be found.

Meanwhile, the Singaporeans were growing concerned about their situation. As far as they were concerned, their responsibility had been to get the hijackers out of Singapore. That was done. They were now worried that they were being left out of the negotiations and potentially forgotten about, and they might end up joining the hijackers on a flight to a second country, with a good chance of turning into hostages themselves.

Then, six hours after they had landed, a convoy of cars turned up at the steps of the aircraft. Rough, militant-looking men, armed with revolvers and hand grenades, exited the cars and boarded the aircraft. What was going on here? It turned out that they were the PFLP hijackers from the Japanese Embassy. The siege was over. South Yemen (now a part of Yemen) had agreed to take them. Once on board, completely ignoring Clarence and the other Singaporeans, they made their way to the rear of the aircraft and had a lively reunion with the four Laju hijackers. Big hugs all around. It was only at this stage that the Laju hijackers learnt of their PFLP comrades' efforts to secure their flight from Singapore to Kuwait.

The Singaporeans looked at one another uncertainly. They were still on board the aircraft that was due to fly off with this expanded group of terrorists. Then a while later, the Kuwaiti Foreign Minister boarded the aircraft and told the Singaporeans in a rather blunt manner to get off the aircraft. And so they did.

After a short time in the VIP lounge of Kuwait International Airport, Clarence and his colleagues handed over their weapons (which they never saw again) and were driven to a hotel. They were booked on an evening flight back to Singapore, and had some time to kill. So, after washing up, they headed off to a bazaar. Nathan gave them some pocket money, and they became tourists for the afternoon – albeit ones with a Kuwaiti security detail following them at a distance. Then later that night they flew back to Singapore on a regular commercial flight, via Bahrain.

Their mission was complete.

————————

The bombings of the oil tanks on Pulau Bukom, and the subsequent hijacking of the Laju, was a first for Singapore. The fact that Middle East based terrorists had come to Singapore to highlight their cause seemed a little strange at first glance. There were a number of theories as to why Singapore was chosen, most being related to oil. At the time, Singapore was the third largest oil refinery in the world, and the Shell Refining Company had a large operation on Pulau Bukom (hence it is sometimes called Shell Island). The 1973 World Oil Crisis saw oil prices quadrupled within a few months, contributing to a stock market crash and global recession. So, a successful attack on this third largest refinery in the world would likely put further pressure on oil prices, and lead to even more stress on the teetering world economy. There were also theories that such an attack would disrupt the flow of oil to South Vietnam (and the allied American forces), which was still at war with the North Vietnam, whose goals of anti-imperialism, socialism, and anti-America, were very much in line with the PFLP and the JRA. So Singapore itself was not really a target and interestingly at the end of it the hijackers seemed to be quite apologetic to their Singapore negotiators.

The Laju hijacking was the first time Clarence was involved in a real mission while being a family man. Judy and their two children had no idea what he had been doing during the seven days. They just assumed that he had been off on a regular training exercise. That happened from time to time. Sometimes he would tell Judy where he was going, but in most cases he would just disappear for a few days, and she and the kids would have no idea where, or for how long, he was going to be away for. So it was only when Clarence returned to Singapore and appeared on the national television news, with the rest of the team who had flown to Kuwait, that she first found out what he had been up to. She had been completely in the dark. Which was perhaps a good thing.

Chapter 24
Vietnamese Boat People

A number of times throughout these stories from Clarence's life, I have made reference to the Vietnam War, or the American War as the Vietnamese refer to it. That war began in 1955 and lasted through to 1975, with the fall of Saigon to the North Vietnamese forces on 31st April 1975. It was a brutal war, with devastating effects on the local population. And on the Americans, who were the main foreign power involved directly in the campaign.

As the North Vietnamese and Viet Cong made gains further south, many people from South Vietnam, sensing that the end was inevitable, began to escape the country via sea on whatever boats they could get. Some managed to convince owners and captains of larger ships, oil tankers and coastal cargo ships, to take them out. Many, generally poorer people, had to make do with simple small fishing vessels that were not designed for the high seas or large numbers of people. These boats headed in all directions: west to Thailand; east to the Philippines; north to Hong Kong; and south to Malaysia, Singapore and beyond.

A few days following the fall of Saigon, an SOS signal was picked up from one of these ships approaching Singapore waters. The arrival of a vessel named Truong Hai, with 284 people on board, was the first in a wave of boats that would enter Singapore waters over the following two weeks, seeking help.

With the arrival of these boats, the Singapore government took the position that the country could not afford to take in refugees. The island nation was too small and still too young to handle such a large influx.

What's more, many of these boats intended to sail further to places like Australia and the Philippines, where they believed the Americans were waiting to take them back to the US. But the Singapore government did realise that they had a humanitarian obligation to help. So they allowed these boats to harbour in Singapore waters for a few days, during which the authorities would provide fuel, food, water, and medical assistance to them so that they could continue their journeys in a better condition than which they arrived.

———————

It was initially the role of the Marine Police to manage the boats when they first began arriving. But, having a small fleet at the time, the situation very quickly became too big for them. Soon the Singapore Navy, and soldiers from the 2nd Singapore Infantry Brigade (2 SIB), were tasked to assist.

At this time, Bedok Jetty, a civilian jetty jutting out 250m from the south eastern coast, near the now popular Laguna food centre, had already been built, and this became the berthing post for many of the Singapore vessels involved in servicing the refugee fleet from Vietnam. The land around the jetty, now the East Coast Parkway, was newly reclaimed land that had not yet been developed and were large grassy fields at the time. 2 SIB were tasked with setting up a makeshift camp there to manage sick people requiring medical attention, and from which to distribute food and water. From the jetty, the soldiers from 2 SIB would be ferried out to the refugee fleet on Marine Police, Singapore Navy, and Singapore Harbour Board boats, to ascertain what assistance each refugee boat required. Medical officers were part of these teams, and they would provide aid to the sick or injured on the boats, and send the more serious cases to the camp on shore. Engineers were also sent out to check on the seaworthiness of the vessels, to fix what needed to be fixed, and to condemn those deemed too unsafe.

A problem soon arose. As a group of 2 SIB soldiers approached one of the larger boats, grenades were thrown at them and they were warned to stay away and were prevented from boarding. This was a complete surprise. The unarmed soldiers were there to provide a humanitarian service, yet weapons were being hurled at them. Before long, Clarence received a call to meet Minister Goh at the Ministry of Defence operations room at Dempsey. He was ordered to board and take over the vessel concerned, then to conduct an inspection of all the ships seeking assistance from Singapore.

———————

After putting his team together, Clarence and his men devised a plan to take control of the vessel. This was one of the larger vessels and access to it was via a gang plank which, given the occupant's hostility, was kept up most of the time. It was not possible to do a raid on the boat using ladders as the armed personnel onboard had demonstrated they were quite willing to shoot at the soldiers. However, earlier that day, a delegation of "officials" from some of the boats, including this particular one, had gone to shore to meet some Singapore officials. When it was time for them to return to this boat, Clarence took the opportunity to join them on the ferry boat, along with twelve of his men. As the ferry approached the vessel, the soldiers kept themselves out of view. Then, as the gang plank was lowered, Clarence and his men rushed up the gangway and led his men directly to the bridge, catching the crew completely by surprise.

Clarence was now in charge.

On the bridge of the vessel were the ship's captain, a man in a T-shirt, plus a Catholic priest, wearing his clerical collar. Clarence spoke to the captain, informing him that he was there to disarm his men and to collect their weapons. The captain replied in Vietnamese, making out that he knew no English. Suspecting that the priest will have been able to speak English, Clarence addressed him. Having recently converted to Catholicism himself, Clarence used this as a way to break the ice with the priest. But still, no English was forthcoming. Clarence found this a little strange. Then he noticed the man in the T-shirt had, on one of his fingers, a ring from the US Marine Corps. So he addressed T-shirt Guy, telling him that he recognised his ring and that he must have trained at Fort Lejeune. Since Clarence had also trained in the US, at Fort Benning, he knew how the system worked and that T-shirt Guy should have known a little English. But T-shirt Guy said nothing. Clarence was starting to get quite frustrated, and he looked angrily at the three men.

Eventually, the priest spoke. He informed Clarence that T-shirt Guy was a general in the South Vietnamese Army and the head of an army division, and hence very senior.

"Why didn't you respond?" Clarence asked the general. If he had, Clarence would have paid him his due respect. "I'm here to disarm your men and to collect all your weapons. I've been ordered to take whatever action necessary, so you should not resist," he continued. There was a pause as the two men looked at each other.

"Ok," the general finally said. "I do not want to fight anymore." He then instructed his men to put down their weapons and follow Clarence's instructions.

Looking out the front of the bridge, Clarence noticed an armed man standing by a door on the deck, as if guarding it. That would be an obvious place to start looking for more weapons, he surmised. It certainly did turn out to be where all their goodies were kept. Besides a large stash of weapons, there was a lot of valuables like silverware and photos in frames. After removing all the weapons, he ordered the general's men to take him around the boat. Clarence wanted to search every nook and cranny. They found more valuables, silverware, framed photos, and a massive amount of rice – a very important commodity for a ship that would be at sea for an indeterminate period of time.

All the soldiers on this vessel were from the marine division of the South Vietnamese Army. Many of them were obviously well off. They had brought their families and as many possessions and as much money as they could carry, no doubt aware that they were starting a new life in a new country.

Once the boat was secured and he was happy that there were no more weapons onboard, Clarence and his team moved on to the next boat, conducting the same operation. As each vessel was confirmed clear of arms by Clarence and his colleagues, the distribution of food and water, and medical assistance followed. Communication with the Vietnamese was difficult, but on one boat, a young Vietnamese officer, who spoke good English, ran up to Clarence and offered to be his interpreter. So that problem was solved pretty quickly.

Some of the boats, particularly the smaller fishing boats, were overcrowded and often unseaworthy. So, Clarence moved some of the passengers to bigger ones. It was a challenge, though. The people on each boat already knew one another before they left Vietnam, or had bonded during the trials of their journey south. Some of these groups did not take too well to outsiders being thrust upon them, and were very hostile to these new arrivals. While Clarence never witnessed it himself, he heard from other colleagues that some of the new passengers were pushed overboard (luckily in view of the Singapore soldiers, who were able to rescue them).

To resolve this, he decided to jumble up the boats somewhat (ensuring not to break up family groups), effectively breaking up the stranglehold of the existing communities. Then, to ensure any simmering hostilities were subdued, Clarence mobilised more commando units so that every boat had a section of soldiers keeping watch. It was, alas, a security detail that could only be maintained while the ships remained in Singapore waters.

———

After a few days, Clarence returned to one of the boats that he had secured earlier to see how things had settled. As he boarded, a distressed elderly lady approached him. She tugged his arm, showing him a US$1 bill, and said something in Vietnamese. "She is asking for milk," the interpreter relayed. Clarence was puzzled. They had already given enough supplies, including milk, to this boat for free. There should have been plenty to go around. Through his interpreter, he learnt that the captain of the boat and his first mate, both officers from the South Vietnamese Army, were selling the supplies provided to them.

This was not good. The policy for food distribution had been to give the food to the captains, who would be responsible for its distribution to their passengers. That structure had obviously broken down on this boat.

Clarence told the woman not to worry as he would apprehend the culprits. The woman warned him that they were armed, so Clarence gestured at two of his men to follow him. Speaking in Malay so that the Vietnamese wouldn't understand him, Clarence told his men to train their weapons on them as they approached the two men. "Hand over your weapons," he ordered. "You are going to be moved to another boat." As Clarence and his team led the men away, everyone else on board began clapping and cheering. The ruffians were split up and put on separate boats.

———————

Operation Thunderstorm, as this mission was known, lasted for 13 days. As each boat was refueled, replenished with food and water, checked and fixed for seaworthiness, and all the passengers considered well enough to continue their journey, they were sent on their way. More than 8,000 refugees passed through Singapore waters on around 64 boats.

Many of the boats seemed to know where they wanted to go, and had no intention of staying in Singapore. Some headed for Subic Bay, north of Manila in the Philippines, where they had heard that US ships were waiting to take them to North America. Some continued to Australia, island hopping their way along the Indonesian archipelago, before crossing the Timor Sea.

It was a busy time for Clarence and his commando colleagues, and all who had been mobilised. The situation required a lot of creative thinking and presented many of the soldiers with unique experiences. One of Clarence's NCOs assisted with a childbirth on one of the boats. Clarence worked with one of the harbour masters to find a way to reduce the effect of the smell of residual fumes for the passengers on the deck of the oil tanker that they were travelling on. During those two weeks, Clarence spent most of his time on the water, and by the end of it he had that wobbly sea legs feeling that sailors are only too familiar with.

The whole experience moved Clarence greatly. Working with the poorer people in the smaller fishing boats, whose only possessions were the shirts on their backs, he saw how tired, hungry, and thirsty they were when they first arrived. He saw how they were often mistreated and abused by those wealthier and wielding power on the ships. There was a clear hierarchy on some of the boats. The senior officers were often comfortable and commandeering the kitchens on the larger vessels, while the poorer folks lived under tarpaulins on the decks and had to make do without access to the kitchens. On one boat, Clarence noticed some folks on the deck eating uncooked rice mixed with condensed milk. He quickly rectified this situation back in the camp by Bedok Jetty.

While the departure of the last boat from Singapore waters on 14th May 1975 marked the end of Clarence's involvement with the Vietnamese boat people, people continued to trickle out of Vietnam over the following years and make their way to other shores around the region. 1978 saw a large increase. In response to this later wave of refugees, a proper land-based refugee centre was set up that year in Singapore by the United Nations High Commissioner for Refugees, to process many of these arrivals and fly them on to adoptive Western countries. The commandos were not involved in these later situations.

Operation Thunderstorm was "an experience that would lie in my heart", Clarence would later say.

Chapter 25
Always a Commando

The Laju hijacking and Operation Thunderstorm were arguably the last high-profile events that Clarence was directly involved in. There was a lesser known event in October 1977 that saw Clarence again working with the Minister of Defence, Dr Goh Keng Swee, in yet another hijack case. In that incident, four Vietnamese hijackers had taken over a Vietnamese Airlines DC-3 that was on a domestic flight out of Ho Chi Minh City, and diverted it to Singapore, via U-Tapao airport in Thailand. They were seeking asylum outside of Vietnam. In the process, during the flight two Vietnamese officials on board were killed. Commandos were placed on standby at Seletar Airport, where the aircraft landed, in case they needed to rescue the hostages. But the negotiators managed to resolve the situation with the hijackers giving themselves up without further bloodshed.

While there were no further high profile events during the mid to late 1970s, he was certainly kept busy with the continuing development of and growth of the commandos.

Then in 1978, after nine years as a key member of the team that had built the commando unit from scratch, the time came for Clarence to hand the reigns of the 1st Commando Battalion over to a new face, and to take on a new role as the commander of the 2nd Singapore Infantry Brigade (2 SIB). He would spend eighteen months there before undertaking another 18-month posting to 5 SIB. Both these posting were very different to his experiences with the commandos. 2 SIB was purely infantry, and 5 SIB was a reserve brigade. But they both had their interesting and unique challenges.

During these three years away from the commandos, Clarence remained a commando at heart. As is the practice for vocational roles like commandos, he continued to wear his red beret and his commando-related badges, including those from the US Ranger and Airborne.

Following these postings he was posted back to the commandos as its commandant. Clarence would spend a further six years back with his home unit.

———————

Throughout these early days of the Singapore army, a great deal of ingenuity was required by everyone involved. Throughout his career Clarence demonstrated this many times, and perhaps one good example was on the parachuting front.

When he first returned from his US Airborne Course in the US, the army did not have a parachute unit at which he could continue to hone his skills. In fact, the only place to jump at the time was through a sports club run by the British Army's Joint Services Sports Association. With the withdrawal of the British Army from Singapore, the Joint Services Sports Association was handed over to the Singapore Army Sport Association, with the parachuting section placed under the commando unit. Clarence and some of his colleagues took over this club, renamed it the Parachute Association of Singapore, and used it to introduce the regular commandos to parachuting. Being a sports club, they had to do all the activities outside of work hours, so training was conducted during weekday evenings and the jumps were made in the weekends.[34] It also

---

34 It would not be until 1974 when, with the help of an officer and a warrant officer from the New Zealand Army Parachute Training School, that a dedicated army parachute training school was set up in Singapore under the commandos, so that all commandos could learn how to do military parachuting.

Freefalling over Singapore

Practicing formation jumps over Seletar. The Strait of Johor, separating Singapore from Malaysia, can be clearly seen, along with the Causeway connecting Singapore to Johor Bahru. Clarence is in black on the far right.

meant they could not do any military jump training, so they had a lot of fun doing free-fall jumps instead. Free-falling is where jumpers jump from a higher altitude, say, 10,000 feet, and fall freely down to around 3,000 feet before opening their parachute. During the free-fall phase they perform aerobatic manoeuvres, or set up various formations with other jumpers.

Once Clarence and his colleagues became competent at these formation jumps, they put on a few demonstration jumps for the Ministry of Defence, who were very impressed and encouraged them to continue. They even started doing jumps at some events for the general public. In those days, they only had access to round parachutes, which are pretty limited in their directional control. But being the resourceful man he was, when Singapore Airlines asked his team to perform at the opening of a new aircraft hangar, he managed to convince them to pay for some new square parachutes, which provided much better directional control.

Over the years of my listening to Clarence's stories, and in speaking to others who knew him from his time with the commandos, I have the distinct impression that parachuting was an activity that he particularly enjoyed. And he certainly got to do a lot of it.

In late 1971, Clarence took his parachuting skills to another level and spent some time with a group known as the Golden Knights, in the US. These full-time parachutists are the US army's demonstration and competition team, more formally known as the United States Army Parachute Team, and their job is to impress crowds through jumping at shows and competitions. Still in existence today, they do some pretty impressive aerobatic stunts while free-falling through the air. Jumping with these guys was far more intensive than what he had done up until then. They would begin their day at sunrise and jump all morning. An aircraft would take them up, then they would jump. Once back on terra firma, they would gather their parachutes, pack them back up, and head

back up in the aircraft to do it all over again. Up and down all morning.
After lunch, he and his fellow jumpers would sit around and watch
a movie of their morning jumps, discuss their manoeuvres, then talk
about their jumping plans for the following day. They lived, breathed,
and ate jumping.

Clarence jumped all throughout his career, amassing over 1,300
jumps. It is an activity that has pretty serious risks associated with it, but
he was able to come out of all those jumps with only one broken foot,
sustained during a routine jump at Sembawang airforce base when he
slipped on some wet grass while landing. It happens.

Marjorie recalls going out to the airfield in the weekends, when
she was young, to watch him jump. Clarence would bring her along,
and while he was up in the air the rigger girls, the team responsible
for that very important task of packing the parachutes, would keep her
entertained. She obviously caught a bit of the bug herself and tried her
hand at it during her posting to New Zealand, even doing a free-fall
from 10,000 feet on her first jump.

By the mid-1980s, Singapore, New Zealand, and Australia already had
long established military ties with each other. The Australians were
heavily involved in the defence of Singapore against the Japanese in
early 1942, and both New Zealand and Australia had maintained some
form of presence in Singapore in the years following World War II.
Both their armies had fought, and lost men, in the Emergency and
the Confrontation. Admittedly the actual fighting in those campaigns
was not on the island of Singapore itself, but Singapore was a base for
many of them before they headed off into the jungles of Borneo and
Peninsula Malaysia.

The Australians pulled their last troops from Singapore shores in
1974, but the establishment of the Five Power Defence Arrangements

had obligated these three countries (plus Britain and Malaysia) to consult one another in the event that either Singapore or Malaysia should be attacked by a foreign army. The New Zealanders actually hung around quite a while longer, with the 1ˢᵗ Battalion Royal New Zealand Infantry Regiment only returning to their homeland in 1989. Additionally, Singapore had been conducting large-scale training exercises in Queensland since the mid-1970s, and Australian and New Zealand instructors were conducting courses for Singapore's growing army.

Given the strong history, and ongoing military collaboration between Singapore and these two countries, it should not be surprising that the island nation had a Defence Adviser based at the Singapore High Commission in Canberra. And it was this role, a diplomatic posting as Singapore's Defence Adviser to Australia (and New Zealand), that would end up being Clarence's penultimate posting as an officer in the Singapore Armed Forces.

In November 1987, with Judy and Marjorie, now 16 years old, in tow (His son, Melvin – Kuku Mel – stayed behind in Singapore to complete National Service), he headed off to assume this new posting at the Singapore High Commission in the Australian capital, and a role that was arguably as different as he could get to all his military work so far. The ultimate in non-field-related positions: dinners, diplomatic functions, black tie events, lots of smiles and handshakes and pleasantries. And golf. But it was all work. Technically. Much of his time was spent negotiating for ongoing access to these countries' land for training exercises, and opening up new areas. During his time he helped to gain access for Singapore forces to Rockhampton, Pearce Airforce Base, and Amberley Airforce Base in Australia and the Waiouru army training area in New Zealand.

The family spent four years in Australia before returning to Singapore in February 1992.

When he did return to Singapore following their time in Canberra, Clarence was appointed to the role of Senior Project Officer in the Ministry of Defense. However, shortly after returning, he was approached with an offer to run the Singapore office of a defence company. This gave Clarence cause to stop and rethink his plans. He had recently celebrated his 51st birthday, and for some time now had been considering the idea of trying something completely new. Given his age and his length of service, he was eligible for a pension, and this seemed like the perfect time to take that leap. So he accepted the offer.

Thirty-three years after starting his military career as a part-time solider with the Singapore Volunteer Corps, he handed in his notice and was approved for early retirement from 1st July 1992.

Clarence, your Kong Kong, was a civilian again.

Clarence and Judy hosting the Singapore Armed Forces Day function
at the Singapore High Commission in Canberra, 1989

Closing Letter

Dear Emma and Luke,

When I think of all the stories that I have had the privilege of hearing from your Kong Kong over the years, I find it interesting that most of them, if not all, were either from his childhood or from his days in the army. While he worked for a number of years in the commercial world following his retirement from the army, I guess the stories of those business days were not as exciting, even if more recently, in his early 70s, he was test flying an aerochute around the vineyards of Victoria, Australia, with a view to selling such aircraft throughout South East Asia.

This book in no way contains all the tales that he has told me over the years. There are more. And there are no doubt tales that I have not yet heard. Tales that he might tell you himself. For now, as you and he continue to enjoy your childhoods, he is happy playing with you and teaching you new games and tricks from his kampong days, such as making kites, stringing rubber bands together to make skipping ropes, or cobbling together rubber-band-powered cars. As you grow older and better able to understand things, I am sure that he will begin to tell you stories himself.

I first was made aware of Kong Kong's military reputation soon after I met your Mummy in 1996, during her time in Wellington. It was not Mummy herself, but her other Singapore friends who told me about him. So even before I met him, it was apparent to me that he was a man of stature in the Singapore army, particularly amongst the Singapore boys of my generation, all of whom at that time were only a few years out of National Service and would probably have heard of him through that.

On a later occasion, I learnt a little more about him through a rather special mutual connection that Mummy and I unknowingly shared. One evening, we were doing the dishes at my family home in Wellington with our parish priest and good friend of the family, Father Geoff Broad. He began telling Mummy about the time he spent in Singapore as a chaplain to the Royal New Zealand Navy. As the two chatted further, we soon discovered that Father Geoff was the vice-captain of the Sembawang Golf Club when Kong Kong was the captain. They had known each other and played golf together. Naturally, given this connection we had to ask Father Geoff to concelebrate our marriage ceremony in Singapore a few years later. When he was in Singapore for the ceremony, Father Geoff visited the golf club with Kong Kong, and he subsequently told me that Kong Kong was a very different man to the one he knew from his army days. He had known Kong Kong as a typically serious military officer, but, as a civilian, he was a much more relaxed man. The man I met back in August 1998, a number of years since retiring from the army, was most definitely the latter.

While he may have been a typically serious military officer during those years, I also have the impression that he was a greatly respected one who was considerate of his men. To see some of his old soldiers come and re-introduce themselves to him when he is out and about, in places like hawker centres and coffee shops around Singapore, is evidence of this. You too might see this from time to time when he takes you out. Each time, I am impressed by the effort he makes to recall the man's name and face, the years he was in the unit, and to ask what he is doing now. I get the impression that he was always very much an officer for his men, and when time and circumstance allowed, he would join them on their runs or out in the field. In the words of some ex-SAF commandos I have met, those who served as junior soldiers when Kong Kong was at the top: "He was not a paper commander." "He was a leader who could be trusted to be there for his men when things went wrong." "A man of action, and not words." A true field officer. And for this he was very much respected.

There is a great humility in the man. Perhaps a humility one might consider to be the trait of all commandos? While he has been supportive of me writing these pages, he was always conscious that he did not want to be painted as some hero. Like those around him, he simply did the job he was tasked to do. And, from those around him, those other pioneers that helped build the Singapore army, the commandos, and even Singapore itself, he does not wish to be singled out. He was part of the team, and there were many others involved in the work he did.

While he spent 33 years in the army, it is the 13 years that he spent with the SAF Commandos that defines him the most. Even now, almost thirty years after leaving "the unit" he still holds an immense pride and love for the commandos, and he still stays connected with them through various functions. As the adage goes, "Old soldiers never die, they just fade away."

The commandos' motto remains with him: "For Honour and Glory".

I cannot end this book without a final mention of your Mama, Kong Kong's supportive wife. Whether she expected it or not, when she married him back in 1968 she took on a big mantle. As mentioned, Kong Kong would often go away on exercises, leaving Mama at home looking after the kids by herself. Most of these times she would not know how long he would be away, nor what he would be doing. All Kong Kong was allowed to tell her was that he was leaving for a while. The Laju incident was an example in how his absences may not simply be for exercises or training, but actual missions that carried significantly higher risks. It was always a concern for her, worrying about what risky activities he was getting himself into.

Soon after your Mummy was born, Mama had to deal with Kong Kong heading to the US for 10 months of Special Forces and further parachute training (his stint with the Golden Knights), which is quite an extended period to be left alone with two very young children. Not wanting her young baby to forget her father, every day during those months she showed your Mummy a photo of him. It was a technique that obviously worked. As soon as she spotted Kong Kong at the arrival hall of Paya Lebar airport upon his return from the US, your one-year-old Mummy ran to hug her father (she had just learnt to walk).

When Mama and Kong Kong returned to Singapore from Australia in February 1992, they moved into a house on Kembangan Hill, one which had been their home since around 1985. But this was not a Kembangan, nor a house, that was in anyway recognisable to the one Kong Kong knew from his youth. Singapore had changed greatly since those days, including geographically. The homestead he had grown up in was long gone. So, too, was the rubber plantation, and the vegetable gardens that had replaced the rubber trees during the Japanese years, and the squatters who had come following that occupation. Long gone was the pig pen and the pond from which he caught fish for the family meals, and the trees he climbed to pick fruit. Long gone was the Boyanese community at the southern end, and the Chinese farmers along the eastern side of the old estate. And the kids from these communities with whom he had played around the estate, and developed his early sense of adventure. Long gone, too, was much of the dirt that had formed the hill itself.

The estate of his youth was no more. In its place stood tightly packed low-rise, private terrace and semi-detached houses. Just inside what used to be the southern border of the property, ran a raised section of the Mass Rapid Transit (MRT) train line, with the large Kembangan MRT station now taking centre stage of the southern vista. Sealed roads and traffic islands now traversed the area of the old estate. At least some of the road names remained: Jalan Kembangan, Lengkong Tiga, Upper East Coast Road. A hundred metres north of their current home, through the approximate location of where the old homestead had once sat, ran the eight carriageway Pan Island Expressway. Just north of that stood the HDB estates in Bedok, and, beyond them, the newly created Bedok Reservoir. There was no longer a view across the Singapore Strait from the hill, as the hill no longer existed. Much of the dirt from here, and the Bedok Reservoir area, had been bulldozed and carted away via conveyor belts for land reclamation along the southern shore, a few blocks away, to form what is now the land around Marine Parade and the East Coast Park (and other areas). About all that remained from his childhood home was the Siglap Canal, the longkang that once marked the western border of their family estate, though even that had changed with its dirt banks and bed having been replaced by concrete walls and floor.

Things had greatly changed on the land, to the land, and to the skyline of Singapore, since Kong Kong's birth in 1941. Over the decades, all over the island, villages and kampongs and estates had been bought up and cleared by the government to make way for urbanisation and the creation of new residential and industrial zones. Many families that had been living in poor, dilapidated housing, where access to amenities that we take for granted today was minimal, were moved into the new, modern, public HDB flats, that came with running water, electricity, gas for cooking, and hygienic toilets. Eventually the land on Kembangan Hill was needed as a part of this re-development, and in 1972 the family estate was sold to the government.

The benefits of this urbanisation process to Singapore, as a fledgling nation that was fast turning into the economic and social "miracle" that it is today, are undeniable. But it came at a price. One that Kong Kong laments about from time to time, particularly as he watches the two of you grow up. And that is the loss of the carefree days of youth. The carefree days that he was able to enjoy. There is little opportunity for kids like yourselves to run around and climb trees, go exploring and hiding in the bush with your friends, to catch birds and insects. To play outdoors and to be in touch with nature. Sure, there are opportunities to visit numerous parks around the island, but to have it accessible on your very doorstep – that was something truly special.

The morning on which I first sat down to think about this closing letter, I went for a run by the beach at East Coast Parkway to clear my head and contemplate some ideas on how to finish this work for you. I stopped for a moment where the Siglap Canal emptied into the sea. In Kong Kong's school days, this same canal emptied itself 600m north of where I was standing, right next to where Saint Patrick's School still stands. I looked across the Strait of Singapore from this spot, toward the island of Batam around ten miles away with cumulonimbus clouds towering above it, and the myriad of ships parked in the anchorage off shore. Looking west, I could see the office towers of the Shenton Way Central Business District, and the cranes of the wharves near where Kong Kong had first started working. Looking east I could see aircraft taking off from Changi, with every flight being an international one, connecting Singapore with the rest of the world. As I continued my run, I saw others out for their morning walks and runs, or doing tai chi or yoga along the beach front. People of many races: Chinese, Malay, Indian, Eurasian, Caucasian, and no doubt a few Peranakan. That morning's run was a reminder, if ever it was needed, that Singapore still is the multi-racial, multi-religious hub and centre of trade and commerce that it has been for almost two centuries. Singapore has experienced many changes over the years, but in many ways it is still the same.

As I continued my run, I bumped by chance into Kong Kong himself, who was also out for his morning run along the beach front. We stopped for a moment and chatted. He showed me a bag of berries that he had just picked from a bush near the magnolia trees just to the east of Bedok Jetty. He gave me a couple, saying they tasted a bit like blueberries, which turned out to be fairly accurate. As we continued on our separate ways, I could not help but think how Kong Kong had also experienced many changes over the years, but that in many ways he was still the same.

And maybe here is a lesson for all us: Like many men and women of his generation, Kong Kong was an ordinary man, a regular kampong kid, who, through hard work and making the most of opportunities, went on to achieve extraordinary things in his career. It is a lesson that, while we are all dealt different cards in life, through hard work and perseverance we can achieve success and enjoy great experiences in our own way.

And when success does come your way, whatever that success may be and however you may measure it, it is important to never forget from where you came, for that is perhaps where our true selves lie. And the simplicity of that place might just be where you find your greatest joy.

Yes, Kong Kong has achieved great things and has had an adventurous life. Yet after all that, he remains a humble man, true to who he has always been.

Still running, picking wild fruit, connecting with nature.

Still the kampong kid.

Love,

Papa

Clarence standing next to the statue of the Winged Stiletto, the commando formation's insignia.

Lieutenant-Colonel (Rtd) Clarence Tan Kim Peng was a platoon commander in the 1st Singapore Infantry Regiment (1 SIR) from 1964–65. He was promoted to Captain while attending the US Ranger and US Airborne courses. He was subsequently promoted to Major in 1969, and became Commanding Officer of 4 SIR. Also from 1969 he was pivotal in the early work of establishing the Singapore Commandos Unit and would ultimately become its first commanding officer. By 1978, he had been promoted to the rank of Lieutenant-Colonel. In 1978 he was transferred from the Commandos to be the Brigade Commander of 2 SIB, then subsequently of 5 SIB, before returning to the Commandos in 1981 as Commandant of the School of Commando Training. From 1988 to 1992 he was Defence Adviser to Australia and New Zealand.

During his military career, he has been awarded the Long Service Medal (Pingat Bakti Setia), the Public Service Medal (Pingat Bakti Masyarakat), and the Public Administration Medal (Military) – Silver (Pingat Pentadbiran Awam (Tentara) – Perak) by the Singapore government; and the Singapore Armed Forces Long Service and Good Conduct (30 Years) Medal, the Singapore Medal, and the Confrontation Medal by the Singapore Armed Forces.

Lieutenant-Colonel (Rtd) Clarence Tan Kim Peng retired from the Singapore Armed Forces on 1st July 1992.

Bibliography

In order to provide context to the events of Clarence's life throughout this book I have included a very broad overview of some of the pertinent cultural aspects and historical events that affected Singapre, Malaysia, and the surrounding South East Asia region. The region's history is fascinating and I would strongly encourage you to read further elsewhere to gain a deeper understanding of it. There is much out there to refer to and, among others, I have found the following books, videos, and websites, to be very useful in my research.

Publications

Chapman, F. Spencer D.S.O. *The Jungle is Neutral: A Soldier's Three-Year Jungle Escape from the Japanese Army.* Marshall Cavendish Editions, 2014.

Cheo, Kim Ban, and Muriel Speeden. *Baba Folk Beliefs and Superstitions.* Landmark Books Pte Ltd, 1988.

Chua, Mui Hoong. *Pioneers Once More: The Singapore Public Service 1959–2009.* Straits Times Press and Public Service Division, 2010.

Conceicao, Joe. *Singapore and the Many-Headed Monster: A new perspective on the riots of 1950, 1964, and 1969.* Horizon Books, 2007.

Grenfell, Russell. *Main Fleet to Singapore.* Oxford University Press, 1987.

Jackson, Robert. *The Malayan Emergency & Indonesian Confrontation: The Commonwealth Wars 1948-1966.* Pen & Sword Military, 2011.

Lee, Kuan Yew. *From Third World to First: The Singapore Story: 1965–2000.* Harper Collins Publishers, 2000.

Lee, Kuan Yew. *The Singapore Story: Memoirs of Lee Kuan Yew.* Marshall Cavendish Editions, 1998.

Lim, G. S. Catherine. *Gateway to Peranakan Culture.* 4th Ed., AsiaPac Books Pte Ltd, 2005.

Menon, Ramachandran, editor. *One of a Kind – Remembering SAFTI's First Batch.* 2nd Ed., POINTER, Journal of the Singapore Armed Forces, SAFTI Military Institute, 2015.

Nathan, S. R., with Auger, Timothy. *An Unexpected Journey: Path To Presidency.* Editions Didier Millet Pte Ltd, 2011.

Ricklefs, M. C. *A History of Modern Indonesia since c. 1200.* 4th Ed., Palgrave Macmillan, 2008.

Tan, Chee Beng. *The Baba of Melaka: Culture and Identity of a Chinese Peranakan Community in Malaysia.* Pelanduk Publications (M) Sdn Bhd, 1988.

Videos

"Riding the Tiger: The chronicle of a nation's battle against communism." Produced by Singapore Ministry of Information and the Arts, 2001.

Websites

National Library Board (Singapore). *HistorySG: An online resource guide.* eresources.nlb.gov.sg/history

National Library Board (Singapore). *Singapore Infopedia.* eresources. nlb.gov.sg/infopedia/

Acknowledgements

Where does one begin? There have been so many to whom I have turned for assistance and support for various reasons throughout the long iterative process that the writing of this book has been.

First of all, Deputy Prime Minister and Coordinating Minister for National Security Teo Chee Hean. Thank you for accepting our request to write the Foreword. It is a tremendous honour for Clarence, and for myself.

To Mr Teo Eng Dih, Special Assistant to Deputy Prime Minister and Coordinating Minister for National Security, for your valuable assistance. And to MINDEF for their suggestions.

To She-reen Wong and Rachel Heng, my editors at Marshall Cavendish. Thanks for your patience in working with this novice writer. I am sure after reading the first few pages of my initial manuscript you will have thought, "Sigh, we have a bit of work to do here!"

To Alvin Mark Tan for your wonderful illustrations. Thank you so much for coming on board.

To Sylvia Khoo, a personal friend and a Friends of the Museum docent at the Peranakan Museum (and other museums in Singapore), who not only guided Clarence and myself around the Peranakan Museum and in doing so further educated me on many aspects of this culture, but also gave me invaluable feedback on the sections of this text covering the Peranakan culture itself.

To Paul Tan, a Singapore poet, who provided some pointers early on in this process. John Teo and Noel Cheah for reviewing the manuscript. And Kerry Pereira, Alan OwYong, and Wing Chow, from the Nature Society of Singapore – for helping with a few questions I had concerning Singapore birds.

And to all those friends who lent me their ears, gave advice, took photos, made introductions, acted as international couriers, or simply joined me for a coffee when I needed a break – Amanda Soon and Edmund Kok, Janice Yong, Colin & Ai Swan Chan, Mark Puhaindran, Benjamin Lee, Yumi Ng, James Ho, Fawzy Fadzlillah, Melvin Tan, David Yeoh, Rob Macdonald, the Lims of Redwood City, and the Saint Brigid School community of San Francisco.

Then to my mum and dad back at Omahanui in Levin, New Zealand – the most widely read people I know. I know you will have had no qualms telling me to stop dreaming and get back to a real job if you felt that this project was a waste of time. But you did not – so I took that as an encouragement to carry on. Thank you.

To Judy, my mother-in-law. Thank you for your support to me over all these years since I first entered your family. And thank you for letting me have access to Clarence for countless hours as we worked on this project. You can have him back now!

And, of course, to Margie, my dear wife. What can I say? Never once did you question this. It is your sacrifice for which I was determined to see it through. Love you more!

And, finally, to my father-in-law, Clarence Tan himself. It is a daunting undertaking to present one's life to the world, perhaps even more so when it is written in the words of your son-in-law. I think that it is fair to say that this has been an endeavour that neither of us really considered in its entirely when we first embarked on this journey. I will always be grateful and indebted to you for taking that leap. I hope these pages do justice to your legacy.

Thomas A. Squire was born and raised in Wellington, New Zealand, where he met his wife, a Singaporean working in Wellington at the time. Upon following her back to Singapore, he immediately became fascinated with the history of his new home. It was conversations with his father-in-law, a retired army officer, about his life that was the genesis of this book. A pilot and mathematician by training and a tech worker by trade, he has lived in Singapore for more than twenty years.

Always A Commando is his first book.